AF540509

REDISCOVERING GANDHI

VOLUME IV : Consensual Democracy: Gandhi on State, Power and Politics

Series Editor: ***Prof. R.P. Misra***

Vol. 1. Hind Swaraj: *Gandhi's Challenge to Modern Civilization*
—R.P. Misra

Vol. 2. Ahimsa: *The Way to Peace*
—Jonathan K. Crane & Jordi Agusti-Panareda

Vol. 3. Satyagraha: *Gandhian Approach to Conflict Resolution*
—Jai Narain Sharma

Vol. 4. Consensual Democracy: *Gandhi on State, Power, and Politics*
—Ashu Pasricha

Forthcoming Volumes

Vol. 5. Humanizing Science and Technology: *Some Case Studies*
—Vinnie Jauhari and Parul Goyal

Vol. 6. Truth is God: *Gandhi's Search for Religion of Religions*
—R.P. Misra

About the Author

Dr. (Miss) Ashu Pasricha is a faculty in Gandhian Studies at Panjab University, Chandigarh. She has many books to her credit including Gandhian Approach to Integrated Rural Development; Public Administration: Discipline and Dimensions; Peace Studies: Discipline and Dimensions; WTO, Self-reliance and Globalisation; and Consensual Democracy: Gandhi on State, Power and Politics. Also, she has published a number of research papers in various Indian and foreign journals of repute.

Gandhian Studies and Peace Research Series-25

REDISCOVERING GANDHI

Series Editor
Prof. R.P. Misra

Volume 4

Consensual Democracy

Gandhi on State, Power and Politics

By
Ashu Pasricha
Department of Gandhian Studies
Panjab University
Chandigarh

In Collaboration with
GANDHI SMRITI & DARSHAN SAMITI, NEW DELHI

Published by
CONCEPT PUBLISHING COMPANY, NEW DELHI-110059

ISBN: 13-978-81-8069-374-8 (Series)
ISBN: 13-978-81-8069-673-2 (Vol. IV)

First Published 2010

Published and Printed by

Concept Publishing Company Pvt. Ltd.
Regd. Office:
A/15-16, Commercial Block, Mohan Garden
New Delhi-110059 (India)
Phones : 25351460, 25351794, *Fax* : 091-11-25357109
Email : publishing@conceptpub.com
Website: www.conceptpub.com

Editorial Office:
H-13, Bali Nagar, New Delhi-110 015, India.

Cataloging in Publication Data--*Courtesy:* D.K. Agencies (P) Ltd. <docinfo@dkagencies.com>

Pasricha, Ashu, 1967-
Consensual democracy : Gandhi on state, power and politics / by Ashu Pasricha.
p. cm. --
(Gandhian studies and peace research series ; 25) (Rediscovering Gandhi ; v. 4)
Includes bibliographical references (p.) and index.
ISBN 9788180696732

1. Gandhi, Mahatma, 1869-1948--Political and social views. 2. Democracy--India. 3. India--Politics and government--1919-1947. I. Title. II. Series: Gandhian studies and peace research series ; 25. III. Series: Rediscovering Gandhi ; v. 4.

DDC 954.035 22

Preface

Throughout our lives we are members of different groups or associations, from families neighbourhoods, clubs and work-units to nations and states. In all such associations, from the smallest to the largest, decisions have to be taken for the association as a whole: about the goals to be pursued, about the rules to be followed, about the distribution of responsibilities and benefits between members. These can be called collective decisions, in contrast to individual decisions taken by people on behalf of themselves alone. Democracy belongs to this sphere of collective decision-making and equality of rights in the exercise of that control. To the extent that these principles are realized in the decision-making of any association, we can call it democratic.

Today the idea of democracy is triumphant; the model is in principle embraced in most countries the world over. You may say that the very word democracy has been hailed and misused earlier in history. The most repressing and totalitarian regimes have tried to mask themselves as "real" or "people" democracies. What has happened, however, is a historical demasking of these false pretences.

Even those governments which were most authoritarian called themselves democratic. Hitler's Germany was based upon overwhelming popular mandates, and so could be called democratic. Since the Russian Revolution of 1917 the Soviet leadership has called itself a true democracy—presuming that non-Soviet governments were false ones. Mainland China calls itself a People's Democracy. A citizen of another state may call his government a 'guided democracy', which is a contradiction in terms. Obviously the word evokes a positive reaction in people all over the world. No government which openly holds itself to be undemocratic could hope to win general approval at home or abroad. With this perspective in mind the present volume has been written.

Contents

Preface v
Editor's Foreword by ***Prof. R.P. Misra*** ix
Acknowledgements xxxiii

1. Introduction 1

2. Concept of State 5

3. Doctrine of Power 31

4. Concept of Politics 57

5. On Democracy 78

6. Human Rights 106

7, Nationalism and Internationalism 146

8. Doctrine of Means and Ends 172

Bibliography 196

Index 207

Editor's Foreword

To many the greatness of Mohandas Karamchand Gandhi lay in his freeing India from British colonialism nonviolently. He has rightly been called 'Father of the Nation' by India's top evolutionary Netaji Subhas Chandra Bose. Not many, however, appreciate that the freedom of India was only a milestone in his ultimate goal of getting humanity rid off the scourge of violence which in its most virulent form manifests itself as war, and to usher in an era of peace and harmony. The method Gandhi adopted was unconventional: it was not the brute force humanity has been used to since times immemorial; it was *satyagraha*, 'to stand fast against untruth' represented by violence in thought, words and deeds. He experimented with this new found weapon, in South Africa during the first-two decades (1893-1916) of the twentieth century, and then in India since 1916 to lead the country to freedom from colonial exploitation in 1947. India, for Gandhi was a laboratory to test the efficacy of nonviolence in subduing violence. His concern was humanity as a whole and he was ready to launch movements to free the oppressed people the world over from political, economic and social slavery when the very forces he tried to subdue with the weapon of love, took him away from this world leaving his legacy behind for the future generations to carry it forward.

Twentieth century was a watershed in political configuration of the so-called modern world. It was a century of freedom, freedom from European colonialism, and freedom from imperialism and feudalism, and freedom from the shackles of tradition and religious fundamentalism. In fact, the process began in eighteenth century, when the USA became a free country in 1776, and Mexico secured its independence from Spain in 1812. Lenin in Russia overthrew the Czar and brought the working class to power in 1917. Mao accomplished a similar mission in China in 1948. And Gandhi led India to freedom from British colonialism in 1947.

Among all the revolutionaries who led their motherlands to freedom, Gandhi stands out as a unique freedom fighter. His way of accomplishing his mission was unique and the goal he set before him was also unique. While others subdued their adversaries by using the same force that their adversaries used, to enslave their countries; Gandhi did not hurt his adversaries physically or even psychologically, he melted their hearts by suffering and addressing to their human conscience. Further, Gandhi's vision was far wider and larger; he not only wanted to free India from British colonialism but also to free humanity from the scourge of war. Inspired as he was by Indian civilization and its two basic tenets—*shanti* (peace), and *vasudhaivakutambakam* (whole world constitutes one joint family), he wanted India to be free so that it could become an instrument of freeing humanity of the scourge of violence appearing as greed, hatred, poverty, inequity, discrimination, conflicts, wars, and exploitation of nature and fellow human beings.

Gandhi was a visionary, thinker, social reformer, politician, educator, applied theorist, and above all, a man of action *(karmayogi)* who believed in *nishkam karma* (performance of duty unmindful of the outcome). He was a systems man and saw parts as inseparable elements of the whole all the way from the universe to the invisible atom. As such he considered the political system as a subsystem of the larger social system inseparably interconnected both horizontally and vertically. Political decisions impact economic, natural and other parallel sub-systems, and are at the same time impacted by them. Water-tight compartmentalization and departmentalization of the society lead to a number of unexpected and unintended consequences. Unlike other political thinkers, Gandhi did not see political system independent of other systems.

He considered individual human being as the core around which are built the other aspects of human endeavours manifested as economy, ecology, polity, technology, etc. He compared the spatial configuration of the world with Oceanic Circles with individuals forming the core. Around the Core are, families, small communities, and then are the larger circles like development blocks, districts, States (in India) and nations. Nearer the Circle to the Core, stronger, smaller, and more important it is for it is with these that the individual interacts more frequently and hence is influenced by it. Gandhi envisaged a spatial order in which the individual living in a family ought to enjoy maximum autonomy, of course, with maximum interdependence. In Gandhi's scheme of things, the individual living in a family which in turns makes a community, call it village or neighbourhood, that should be marked with maximum autonomy in social, economic, political and cultural matters. Outer the Circle less powerful it is so that the world government as and when it is formed, should interfere with the inner circles only to strengthen their autonomies; to check any abuse of human rights; and stop conflicts and wars.

There is a lot that Gandhi had to say on what is now known as development. He laid emphasis on human development with equal stress on inner and outer development. By inner development, he meant moral, intellectual development; and by outer development, he meant economic, social, political and technological development. He considered the latter unaccompanied by the former, a dangerous proposition. Since he was a practical theorist, he started his experiment of inner development on himself first, and the outer development on the people of India. To begin with, he tried to subdue the animal in him; he rejected war as the means to bring peace, and became a votary of truth and nonviolence. His life was full of love for everyone: his *ashramites* or adversaries, and he demonstrated that an ordinary man living with just five most basic possessions: a loin cloth to cover the body, a watch to keep track of the time, a pair of spectacles, a pair of sandal, and a stick for support while walking, could rise far above the richest, most educated, and most powerful human beings. Righteous path he treaded gave live demonstration to people the world over that the evolution of humans to the higher levels of consciousness depends on themselves, not on the 'survival of the fittest'. He forced a mighty British Empire to quit India, not by killing the British, but by using the soul force of love. No wonder then that the United Nations has declared October 2, his birthday, as the International Day of Nonviolence. He is honoured today, not only because he was a political leader who led India to freedom and democracy and set the ball rolling for the freedom of other enslaved nations of the world but also and more importantly because he discarded the use of brute force in human relations and gave practical demonstration of nonviolence as the means to bring peace and harmony in the world.

Gandhi presented to the world a new vision of the future: a vision of *vasudhaivakutambakam.* He was a politician yet a spiritual leader, an economist, social reformer, ecologist, moralist and scientist all combined into a single whole, otherwise called Mahatma Gandhi. His politics was not designed to garner power; it aimed at distributive justice, good governance, democracy wherein even the poorest and the weakest had a stake, and conflict resolution without the use of force. Gandhi warned humanity against impending environmental crisis; and the atmosphere of violence that prevails today all over the world. In Gandhian praxis, politics, economics, sociology, religion, ethics, science, and technology were not independent of each other; they formed part of a common whole – the means to help man step into the higher level of consciousness in his evolutionary journey from animal to human and then on to better human being until he attained self-realization, i.e. knowing oneself as servant of the humanity. Complete adherence to truth and nonviolence would carry man to his ultimate destination, said he. And closer man is to that destination nearer he is to peace and harmony, both inner and outer.

Asked to give a message to the people, Gandhi replied 'My life is my message'. Elsewhere he asked people to avoid seven major sins that plague humanity. They are:

'Politics without Principle;
Wealth without Work;
Pleasure without Conscience;
Knowledge without Character;
Business without Morality;
Science without Humanity; and
Worship without Sacrifice'

Unfortunately, in the so-called modern world, none of these sins are the objects of abhorrence. Gandhi's 'modern' world would have nothing to do with them for they come in the way of positive human relations. That is why his reply to the question: What do you think of the modern world? Gandhi responded 'It is a good idea.' He worked towards this idea all through his life. The modern world was, however, so bitten by modernity, that it did not allow him to complete his journey of life; he was assassinated on January 30, 1948, just 148 days after he freed India from the clutches of colonialism. But the soul force that he used to free India has remained alive and is getting stronger as time goes. If the results of 2009 parliamentary elections in the USA and India are any indicators, Gandhian values are at work, even if unnoticeably, to cleanse humanity of the seven sins mentioned above.

Gandhi compared humanity with an ocean with innumerable waves emanating from a centre (oceanic circles). Nearer the centre a circle is, smaller it is in size but stronger in force. Contrariwise, larger the circle, weaker it is in force. All the circles are interconnected and interdependent, small or large. None exists in isolation. In the ocean of humanity, the individual constitutes the centre of the circle. Around the individual are the circles of family, community (village or urban neighbourhood), regions, nations and finally the world (the ocean). They together form a system. Each circle is important, but closer to the centre it is, more powerful it has to be. How strong the circles would be, would depend on how strong the force emanating from the centre is. If the outer circles are strong and the inner ones weak, a Black Hole or whirlpool would come into being and everything would be devoured by it. Looking from this perspective, the individual is the centre. It is he, including the institutions he creates, who shapes the outer circles. If the world is devoid of peace today, it is because the individual is not at peace.

We can understand the systems approach better by comparing the world with human body. So long as each cell and organ of the body is healthy and maintains lateral and vertical interrelations without violating the laws governing their functioning, the body functioned well. Once these laws are violated or individual cells or organs get infected, the body gets sick. Each element of it functions autonomously, produces its own energy, and cleans itself of any polluting elements, and thus keeps itself in good health. The autonomy is, however, qualified by inter-dependence with the sub-systems above, and below, and the overall system. There is a threshold limit within which malfunctioning of cells and organs of our body, for example, can be managed by the body system. Once the threshold is crossed, the body gets sick. If appropriate corrective measures are not put in place, the system degenerates and comes to an end.

Applying this analogy to political system, the subject matter of this book, we see it as a highly complex sub-system of the larger social system, and at the same time having a number of sub-systems within it. The building block of the system is the individual. He is the key figure in a democratic political set-up. The quality of the governance depends to a great extent on the quality of the people; the knowledge they possess and the values they cherished. In a truly democratic set-up, it is always possible to change and improve the political institutions and educate the people. It is just the other way round when the government is not representative of people and the main concern of the state is to keep its power intact rather than the welfare of people. Gandhi saw the British Raj in India as anti-people; on the surface, it looked glamorous but in reality it was corrupt and antinational. Gandhi aroused the conscience of people against it and made them see how they themselves were responsible for their slavery. British did not occupy India; Indians invited the British to rule over them, said he. He fought against the British Raj, and at the same time prepared the people to take over the leadership of the movement he launched and to ready themselves for *swaraj* (rule over the country by ruling over themselves) once the British were gone.

It would be unfair to confine Gandhi to the sphere of politics: for him politics was one and only one of the means to transform India and its people into a morally, culturally, and socio-economically strong nation, Gandhi gave priority to freedom of India because British colonialism was immoral and also because I came in the way of India making its due contribution to the progress and happiness of the world.

This is the message of Dr. Ashu Pasricha's book entitled *Consensual Democracy: Gandhi on State, Power and Politics.*

Essence of the Book

The book focuses on Gandhi's concept of state (chapter 2). Here it points to the five main factors that influenced his views on state: the concept of *dharma* (duty); morality as guiding principle; the liberal tradition he acquired from western countries; humanism he inherited from his family tradition; and his role as the undisputed leader of India's struggle for independence. For him, self-realization was the goal of all human beings and it was the responsibility of the state to create conditions in which the citizens of the country without any discrimination are able to move in that direction. He debunked modern (western) civilization as satanic because it took man away from the path of self-realization.

In a way Gandhi had a streak of anarchism in him. He considered the state as the engine of violence and for him the government that governed the least was the best government. Man, he thought, was evolving into a super-conscious being and a stage would come when he would not need the state to protect his rights. He was thus the protagonist of a divine kingdom (Ram Rajya) inhabited by enlightened human beings. It is our responsibility to make the transition from colonial and feudal governance to Ram Rajya as smooth as possible undeterred by the roadblocks that come in the way.

Gandhi was thus the spokesperson of moral sovereignty and the sovereignty of the people who are easily swayed by mundane self-interest. For him, spiritual authority (inner voice) was far more powerful and legitimate than the temporal authority of the state. He did not, therefore, work for the abolition of the state; he worked for strengthening the power of the people. Once India got political freedom, he started working to strengthen the power of the people to counter the state power. He wanted the Congress party under whose banner the people were mobilized to fight against the mighty British Empire to convert itself into a Servants of People Society and thus to develop a counter-force of moral authority to keep the power of the state in check. Incidentally, this is what has now emerged as civil society initiative.

Gandhi's concept of nonviolent state was concretized in the idiom of the common man as *Swaraj* and *Ramaraj*. What in essence it means that the people should govern themselves and the state as their representative should function only with the consent of the people. It should be the responsibility of the state to create condition in which people take the responsibility of governing themselves and to ensure that human rights of all are protected and all performed their duties towards others without being asked to do so as mother performs her duties to her offsprings joyfully. Naturally, this would be possible only in a nonviolent society. Unless *ahimsa* (nonviolence) becomes the source of power of the individual and the state, *Ram Rajya* would not be realized. *Ramaraj* means a state, which derives its power from self-disciplined populace. In such a state the question of violence by the state does not arise, nor does arise violence by individuals imbued with the spirit of *swaraj*.

A government, which governs the least, would emerge only when the power of the state is decentralized all the way to the individuals and small communities 'If India is to evolve along nonviolent lines' (*Harijan*, December 30, 1939). Concentration of power at the top leads to dictatorships or capitalism. To Gandhi, "the power that comes from service faithfully rendered ennobles, Power that is sought in the name of service and can only be obtained by a majority of votes is delusion and a snare to be avoided" (*YI*, 11-9-1924). The power that comes from the force of arms or votes without service is accompanied by violence and it always leads to more violence.

The state as it is constituted today, represented violence in undiluted and organized form. It is not possible to abolish the state, but it is definitely possible to curb the power of the state by decentralization of power. The material and moral development of the people is possible only in the decentralized system of governance. Since the power ultimately lies in the hands of the people, it must rest with the people. And this can be achieved far more under a decentralized than centralized system.

Religion and Politics

Gandhi was aware of the desire of man to have power and glory. In fact that is one of the traits that distinguish him from animals. The relation between the state and the power to govern is so close that political science has always considered power "as the axis around which the social commonweal spins". Gandhi challenged this notion of power politics and used *satyagraha* as an alternate source of power to challenge one of the most powerful military and political power of his time. Thus he brought religion and politics closer. Gandhi did not mix religion and politics but he did use the universal principles of all religions to purify politics. He said once "...politician in me has never dominated, it is only because politics encircle us today like the coil of a snake from which one cannot get out..." (*YI*, 12-5-1920, p. 2) Gandhi decided to wrestle with the snake, consciously earlier and unconsciously later. And this he could accomplish by bringing politics and religion close to each other. The reader should know that by religion he meant *dharma* or morality, which cuts across all religious traditions. For Gandhi religion and spirituality were coterminous for they had a common denominator, i.e. morality which in practical terms means adherence to truth and nonviolence. If religion deviates from morality, it does not deserve to be called so. He abhorred the exploitation of religion for political purposes. His concept of God and religion were essentially *Upanishadic*. He, therefore, had no interest in rituals; his interest lay in right thinking, right speaking and right conduct.

That is why Gandhi did not want religion to be separated from politics. In fact he based his political activities on the well known tenets of *dharma*. "For me the road to salvation lies through incessant toil in the service of my country and of humanity. I want to identify myself with everything that lives. In the language of the *Geeta*, I want to live at peace with both friends and foes. So my patriotism is for me a stage in my journey to the land of eternal freedom and peace. Thus it will be seen that for me there are no politics devoid of religion.

They subserve religion. Politics bereft of religion are a death trap because they kill the soul." ('My Mission', *Young India*, April 3, 1924).

All those political parties of India, which use religions to serve their political ends would do well to study Gandhi's concept of religion and stop dividing people on religious basis. It would be great indeed if the enlightened leaders of all religions come together to find common ethical values which cut across all religions and faiths and jointly propagate those values. This would unite the people and purge the anti-social elements that infest all political parties of India today.

Gandhian Secularism

While Gandhi advocated politics impregnated with moral values, which he termed as religious values, he did not stand for secularism that some parties in India practice today. He was the votary of keeping state independent of religion but not free from values on which various religions of the world are based such as Truth and Nonviolence. He did not want the state to interfere in matters of religion. Let people follow the religion they wanted; it is their personal matter. He did not accept the concept of state religion either. In his own words, "I do not believe in state religion even though the whole community had one religion...There were in reality as many religions as minds. Each mind has a different conception of God from that of the other ...This did not mean that the State Schools would not give ethical teachings. The fundamental ethics were common to all religions."

The state has no religion but it did not mean that it had no morality. It would be only proper for the state to teach moral and ethical values through its educational institutions. Carrying it further, it would be the duty of the state to keep immoral individuals away from politics. Their place must be in the jail, not in national parliament and state legislatures. If there is moral down in all Indian politics, it is partly because of the mixing of denominational religion with politics and partly because of the total rustication of morality from politics. Politics that is impregnated with immorality, with greed and self-aggrandizement, and with tendencies to amass wealth and power is not a truly secular politics. And, of course, it is not a religious politics either.

India removed ethics and morality from educational curricula in the name of secularism. Gandhi had laid great emphasis on basic education tuned to enriching the mind, training in skills, and making children sensitive to human values. It was a complete departure from what Gandhi had emphasized. The prevailing environment of violence in the country has to a great extent resulted from the neglect of religious education

Gandhi on Democracy

Government of the people, by the people and for the people is democratic, so says the textbook definition. If the 51 percent of the people vote for a government, it would be a democratic government. Gandhi never agreed with this definition of democracy. He considered it as a façade of democracy to do undemocratic acts as the British did when they occupied India. First, majority is not always right. Most of desirable social, economic, and political changes in the society have been triggered off by those who were in minority. Second, true democracy must be participatory to truly represent the will of the people. Third, democracy should not cross the perimeter of morality, i.e. it would give no place to manipulations, hypocritical professions, lies and above all corruption. Military and police may be important for external and internal security but democracy must aim at system without either of them. The people should be their own watchdogs.

Gandhi was not very enamoured of the electoral system of western democracy as the mechanism to determine the will of the people. He repeatedly said that parliamentary democracy is not immune to corruption. If we look at the Indian democracy as it is today he was perfectly right. He checked democracy from falling in the hands of those who were powerful in money or muscle power and wise, and he wanted to introduce several innovations. To begin with, he wanted democracy to be democratized. It "is an impossible thing until the power is shared by all... Even a pariah, a labourer...will have his share in government." Its base should be the enlightened individual and cohesive local community; the apex should be narrow with limited functions. And to achieve this, nonviolence must be accepted as the religion of the state. "True democracy or *swaraj* of the masses can never come through untruthful and violent means, for the simple reason that the natural corollary to their use would be to remove all opposition through the suppression or the extermination of the antagonists. That does not make for individual freedom. Individual freedom can have the fullest play only under a regime of an unadulterated *ahimsa*." (*Harijan*, May 27, 1939)

The means to counter the evil in general and power seekers in particular was *ahimsa*, which in operational terms meant *satyagraha*. People must be tolerant; they must respect the right of others to hold their opinion even if the opinion so expressed was unpalatable. Everyone should have the right to profess the religion of his choice without let or hindrance. State must be secular in this respect but not in spiritual matters.

Gandhi wanted the Constitution of free India to be flexible enough to allow change to meet the needs of the time. The head of the state should be a humble and honest person who can inspire confidence in the government. "I would rejoice to think that we had a *mehtar* girl of stout heart, and of crystal like purity to be our first president." The legislators should be true representatives of the people. The laws passed by them should be in consonance with the wishes of the people. He did not want the Indian parliament to be like the British House of Commons. The executive should be chosen from amongst the legislators and the courts should have right to scrutinize what the executive does. Thus he wanted the judiciary to be the final arbiter.

Gandhi advocated a federal system of governance in India. The governor who would be the head of each province (State) would have the following qualifications:

1. He should be teetotaler;
2. He should be creative and constructive;
3. He should not live ostentatiously;
4. He should work for the underdog;
5. He must be morally strong; and
6. He should know the national as well as the provincial language.

In free India, Gandhi envisaged each village to be a republic with full powers to manage its internal affairs.

Gandhi knew that power corrupts and absolute power corrupts absolutely and, therefore, politics should be purified by service and decentralization of power down to the individual level. He wanted a band of constructive workers to function as a check on those who held political power.

Meaning of Development

The term development was not current in Gandhi's time. What was current was economic progress, which for all practical purposes meant 'industrialization' on European and American lines. Gandhi not only opposed the imperialism of the West but also its economic and social development processes. He was not enamoured of industrialization, for he saw a close relationship between western style industrialization and colonialism. He was not a *status quoist*. He was a revolutionary of a special brand and wanted India and other developing countries to adopt a new approach to progress.

Unlike the concept of economic progress as understood in the West, Gandhi broadened the meaning and called it human progress. The first and primary goal of progress is to take man to a higher level of consciousness so that he becomes a better human being. And this objective could be achieved not by becoming a saint but by living in the society and working for the progress of each individual singly and collectively to attain higher level of life and living. Higher levels of life meant spiritual progress and higher level of living meant material progress. Gandhi considered the two as two sides of the same coin. Material progress without spiritual progress would produce a society of *thugs* and spiritual progress without material progress will produce a society mendicants.

After the Second World War the term industrial progress was replaced by economic development because the developing countries needed agricultural and social progress too. Soon, 'economic' was taken off because 'development' meant economic anyway. So, development as it is understood today has only one dimension, i.e. economic. It is presumed that other developments—social, political, ecological and cultural—will automatically follow if the level of economic development is high.

We thus see a great divergence between the meaning of progress as envisaged by Gandhi and the one envisaged by the post-war development in India. Gandhi wanted economic, political and social progress to boost spiritual (moral and ethical) progress of man. And if the spiritual and material progress went hand in hand then there will be peace and prosperity. People will cooperate with each other for a common good; they will help and support each other. There will be no inequity and disparity in development: interpersonal, inter-group or inter-regional. At the global level too the rich nations would help the poor nations and in due course of time there will be no poverty and exploitation in the world.

Gandhi's thesis on development was ignored in India. The country followed the western path of industrialization and did make some notable progress. Perhaps, it was necessary for India to keep the Gandhian concept of development at bay for the time being. It was the question of survival of the nation. Had the American food aid not come, there would have been a great famine in India? India's economy was totally shattered, and the country had to rebuild everything. When Nehru declared the new dams and new factories as the 'modern temples' he was right. Even Gandhi would have approved of this and he approved of the Indian forces marching to Jammu & Kashmir to save the valley from the onslaught of the marauders from across the western border.

Now after more than half-a-century of practicing western model of development, not only we in India, but people the world over realize that the El Dorado of happiness is beyond reach. Poverty, unemployment, exploitation, diseases, ignorance and conflicts afflict the world more than ever before. Regimes fall, ideologies disappear, theories lose their meanings, and methodologies become ephemeral. How long the strategy of globalization, privatization and liberalization would last, we do not know. But we do know that its traps are not inferior to those of the former strategies; in fact they are more powerful. It may lead to far more serious economic, social, ecological and political problems than we have ever faced unless corrective measures are taken well in advance and are built in the very process of the implementation of the strategy.

What are the corrective measures? The main spring of the corrective measures lie in Gandhian praxis. India would become a developed country even if a quarter of its population fails to get two square meals a day. The way development is measured, can absorb this gap. As in 2005, our development strategy is biased against the poor in several ways. Most of the poverty eradication programmes benefit the rich more than the poor. No matter which sector one looks at, the rot is glaring. While the nation grows, the poor decay. We may attain 10 per cent GDP growth in not too distant a future. In the mean time the gap between the rich and the poor would also grow fast enough to compensate for the progress we make on the national front.

Even such lofty concepts like Human Rights have been corrupted. How can the poor and deprived fight for their rights? There is need to go beyond human rights and proclaim basic human duties too. It is the duty of each and every individual to protect human dignity. What is more undignified than to live in poverty under the very nose of those who fight for the human rights? And in a society where everyone is trying to knock down the other, the chance for an egalitarian society ever emerging is practically ruled out. Unless the dignity of the individual gets as high a priority in governance as economic progress, there is no hope for sane society developing in the foreseeable future.

As Prof. Pasricha has put it, "In a well-ordered society then self-respect is secured by the public affirmation of the status of equal citizenship for all; the distribution of the material means is left to take care of itself in accordance with the idea of pure procedural justice." Gandhian approach to development is the only sure way to ensure human dignity and to get over the emerging problems of poverty, inequity, immorality and violence. In this approach economic progress is used as means to achieve human progress. This approach is well reflected in concepts like 'growth with redistribution', 'new international order', 'basic needs', 'Latin American Model', 'Club of Rome Report', 'human centred development', 'humanizing development', etc.

Nationalism in a Globalized Economy

The national struggle for independence under the inspiring leadership of Mahatma Gandhi led to fusion of local, regional, caste and religious interests nationalism and it was hoped that India would once again emerge as a nation that would shape the destiny of the world in the long run if not in the short run. Some of the British policies on education, social development, rule of law etc. also helped India integrate emotionally, socially and economically. But the national movement became more oriented to fighting for independence and taking over the reigns of the government from the British in a constitutional way by 1930. But the images of independent India that different sections of the society harboured were not integrated to form broad enough canvas for painting a political scenario.

How the caste, religious, regional and ethnic loyalties would be reconciled, was not given the attention it deserved. The desire to discover the moorings and to bring certain aspects of collective life in tune with the times and the exigencies of the situation, were not strong enough. The tendency to hide the differences under the carpet was very much there. That is how religion got politicized. On a medieval social base, it was difficult to erect a twentieth century political edifice. After the attainment of independence all these issues would be taken care of in a democratic manner, was the general thinking. Gandhi alone was involved in creating a united cultural and social base for *swaraj* to be lasting and marked with *Satyam, Shivan* and *Sundaram* (truth, goodness and beauty). But his message was drowned in the noise of political struggle, which was essentially political.

The leadership of the freedom movement was in the hands of western educated liberals who wanted the British to hand over the reign of the government to them and get lost. They had a firm faith in democracy but not very oblivious to the fractured social order, which the country was going to inherit from the British. The internal discards had already surfaced in the form of religion, region, and caste based political identities wanting to secure political power even if it meant the division of the country. He, Gandhi, alone offered a new ideology that cut across all boundaries including international. "I want India's rise so that the whole world may benefit. I do not want India to rise on the ruins of other nations", said he in 1925 (*YI*, 12-3-1925, p. 88). "My mission is not merely brotherhood of Indian humanity. My mission is not merely freedom of India, though today it undoubtedly engrosses practically the whole of my time" (*Young India*, 4.4.1929). There was no antagonism between nationalism and internationalism in Gandhian praxis, for the politics underlying them both was bounded morality.

From Politics of Power to Politics of Empowerment

In Gandhi praxis *rajniti* (politics) means different from what the term politics connotes. *Rajniti* means governance system, which is based on certain ethical principles. Included among them are: purity of means in achieving one's ends; welfare of all, not just the welfare of the majority; and service before self. Gandhi did not accept dichotomy between means and ends. The contemporary schools of political thought laid emphasis on the goal rather than on the means to achieve the goals. If the goals were good, any means would be legitimate. If freedom of India was a desirable goal, any means could be used to secure it. Gandhi being an absolute moralist, he concentrated on the purity of means, for that would ensure the purity of the results, if not the subjective goals set by the individuals or society. If the goal is impure, it could not be achieved by pure means and if the means were impure, the results would turn out to be impure. For Gandhi end did not justify the means, as is the case with most political thinkers. 'As the means so the ends', said he.

Self-realization is the goal that man should try to attain. It could be achieved only through self-purification, which in essence means an ethical discipline. "... he who is not prepared to order his life in unquestioning obedience to the laws of morality, cannot be said to be a man in the full sense of the world." This ethical outlook is the backbone of Gandhi's political philosophy. Moral discipline is the most important means of social reconstruction. It is here that Gandhian philosophy differs from that of socialism and fascism, which aim at capturing the political power by hook or crook.

Gandhi did not subscribe to the dictum of greatest good of greatest number for it meant tyranny for 49 per cent for the comfort of 51 per cent or the luxury of still few. He believed and worked for the greatest good of all. And this could be best achieved by service rendered to each other. And he summarily dismissed use of force as a means to achieve any end no matter how noble it may be.

Is Indian Democracy Gandhian?

India is the largest democracy of the world. So far it had ten general elections the latest being in May, this year (2009). The number of voters exceeded 700 million. They cast their votes at over 80,00,000 polling booths, the elections were held in five phases to enable the government to provide necessary security and personnel to manage the booths. More than a million (91.3 million) voting machines were used and the number of people drafted to manage the elections exceeded 6 million. The results of the election were also astounding in many ways. Many of the mafia dons who used to get themselves elected lost; many caste leaders known for all sorts of unethical acts were either cut to size or thrown over board. The election also proved beyond doubt that the people of India have realized that they can make a difference.

India is a democracy in the same way as the USA, UK, and France are democracies. In a world which still has dictators and one party governments, to be the largest democracy of the world gives we Indians a sense of pride. But we know that this is not the type of democracy our founding fathers like Mahatma Gandhi, Jawaharlal

Nehru and B. R. Ambedkar had aimed at. It is not Indian democracy; it is western democracy implanted in India. As the May 2009 elections demonstrated our democratic institutions do not meet the standards set by the Father of the Nation especially. It was an election which could be fought only by the rich. Many rich people bribed the voters and got elected. It was nowhere close to what Gandhi has envisioned.

At mid-night on August 15, 1947, Pandit Jawaharlal Nehru made the well known tryst with destiny speech that not only reminded our glorious past, and struggle for independence but also warned the people of the tasks ahead. The speech is reproduced below, for any tempering with it will corrupt its intents.

> *Long years ago we made a tryst with destiny, and now the time comes when we shall redeem our pledge, not wholly or in full measure, but very substantially. At the stroke of the midnight hour, when the world sleeps, India will awake to life and freedom. A moment comes, which comes but rarely in history, when we step out from the old to the new, when an age ends, and when the soul of a nation, long suppressed, finds utterance. It is fitting that at this solemn moment we take the pledge of dedication to the service of India and her people and to the still larger cause of humanity.*
>
> *At the dawn of history India started on her unending quest, and trackless centuries are filled with her striving and the grandeur of her success and her failures. Through good and ill fortune alike she has never lost sight of that quest or forgotten the ideals which gave her strength. We end today a period of ill fortune and India discovers herself again. The achievement we celebrate today is but a step, an opening of opportunity, to the greater triumphs and achievements that await us. Are we brave enough and wise enough to grasp this opportunity and accept the challenge of the future?*
>
> *Freedom and power bring responsibility. The responsibility rests upon this Assembly, a sovereign body representing the sovereign people of India. Before the birth of freedom we have endured all the pains of labour and our hearts are heavy with the memory of this sorrow. Some of those pains continue even now. Nevertheless, the past is over and it is the future that beckons to us now.*
>
> *That future is not one of ease or resting but of incessant striving so that we may fulfil the pledges we have so often taken and the one we shall take today. The service of India means the service of the millions who suffer. It means the ending of poverty and ignorance and disease*

and inequality of opportunity. The ambition of the greatest man of our generation has been to wipe every tear from every eye. That may be beyond us, but as long as there are tears and suffering, so long our work will not be over.

And so we have to labour and to work, and work hard, to give reality to our dreams. Those dreams are for India, but they are also for the world, for all the nations and peoples are too closely knit together today for any one of them to imagine that it can live apart. Peace has been said to be indivisible; so is freedom, so is prosperity now, and so also is disaster in this One World that can no longer be split into isolated fragments.

To the people of India, whose representatives we are, we make an appeal to join us with faith and confidence in this great adventure. This is no time for petty and destructive criticism, no time for ill-will or blaming others. We have to build the noble mansion of free India where all her children may dwell.

The appointed day has come—the day appointed by destiny—and India stands forth again, after long slumber and struggle, awake, vital, free and independent. The past clings on to us still in some measure and we have to do much before we redeem the pledges we have so often taken. Yet the turning-point is past, and history begins anew for us, the history which we shall live and act and others will write about.

It is a fateful moment for us in India, for all Asia and for the world. A new star rises, the star of freedom in the East, a new hope comes into being, a vision long cherished materializes. May the star never set and that hope never be betrayed !

We rejoice in that freedom, even though clouds surround us, and many of our people are sorrow-stricken and difficult problems encompass us. But freedom brings responsibilities and burdens and we have to face them in the spirit of a free and disciplined people.

On this day our first thoughts go to the architect of this freedom, the Father of our Nation [Gandhi], who, embodying the old spirit of India, held aloft the torch of freedom and lighted up the darkness that surrounded us. We have often been unworthy followers of his and have strayed from his message, but not only we but succeeding generations will remember this message and bear the imprint in their hearts of this great son of India, magnificent in his faith and strength and courage and humility. We shall never allow that torch of freedom to be blown out, however high the wind or stormy the tempest.

> *Our next thoughts must be of the unknown volunteers and soldiers of freedom who, without praise or reward, have served India even unto death.*
> *We think also of our brothers and sisters who have been cut off from us by political boundaries and who unhappily cannot share at present in the freedom that has come. They are of us and will remain of us whatever may happen, and we shall be sharers in their good and ill fortune alike.*
> *The future beckons to us. Whither do we go and what shall be our endeavour? To bring freedom and opportunity to the common man, to the peasants and workers of India; to fight and end poverty and ignorance and disease; to build up a prosperous, democratic and progressive nation, and to create social, economic and political institutions which will ensure justice and fullness of life to every man and woman.*
> *We have hard work ahead. There is no resting for anyone of us till we redeem our pledge in full, till we make all the people of India what destiny intended them to be. We are citizens of a great country on the verge of bold advance, and we have to live up to that high standard. All of us, to whatever religion we may belong, are equally the children of India with equal rights, privileges and obligations. We cannot encourage communalism or narrow-mindedness, for no nation can be great whose people are narrow in thought or in action.*
> *To the nations and peoples of the world we send greetings and pledge ourselves to cooperate with them in furthering peace, freedom and democracy.*
> *And to India, our much-loved motherland, the ancient, the eternal and the ever-new, we pay our reverent homage and we bind ourselves afresh to her service.*

And Dr. B. R. Ambedkar, the chairman of drafting committee of the Constitution of India remarked :

> *On January 26, 1950, we are going to enter into a life of contradictions. In politics we will have equality and in social and economic life we will have inequality... We must remove this contradiction at the earliest possible moment or else those who suffer from inequality will blow up the structure of political democracy, which this Assembly has so laboriously built up.*

Sixty years have elapsed since India became independent. But it has yet to redeem the pledge it made to the people of India in 1947 and 1950. The social and economic inequality that marked India of the colonial days has come down only marginally. The frustration of the people has led to violence in different forms in practically all walks of life. The most extreme form of it is Naxalism. Indian democracy, despite many achievements, is crippled by the entry of mafias, rampant corruption. India had more political equality in 1950 than it has today, six decades later. Today, Indian political system belongs to those who have money, especially those who have black money; the days of any one getting elected as MLA or MP are gone no matter how knowledgeable and service oriented he is. No wonder then, that even the last parliamentary election elected around 150 MPs who have serious criminal cases against them.

Seventy per cent of the Indian electorates live in rural areas; 30 per cent are below the poverty line and of the rest one-third belong to the lower middle class. They are reluctant even to vote what to say of contesting election. True, there is freedom for all to contest, but in real terms this freedom enshrined in our Constitution is limited to those who are *crorepatis* (millionaires). Thus more than ninety per cent of people are practically debarred from contesting elections. Indian democracy is thus a democracy of rich, for the rich and by the rich. The implications of the corrupt electoral process extend to all other sectors of society and economy. These elected representatives join hands to defend each other, even though they may belong to different parties. There is rule under which all candidates have to declare their assets and criminal cases pending in courts. But rarely does any one is honest enough to disclose his ill gotten assets. Many of the candidates have declared crores as their assets but they do not own even a single car. Among the *crorepatis* are 138 MPs of the INC, 58 of BJP, 14 of SP, 11 of BSP and 11 of DMK which together add up to 56 per cent of the MPs elected in 2009. UP, one of the poorest States of India has returned 52 *crorepatis*, Maharashtra 37, AP 31 and Karnataka 25.

Rigging of elections has come back in a big way. Earlier, booth capturing was a common practice. The polling booths were stormed, ballot boxes stuffed with fake ballot papers or filled with water; and many of them were taken away. All this practically stopped when TN Seshan became the Chief Election Commissioner; introduction of voting machines also contributed immensely to fairness in electoral process. With increasing use of black money, the rigging has taken a new and more pernicious form. Now the voters are purchased in open market, as it happened in Tamil Nadu during the last election wherein around Rs. 1000 crore were distributed to entice voters to cast their votes in favour of candidates doling out money.

In a country where one-third of the people live on less than a dollar a day, money matters a lot. If they are prepared to sell themselves in order that they can quench their hunger, they would be more than willing to sell their votes that can fetch a 1000 rupee note. And there is enough unaccounted money stacked in the pillows and mattresses to incite the poor to become immoral. The Election Commission does demand affidavit declaring the assets from each candidate, but it has no say in how these assets were acquired, nor does the government formed by these dishonourable take up any follow-up action. And if someone goes to the court, the case drags on till it is too old to pursue. (P. Radhakrishnan, *Asian Tribune,* June 7 and 14, 2009).

What the elections have demonstrated is not something that can be ignored by the largest democracy in the world. It has already entered the blood veins of Indian democracy and the day is not far off when the country would face not only internal colonialism but also anarchy. Half of the country is already in the grips of Naxalites and it is only a matter of time before they organize urban guerrillas. The externai dangers posed by Pakistan based Islamic terrorists have made Indian cities and public and defence establishments insecure. The time has come for rethinking about the political processes we have followed thus far.

Concluding Remarks

We cannot understand Gandhi and his political philosophy without understanding his synergic paradigm of human development that formed the basis of his thoughts, words and deeds. His measuring rod was two dimensional: the ethical base of the society, and the dignity of the individual. Anything that produced or promoted unethical behaviour or eroded human dignity had to be abhorred. All religions and cultures the world over have tried to ensure morality and human dignity but none has succeeded so far. Without being ethnocentric, Gandhi felt that Indian civilization.

Politics in concrete terms means seeking power to keep the society in order. Power has, however, proved to be highly corrupting and hence humanity has suffered perpetual disquiet or conflict. And this situation will remain so long as power is used for self-aggrandizement, and not for the service of humanity. Adherence to a moral code of conduct would transform politics for power into politics for service.

The mainspring of the prevailing inequity, exploitation, poverty, and conflict is politics devoid of morality. The only way to correct the situation is adherence to nonviolence in its broadest sense. And the Mahatma demonstrated in his lifetime that nonviolence was more powerful than violence. He wanted to unite the people to create a moral force, which could have a check on the society as well as the politicians lest they returned to an immoral path. He passed away before he could initiate and give shape to this movement.

Indian politics today is exactly what Gandhi was trying to save India from. Today, the political leaders who are not corrupt, who have not amassed unearned money and who do not indulge in unlawful and immoral activities have become scarce. Well known mafia dons sit in the Parliament House and make laws for the law-abiding citizens. Corruption involving almost half of the development budget of the central, state, and local governments has made a mockery of government's repeated promises in eradicating poverty, exploitation, illiteracy, diseases, and environmental risks. Even judiciary is no longer immune from corrupt practices.

But not everything is lost. We still have political leaders like the present Prime Minister of India Dr. Manmohan Singh and the erstwhile Prime Minister Sri Atal Behari Bajpai whose stature as honest and upright statesmen cannot be questioned. There is hope. The time has come for all those who love India and its cultural heritage of several millennia to introspect and for the civil society to unite for a common cause, i.e. to replace Indian politics on ethical foundations.

Humanity, for millenniums, has been governed by the power of violence (*himsa*). In fact, it was the continuation of the mode of behaviour man had cultivated in his animal stage of evolution. Many a great man and woman of wisdom emerged on the scene to take humanity on the path of nonviolence (*ahimsa*), such as Ram, Krishna, Mahavira, Buddha, Christ, Zoroaster, Mohammad, Guru Nanak, and Mahatma Gandhi. They did turn the face of humanity from violence to nonviolence, from love to hate and from war to peace. But their teachings were turned into rituals and the essence was lost in the animal past. Their teachings were ritualized into religions which have not shield away from using violence against fellow human beings. Millions of people were killed because they professed a particular religion.

Invading kings and despots killed millions of people as they marched through villages and cities. They wanted to expand their sway over the land and people outside their domains. The religious men were quick to accompany these invading armies with a view to spread their religious beliefs. Very often they teemed with the invaders. The situation has not changed much even in twenty first century. We still have many despotic rulers; some of them in the garb of democracy. Even democracies are not devoid of unethical ways of dealing with crises that grip humanity from time to time. We are now passing through a situation where law and *himsa* have joined hands to govern us.

USA, the most powerful country of the world, both economically and militarily, has a decisive role in national as well as international affairs. Its writ prevails even in the UN forums. It has used military power at will to defend what it considered to be 'right' and 'legal'. Then we have dictators at the national level, who appoint or elect themselves. The people have to suffer them and follow their dictates. In fact, this system of dictators governing the people 'lawfully' goes down to the regional or local levels. Mafias and dons with ill-gotten money bend democracy the way they want. Many of them get elected to parliament and State legislatures by threatening or bribing the people. Huge sums of funds are spent on their security while millions of people in rural areas and urban slums live in misery.

Is there a way out? Yes, there is. The way out lies in the creation of a third force; the force of the civil society, which can oversee the governance system and fight against violence (*himsa*) and *himsa* based law. Gandhi wanted the Indian National Congress to disband itself once the country attained political freedom and to convert itself into *Lok Shakti*, i.e. people's power. It did not happen then but the idea he floated is not dead. The time has now come to revive that idea—not to convert any political party into *Lok Shakti* but to mobilize the people against violence and misuse of power.

Gandhi was the votary of development from within and below. The *Lok Shakti* too has to emerge from within and below. It is the people who have to give a lead. A number of organizations have come forward to expose the misdeeds of the people in power and the shortcomings of the institutions we have created to govern ourselves. Important among them are: National Election Watch (NEW), Association for Democratic Rights (ADR), and Transparency International (TI). And then there are a large number of NGOs and NGIs who play a leading role in pointing to the growing corruption in the country and the sufferings the people have to go through. The defeat of a number of powerful mafias, despite their alliance with practically all political parties of the country, points to a new and emerging positive trend. It is hoped that the people will rise equal to the occasion and defeat at the hustling money power too.

According to B.S. Raghavan (*Hindu Business Line*, Oct. 30, 2004) "For as long as the Transparency International has been publishing the Corruption Perception Index, India has been enjoying the unique distinction of occupying a consistently low grading both for integrity (currently 2.8 on a scale of 10) and human development (127th out of 154 countries). What a fall for a country with such exalted moral traditions enshrined in its scriptures and epics and exemplified by personages such as Mahatma Gandhi, Rajaji and Kamaraj."

India is perceived to be one of the better governed countries in the Third World. We have a functional democratic system of governance. But India is also a different country with a culture that is unique and the way we are managing ourselves falls far short of the standards our forefathers have laid and Mahatma Gandhi in our own times has asserted and reestablished. Gandhi wanted India to lead the world in ushering in a new era of peace and harmony—an era wherein there was no exploitation of nations and peoples; where there was no poverty; and where all irrespective of their sex, place of birth, and economic status could enjoy the dignity that human beings deserve. So long as there are rich and poor, powerful and weak, educated and uneducated, and privileged and unprivileged, there can be no peace.

Gandhi advocated a system of social management wherein all could earn their livelihood and meet their basic needs at a level society could afford. For practical purposes, we should accept the per capita income of the people of a country or region as the floor below which no one should be allowed to fall.

At present the per capita income of India amounts to Rs. 39,000 per annum, i.e. Rs. 3,250 per month. The income of a family of five should be at least Rs. 16,250 per month. Anything below it should be unacceptable. According to the estimates of several organizations, at least half of the population of India earns less than the average income. The disparity income compounded by an education that teaches everything except ethics and morality, has led to an atmosphere of violence in the country. No one except the powerful are safe.

Let me end by saying, that India must return to the Gandhian path; there is no other way to peace, progress, and prosperity.

R.P. MISRA
Series Editor

Acknowledgements

Personal acknowledgements are no easy matters where so many have been kind. My special thanks are due to Professor R.N. Pal, Dr. K.S. Bharathi, Dr. A.D. Mishra, Professor Jai Narain Sharma, Dr. Seema Pasricha, Dr. Rashmi Sharma, Mr. Ajay Pasricha and Mrs Seema Pasricha (Advocate), Anusha Pasricha and Master Hemant Malhotra. Beyond that I can make only an all embracing salute to the galaxy of the scholars whose works I have consulted.

I am also grateful to Prof. R.P. Misra, who inspired me to write this volume and has also very kindly written the foreword. Shri Ashok Kumar Mittal my publisher for his consistent zeal in printing and publication of this volume.

Chandigarh ASHU PASRICHA

1

Introduction

In no department of life has the contribution of Gandhi been so unique and significant as in political both, national and international. At no time throughout history, as we know it, have fundamental moral values, such as truth, non-violence, justice, and brotherhood of man been applied or even recognised as valid in human relations in the political field and more especially in the mutual dealings of organised groups and nations. It is true that moral values are often violated in all spheres of life, especially in the field of commerce and industry. Yet even here the validity of these values has never been questioned. Often businessmen are reminded of their duty to be fair and honest. In highly organised communities, businessmen themselves have devised desirable norms of conduct, which would be fair to the producers and the consumers of goods. Even in societies where no such code of conduct exists, honesty is considered as the best policy. It is not unoften that an honest businessman does as well as, if sometimes not better than, one who uses doubtful methods. Further, businessmen keep their word with one another and fulfil their obligations. Whatever be the actual conduct of businessmen, the validity of the moral law is never questioned. Unfair conduct, even when tolerated, is not applauded.

Reverse is the case in the political field. The very recognition of the validity of the moral law is denied in political dealings. To some extent the validity of the moral values is recognised in a democracy. The more genuine a democracy is the better is the standard of conduct observed in it. As a matter of fact, democracy is based upon the recognition of the dignity of man which functions, not by breaking heads but by counting them, not by the bullet but by the ballot-box. It can be real only when the voter is free from any coercion, exercised by power—social, economic or political. This means that democracy, for its healthy and proper functioning, needs non-violence in the field of politics. It is defiled when there is widespread deviation from the standards of honesty, which is truth.

Gandhi did not consider political philosophy as a distinct, autonomous intellectual system separated from ethics, economics, sociology, etc. He viewed life in its totality. He looked at life *en face,* not in profile. For Gandhi, therefore, there was no line of demarcation between economics and ethics, ethics and politics, politics and economics, etc. This might have been due to the influence of the Indian philosophical tradition. Every problem is discussed by the Indian philosopher from all possible approaches—metaphysical, ethical, logical, etc. This tendency has been called by some thinkers, like Acharya Brajendra Nath Beal, "the synthetic outlook of Indian philosophy."

Any study of political philosophy should start with defining its scope. The first task would be to sort out the elements that constitute it to follow Prof. C. Wright Mills:

(i) A political philosophy is itself a social reality; it is an *ideology* in terms of which certain institutions and practices are justified and others condemned; it provides the phrases in which demands are raised, criticisms made, exhortations delivered, proclamations formulated and at times, policies determined;

(ii) It is an ethic, an articulation of *ideals,* which on various levels of generality and sophistication is used in judging men, events and movements, and as goals and guidelines for aspirations and policies;

(iii) A political philosophy designates *agencies* of action, of the means of reform, revolution or conservation. It contains strategies and programmes that embody both, ends and means. It designates, in short, the historical levers by which ideals are to be won or maintained after they have been won; and

(iv) It contains *theories* of man, society and history, or at least assumptions about how society is made up and how it works; about what are held to be its most important elements and how these elements are typically related; its major points of conflict and how these conflicts are resolved. It suggests the methods of study appropriate to its theories. From these theories and with those methods, expectations are derived.

To examine any political philosophy, then, we must examine it as an ideology, a statement of ideals, a designation of agency or agencies, and as a set of social theories.

Gandhi's political philosophy contains in a way this assortment of elements. Any study undertaken for the purpose of systematizing and giving a theoretical construct to his speeches and writings shall at the outset have to find out the nature of his political philosophy. The rough-hewn social and political theory that he evolved can be traced back to his basic humanistic outlook. He talked often in terms of god, spirit, soul, etc., but in its inspiration the secular consideration played the key role. Though there was for him no antithesis between spiritual and worldly matters, he had certain fundamental beliefs from which he never budged an inch. The basic moorings of his overall world outlook is, of course, to be found in philosophical idealism. But in social and political matters he did not start from *a priori* considerations, rather he looked at the world empirically. An experiment with Truth that he was, it was logical on his part to develop this empiric attitude regarding practical affairs. It is plausible that this was due to the influence of his contact with the Englishmen during his student days and afterwards. For, to be sure, empirical outlook is said to be one of the characteristic features of the Englishmen. But we are not quite certain as to whether Gandhi consciously derived this trait straight from the English source. That does not, however, invalidate our hypothesis. The lack of adequate intellectual system is in a certain sense a defect. But at least from the point of view of immediate effectiveness, this deficiency was evidently an advantage for him. His greatest merit as a thinker, says Spratt, was his eclecticism. Gandhi concerned himself mainly with prescribing practical cures for the evils of the world and so he had necessarily to be pragmatic in his approach.

Belonging to the most modern type of mass leader, Gandhi had to move millions of men. A practical idealist which he was, he undertook for himself the responsibility of translating his life-philosophy into action. As a practical man, he was concerned with taking care of the present. One step was enough for him. As he wrote: "I know only the moment's duty." This pragmatic approach characterizes his political philosophy. But some commentators of Gandhi's philosophy, who find in him a spiritual leader above everything else and who ignore the historical significance of Gandhi, do not share this view. Any analysis, which takes into account the role of Gandhi in its totality can never brush aside his incomparable political realistic acumen. This sense of native realism was reflected in his pragmatic approach. He had no inclination for determining the distant goal by definitions in advance; rather his prime concern was centred upon action in the immediate present. As he himself wrote: "I have purposely refrained from dealing with the nature of Government in a society based on non-violence...when society is deliberately constructed in accordance with the law of non-violence, its structure will be different in material particulars from what it is today. But I cannot say in advance what the Government based wholly on non-violence will be like." The compulsion of practical politics makes a leader pragmatic. For a mass leader has to move about an essentially pragmatic world. Gandhi's credit was that pragmatism did not degenerate into opportunism, as has usually been the case with other lesser men. He was not, much of a pragmatist to deviate from his basic principles of Truth and Non-violence.

This study makes no pretension to being a comprehensive review, of the evolution of the unique personality of Gandhi as a political figure or of his leadership pattern; it does not deal with all aspects of Gandhian theory and technique of action. Nor does it evaluate his role in Indian politics. It may be found necessary to refer to some of the political events only to place his ideas in their background. This study will primarily concern itself with tracing the evolution of his theoretical concepts. The limitation is obvious. But howsoever limited may the scope of the study be, it will fail in its task if it is not taken into account the philosophy of Gandhi. This awareness impels us to go beyond what in modern times is considered to be politics, and discuss, though not in much detail, his views on state, power, politics, democracy, means and ends, human rights, nationalism and internationalism.

2

Concept of State

Like many other Indian leaders Gandhi had considerable difficulty in coming to terms with the modern state. At one level he understood it better than many others. He was trained as a lawyer, had observed it in its developed even if distorted form in Britain and highly corrupted forms in South Africa and India, and as, a leader of the independence movement he had close day-to-day contact with it. He was one of the few to notice that the modern age was unique in assigning the state a most dominant position in society. Having led several anti-racist campaigns in South Africa, he understood the nature of political power and ideology better than most of his contemporaries and knew how the state was interlocked with dominant interests and upheld the prevailing social order. Gandhi, however, had his severe handicaps. As a votary of non-violence he was obsessed with the coercive aspect of the state and could not appreciate its moral dimension until fairly late in life. He was opposed to large-scale industrialisation and did not much understand the economic role of the state. As a moralist he was deeply preoccupied with personal integrity and individual responsibility and had great difficulty in coming to terms with the need for collective discipline and the moral compromises required by membership of the state. As a political leader who had spent all his life fighting against it, he could hardly avoid sharing the rebel's deep suspicion and biased view of it. For these and other reasons Gandhi's theory of the state was uneven, in parts refreshingly original and profound, in others a historical and may be, even naive especially to those who consider state as an end in itself, and not as a means to advance human progress.

But it would be worthwhile to refer to some of the factors, which influenced his political ideas as that would help us in having a correct perspective of Gandhi's political theory.

First, *dharma* is the basic concept of Hindu political thought, broad in its implications and open to several definitions. Sarvepalli Radhakrishnan has defined *dharma* as the complex of influences, which shape the moral feeling and the character of the people and serve as a code of conduct, supported by the general conscience of the people. It is not a fixed code of mechanical rules, but a living spirit, which grows and moves in response to the evolution of man on his journey of superconsciousness on the one hand; and development of society on the other. Two major meanings of *dharma* are that it is a source of political, social and religious duties, which change through time; and that it is an agency of absolute truth executing these duties in the real world of humans. As has been rightly observed by Dr. Paul F. Power, Gandhi made use of both the meanings, but generally tended to understand *dharma* as a universal morality to which the affairs of men and states should correspond, much as the first view suggests.[1] Gandhi, while not accepting the orthodox versions of *dharma* on many vital matters, adhered to the broad traditions of Hindu thought.

Second, his concept of universal morality transcended the Hindu concept in the sense that he assimilated the Christian ethics, and his concept of fundamental morality was a synthesis of the best of the Hindu and Christian traditions.

Third, he was considerably influenced by modern political traditions. As has been noted by Professor Humayun Kabir, he was an inheritor of the liberal tradition, of the tradition of philosophical anarchism and of the collectivization found in the socialist thought.[2]

Fourth, elemental humanism is the essence of Gandhi's attitude to the state.

Fifth, the role that he had to play as the supreme commander of the nation engaged in fighting the mightiest state organization of the world determined his attitude to a large extent, towards the state power-structure.

Keeping this background in view let us proceed to discuss the Gandhian concept of state. This section should be read along with the section on Gandhi's concept of freedom, which would enable us to form a clearer picture of the state he envisaged.

Gandhi considered self-realization to be the ultimate aim of man's life and service of the nearest and the best known of God's creation to be the only way for its achievement. In order to ensure the speedy realization of this objective, he sought to adumberate the features of a well-ordered society. He found modern civilization to be short of the ideal society of his conception and in order to bring the former in conformity with the latter he accepted the state as an indispensable evil. It is, therefore, only in the fitness of things that this hard reality should be duly emphasized before proceeding to the consideration of the essentials, form and structure of the political authority.

STATE AS AN ENGINE OF VIOLENCE

Like Tolstoy, Gandhi regards the state as the organisation of violence. While, Marx and Engels regard it as the agent of the exploiting classes, Tolstoy and Gandhi consider it as the engine of violence. Gandhi was the protagonist of a divine kingdom on earth and hence, necessarily, he was repelled by the resort to force by political institutions. He had in mind the ultimate vision of the perfection of mankind and hence he was hostile to the modern state which, to him, was a mechanical structure representing organised and concentrated violence.[3] We find, thus, that like Gumplowicz, Bluntschli and Franz Oppenheimer as well as the anarchists, Gandhi regarded the state as the organisation of force. Unlike St. Augustine and other Christian Political thinkers, he did not regard political force as the divinely appointed punishment or remedy for the sins of man. Nor did he regard social and political associations and the state as the actualization and objectivization of universal reason or the revelations of an all-pervasive spirit. He was not a conservative historicist so as to identify the existing institutional mechanism with the realized realm of free-will. Neither did he regard the state as being almost the second nature of the individual in the external world nor was he an exponent of the servile cult of state omnipotence.

There is no element of moral spontaneity in the state. Hence, Gandhi had no love for the organised institutions of political power. He accepted, instead, the worth of the plasticity and spontaneity generated by non-violence. The compulsiveness of the commands of the states leads to the destruction of the plasticity and subtlety of personality. Hence Gandhi said: "I look upon an increase in the power of the state with the greatest fear, because, although while apparently doing good by minimising exploitation, it does the greatest harm to mankind by destroying individuality, which lies at the root of all progress."[4]

Gandhi held that violence was evil. Violence includes not only physical coercion but also economic and social coercion. Power of physical coercion belongs to the state. In the modern absolute state there is no limit to the extent of this power. This power of the state to coerce is, according to Gandhi, a kind of organized violence in which lies the essence of the modern state.

Gandhi's characterization of the state as the organ of 'violence in a concentrated and organized form indicates how repelled he was at the omnipotence and the coercive character of the state. As one who believed in the sanctity of the individual and for whom non-violence was a fundamental creed it was but natural that he would characterize the state in such a term. But creed or subjective faith apart, he drew enough lessons from the world he faced—a world where imperialist domination, economic exploitation and racial discrimination were inseparably tied up with political authority.

Objectively considered, the following events and factors might have influenced Gandhi to develop such an attitude towards the state:

(1) His direct experience of the Zulu 'rebellion' (1906). Gandhi's *Autobiography* records that at that time he considered himself a citizen of Natal and he then believed that the British Empire existed for the welfare of the world. A genuine sense of loyalty prevented him from even wishing ill to the Empire. The rightness or otherwise of the 'rebellion' was, under the circumstances, not likely to affect his decision. So he made an offer to the Government to raise a Stretcher-bearer Corps for service with the troops. The offer was accepted. The scene on the battlefront was indeed ghastly and revolting for such a sensitive soul as his. To quote Gandhi "The Zulu 'rebellion' was full of new experiences and gave much food for thought. The Boer war had not brought home to me the horrors of war with anything like the vividness that the 'rebellion' did. *This was no war but a man-hunt*."[5]

(2) General Smuts' 'breach of faith' during the Satyagraha movement (1907-8) for the repeal of the Asiatic Registration Act shocked him emensely. The 'foul play' of this 'heartless man' might have been instrumental in making a deep impact on his thought process.

(3) The vulgarity and monstrosity of British domination and the sub-human existence of the people of this country had struck

> him to the roots of his being and there emerged a rebel who organized and mobilized the non-violent strength of the nation against the 'leonine violence' of the political power represented by the British government.

His encounter with the racialists in South Africa and the British imperialists in India could only lead him to see the essentially violent character of the state.

Gandhi's hostility to the violence of the state may also possibly be due, in part, to the influence of Tolstoy on him. Tolstoy wrote:

> "This superstition resembles exactly the religious one, and consists in affirming, that, besides the duties of man to man, there are still more important duties towards an imaginary being, which theologians call God, and political science the State."

Gandhi's views, while they do not have any significant point in common with the ideas of Max, Stirner and Bakunin, were influenced by Tolstoy's *The Kingdom of God is Within You* (1891), wherein the Russian writer denounced not only war between nations but all manifestations of pugnacity. He felt that the governments, which employed the army were immoral and they served the interests of the exploiting classes to the detriment of the poor and the needy. Tolstoy felt delighted in quoting Herzen's ridicule of modern government as "Chenghiz Khan with telegraphs" which in the present context could be restated as 'Hitler with atom bomb'. He denounced the fourfold technics of intimidation, corruption, hypnotization of the people, and militarization employed by the state engine to buttress its power. He regarded 'the religion of patriotism' as a barbarizing, perverse and evil slogan and felt that to preach unconditional obedience to the state was a pagan doctrine absolutely antithetical to the Christian notion of the unimpeachable superiority of the divine law or love. He definitely felt that there could not be a Christian state. Christianity based on love and the state based on violence are antitheses. Those countries where the claim is made of their having a state based on religion are only the exemplification of sheer power and of spiritual sanction. The disparate conjunction of the temporal and the spiritual, necessarily, results in the death of the latter and the triumph of the former.

In criticism of Gandhi it may, however, be noted that not all state coercion is evil. For example, the coercive power of the state has also been used for common good: in suppressing individual and group coercion; in the preservation of internal and external security; in the maintenance of the system of contracts; and in implementing the general will undeterred by the recalcitrance of the dissentient members.

These, solid contributions of the state make it essential that a more thorough historical and sociological study of the nature of the state be done than Gandhism has provided.

Gandhi's trenchant hostility appears to be directed to the coercive apparatus of the contemporary imperial state, rather than to state in general. It may be argued that if the state were rooted in community-consensus and tried to realize the common social and economic good, he might have toned down the vehemence of his attack.

THE HEGELIAN THEORY OF SOVEREIGNTY

Gandhi would be thoroughly opposed to the Hegelian and Austinian concepts of law and sovereignty. Positive law and the sovereign political structure, due to their ultimate reliance on violence, authoritarian dictates and compulsive commands, do not help the genuine realization of the system of individual rights. Gandhi's conscience revolted against the sovereignty of the despotic imperial state. Sovereignty to him was the magnification of political power, howsoever clothed in legal terminology it might be. The glorification of the sovereignty of the state was a challenge to the moral right of man to shape independently his own destiny. Hence, any concept of the exaltation of the absolute, uncontrolled and illimitable power of the state was, according to Gandhi, an attack on the moral fibre of civilization. He would have agreed that the purified, regenerate will of the community can alone be the sovereign.

Against the absolutist doctrines of Hobbes, Austin and Hegel, Gandhi appeared as the spokesman of the moral sovereignty and of people. His opposition to the concept of sovereignty as propounded by Hobbes, Austin and Hegel would, possibly, have been based on three grounds. First, as a devout theist, Gandhi regards spiritual authority to have a higher validity than the temporal authority of the political ruler. No ruler could claim to set himself up against God. Secondly, as the founder of the science of Satyagraha, Gandhi preached the right of inner conscience to oppose an unjustified law, statute, order, decree, ordinance or proclamation of the state. Thirdly, against the organized power of the legal sovereign, Gandhi stood as the prophet of the moral authority of the people.

Swaraj or Ramaraj

Distinction between Ideal Society and Swaraj. The political goals of Gandhi can be stated to be three:

(i) *Immediate Swaraj for India*: More or less on the lines of western nationalism and representative democracy;

(ii) *Non-violent State*: Marked by the growth of Decentralization (Village Republics) internally and synchronistic with the development of Internationalism. Slowly the non-violent state will be transformed into Pure Democracy and Enlightened Anarchy; and

(iii) Ramaraj or Divine Raj.

In an article in the *Young India,* Gandhi draws a distinction between the ideal society and Swaraj.[6] In the ideal society, there will be no railways, no hospitals, no machinery, no army and navy and no laws and law courts. But he emphatically states that under Swaraj these five entities and institutions, will continue to function. Under Swaraj, laws and law courts will be the custodians of people's liberty and not the bureaucratic instruments of oppression. He visualised that in the future independent Indian State, soldiers will form a "national militia" and would be used not for offensive but only for defensive and protective purposes. It may appear a bit surprising that Gandhi should write that under the Swaraj government, soldiers as national militia, will have a voice in the moulding of the affairs of the nation. In the Swaraj polity, the police will be retained but its character would be changed.

"The police of my conception will, however, be of a wholly different pattern from the present day force. Its ranks will be composed of believers in non-violence. They will instinctively render them every help and through mutual co-operation they will easily deal with the ever-decreasing disturbances. The police force will have some kind of arms but will be rarely used, if at all. In fact, the policemen will be reformers. Their police-work will be confined to robbers and dacoits. Quarrels between labour and capital and strikes will be few and far between in a non-violent state because the influence of the non-violent majority will be so great as to command the respect of the principal elements in society. Similarly there will be no room for communal disturbances."[7]

The Indian Swaraj polity was to be a parliamentary government at least for the time being. There would be a central authority constituted on representative basis. The Swaraj government would be based on popular consent of the largest number of the adult population both male and female. But sometimes Gandhi added some reservations to the concept of universal popular franchise and said that the central power would be based on "universal suffrage exercised by a disciplined and politically intelligent electorate." This latter concept is more qualitative in orientation while the notion of adult suffrage is decidedly more quantitative.

"I would be deeply distressed if on every conceivable occasion everyone of us was to be a law unto oneself and to scrutinize in golden scales every action of our future National Assembly. I would surrender my judgement in most matters to national representatives taking particular care in making my choice of such representatives. I know that in no other manner would a democratic government be possible for one single day."[8]

In an article in the *Harijan*, Gandhi indicated his ideas regarding the "Indian Governor" after independence.[9] He was to base his life on the maxim of plain living and high thinking. He was to be a teetotaler, absolutely removed from caste, creed or colour prejudice and devoted to hand-spinning as a necessary ingredient of bread-labour. He should speak the language of the province wherein he may be posted as governor and Hindustani. He must not have expensive furniture, and "must dwell in a cottage accessible to all." These ideas indicate Gandhi's absolute devotion to the concept of rural civilization for independent India. He would not have sanctioned the craze for splendid American-type buildings that has infected the policy-makers in this poor country.

Non-Violence and State

In spite, of his opposition to the coercive state and its sovereignty, Gandhi did not contemplate the deliberate destruction of the state machine; believed in the final elimination of the coercive state by increasing observance of non-violence in political action. Gandhi had firm faith in the inevitable non-violent society of the future. He regarded violence as contrary to the spirit of India and was of the view that in time the spirit of violence would be extinct.

"The world of tomorrow will be, must be, a society based on non-violence. It may seem a distant goal, an impracticable Utopia. But it is not in the least unobtainable since it can be worked for here and now. An individual can adopt the way of life of the future, the non-violent way, without having to wait for others to do so. And if an individual can do it why cannot whole groups of individual? Whole nations? Men often hesitate to make a beginning because they feel that the objective cannot be achieved in its entirety. This attitude of mind is precisely our greatest obstacle to progress—an obstacle that each man, if he only wills it, can clear away... In that world there will be a faith in God, greater and deeper than ever in the past. The very existence of the world in a broad sense depends on religion."[10]

He believed in the eventual reliability of a non-violent state. He once opined that possibly the Mauryan King Asoka presided over a non-violent state. He wrote: "It is claimed that a state can be based on non-violence, *i.e.,* it can offer non-violent resistance against a world combination based on armed force. Such a state was Asoka's."[11]

According to Gandhi, the non-violent state must be based on the willing allegiance of an intelligent body of citizens.[12] The government in such a state will represent the will and ideals of the overwhelming majority of the people. "If it is expressed non-violently, it cannot be a majority of one but nearer 99 against I in a hundred."[13] Gandhi propounded the concept of a progressively non-violent state.[14]

"I believe that a state can be administered on a non-violent basis if the vast majority of the people are non-violent. So far as I know, India is the only country which has a possibility of being such a state. I am conducting my experiment in that faith."[15] But as a realist, he was not very hopeful of the immediate acceptance of non-violence as a principle of state policy. In August 1946, in a discussion with Shankarrao Deo, Gandhi expressed hope that if a state without a government could ever come into being it would be in India because it is the only country where the attempt has been made.[16]

FUNCTIONS OF THE STATE

In order to speedily realize the ideal of the all round welfare of all, he wanted the state to perform a variety of functions which for the purpose of systematic presentation, may be categorized into the following groups: (i) Protective Functions; (ii) Prohibitive Functions; (iii) Economic Functions; (iv) Educational Functions; (v) Political Functions; and (vi) International Functions.

Protective Functions

In the ideal make up of a nation, Gandhi ruled out the necessity of arms and armed forces not only because he considered them to be ineffective,[17] but also because he thought that they unnecessarily interfere with the free growth of human mind.[18] He was, at the same time, practical enough to admit that even the predominantly non-violent state would need both arms and the armed forces, including the police.[19] These, he rightly thought, should belong to the state and not to any private individual or organization. He recognized the necessity of the armaments and forces for both defensive and protective purposes for he feared that in their absence the people may lose self-confidence.

Gandhi permitted the use of state force for giving protection to the poor, oppressed and the needy[20] against not only the wrong-doers but also epidemics and natural calamities.[21] When such occasions are not in sight, then, their, services would be used for purposes like cleanliness and cultivation. Performing all these and similar functions, the armed forces of the state shall actually constitute a body of reformers—as a body of persons who, like the charioteers of Rama, possess moral rectitude. He wanted the armed forces to be perfectly disciplined and loyal. The qualifications that he desired them to possess are the following:

(1) They must subscribe to non-violence as a creed;
(2) They must be the messengers of peace;
(3) They must have equal regard for all religions;
(4) They must cultivate, through personal service, contacts with the people in their localities or circles;
(5) They must be disciplined, intelligent and educated, impartial and men of character beyond reproach;
(6) They must be whole-time workers; and
(7) They must wear a distinctive dress so that in course of time, they will be recognized without the slightest difficulty.[22]

Prohibitive Functions

Like T.H. Green, Gandhi believed that it is the primary duty of the state to hinder the hindrances to good life. He wanted it to convert the liquor dens into restaurants, supplying clean and wholesome refreshments and providing instructive literature and other recreation to wean the addicts from the lure of intoxicants. He required it to prohibit the manufacture and sale of cigarettes, cigars or *bidis*. He wanted it also to prohibit the use of intoxicants by women and children in particular. He, however, permitted the use of intoxicants for medicinal purposes. He extolled the attempts of various legislatures at prohibitory legislation.

Further, he wanted the state to ban all literature calculated to promote transport and communications.—"He wanted it to own natively cultivate land, so that the articles of universal communalism, fanaticism... ill-will and hatred between individuals, classes or races." He also required it to ban all evil customs and practices, like those of untouchability, *devadasi,* race-prejudice, colour distinctions and uncleanliness.[23]

Economic Functions

Gandhi's attempt at defining the economic functions of the state seems to be based largely on conditions of abnormality. He was either thinking of conditions treated by famine or the terrifying problems which followed the wake of the partition of country. He wanted that the internal economy of a self-reliant and self-supporting state should be strong and so modelled as is to prove no temptation to the exploiter. He required that the government of such a state should effectively deal with the problems that face it, particularly the problems of starvation, shortage of clothing, disease, back of transport and communications, and illiteracy. Further, when as a result of India's partition a large number of refugees came to India from Pakistan, he declared that "it was the duty of both the governments to see to their food, shelter and clothing."[24] He, thus, desired the state to organize its economy so as to ensure to all persons within its territorial limits the bare necessities of life.

He was pre-occupied with the continuing problem of unemployment. He wanted that, in its attempt to provide the basic necessities of life to everyone, the state should wipe out unemployment, that is, find work for all unemployed persons, so that everyone may have equal opportunity of honest occupation of his choice. To him the basic purpose of employment was to secure the necessities of life through the sweat of one's brow. He, therefore, termed this employment or labour as "bread-labour". He declared it to be the primary duty of every government to *"ensure bread-labour for unemployed men and women, no matter how many they are"*.[25] In order to enable the state to fulfil this primary obligation, he permitted it to own and age the 'key' industries, as well as the public-utility services like transport and communications. He wanted it to own and co-operatively cultivate land, so that the articles of universal consumption may be made available to the people, almost free of charge and the labour is saved from exploitation and wastage. He observed: "In the non-violent order of the future, the land would belong to the state, for has it not been said, *Sarv Bhumi Gopal Ki?"* He also desired it to own and manage mines, rivers and forests, and to undertake the regulation of currency, customs and international trade.

Though as a rule Gandhi did not permit mass production through power-driven machinery, he was not against the textile factories and factories for grinding wheat or preserving oilseeds. He also permitted the state to preserve and protect the twin industries of agriculture and spinning and weaving. He insisted on the restricted use of machinery in order to ensure of affairs in which, the middle class people especially the artisans, do not lose their individuality and are not compelled by economic necessity to leave their state in search of a livelihood.

Lastly, he accepted taxation to be an important function of the state. He would allow it to impose, a sort of 'graded' tax on property and agricultural income and to earn profit yielded by the state-owned industries and public-utility services. He would also permit it to collect various charges and fees like the *fasli chanda* (harvest subscription), arbitration fees, grazing charges, fines and, of course, the voluntary donations. However, one thing he would positively ensure, that is "taxation as a whole should stand for the general benefit of the society", and it should in no case hit the common man hard.[26]

Educational Functions

Gandhi was of the firm opinion that a truly democratic institution must provide education to all, so that the character of the people can be moulded; they may get the opportunity to improve and serve themselves; and they may be able to read and write.[27] All this he thought would enable the rulers to find a throne in the hearts of their people.

He not only recognized the importance of the role to be played by parents in the education of their children, but also maintained that outside the home teacher was "the true textbook for the pupil". This was a reaffirmation of his belief in the truth embodied in a Sanskrit verse, which he frequently cited, namely, "Kingship and learning are never equal: A King is worshipped in his own kingdom, but a learned man throughout the world."[28]

Initially, Gandhi was of the view that the education, as a whole, should be optional. His objection to compulsory education was the outcome not only of his personal aversion to compulsion, but also of his belief that "charity should be given...only to one who is desirous of having it".[29] The stem reality of mass illiteracy prevailing in India, however, compelled him to recognize the necessity of "adult education", as well as the seven-year primary vocational education being made both free and compulsory for all children between the age-group of seven to fourteen years. The higher vocational education, however, was to be ensured by the state to all those who aspire for it, provided he who needs the expertise pays for its training too.

Political Functions

Gandhi wanted the state to take care of its subjects, befriend them and be kind to them, so that a harmonious adjustment interests of the individual and the state may not remain a distant reality. It must raise the downtrodden to the "higher conception of duty" and must secure redress for all their legitimate grievances.[30] It must, at the same time ascertain public opinion, consult the people and respect their wishes and sentiments in matters affecting them. Finally, it must promote unity (which is the condition of progress) amongst them and act with firmness and courage.

Being opposed to the rule by ordinance, he desired that the duly constituted legislative assemblies alone should perform the function of law-making. He wanted the legislation to be "plain, unequivocal and definite", for he subscribed to the notion to the uniformity of law and procedure. He also required the legislators to undertake ameliorative measures, simultaneously warning them against indulging in class-legislation.

He wanted the executive of a democratic government to execute the law with a view to realize the people's welfare, rather than to win "the hasty applause of an unthinking public". He also desired it to exercise its power of mercy in the, larger interests of the state. Under abnormal circumstances, on the other hand, he permitted the national executive, to exercise additional powers needed to protect the sovereignty and security of the state. In this context, he once made the following statement:

> There is a maxim, in English law that the King can do no wrong. The convenience of the powers that he is the law in the final analysis. This objection is applicable to all governments alike. And as a matter of fact it is not always objectionable. Thus to lay the ordinary law on the shelf. Sometimes adherence to ordinary law is itself open to objection. When the authority charged with and pledged to the public good is threatened with destruction by restraints imposed upon it, it is entitled in its discretion to disregard such restraints. But occasions of such a nature must always be rare. If the authority is frequently exceeding the limits set upon it, it cannot be beneficial to the common weal.[31]

Though Gandhi was of the considered opinion that the decision of a third party (acting, as a Judge or an arbitrator) is not always right, he wanted the people to leave it to their government to secure for them justice, which, he thought, must be generous, inexpensive, expeditious, incorruptible, dispassionate and impartial. Subscribing to the notion of the separation of judiciary from both the executive and the legislature, he wanted the judges to confine themselves to the interpretation of laws as passed by the appropriate legislatures and not to meddle with their making or execution. He, further, wanted that they should interpret law in strict accordance with its letter, for the law does not accept the intention of its framer outside what the text bears. Finally, he desired the courts to review executive and legislative measures, but not their own judgements.

International Functions

Gandhi did not restrict the field of state activity to the territorial limits of the state, that is, to the man-made frontiers, for he thought, that "God never made those frontiers".[32] To him, the whole universe was the individual writ large. He subscribed to the maxim of *yatha pinde tatha brahmande* (What is true of the individual is true of the universe). He believed in the possibility of the world being one day united under one government. He said: "Assuming that the national government is formed, and if it answers my expectations, its first act would be to enter into a treaty with the United Nations for defensive operations against aggressive powers".[33]

Gandhi frequently sought to adumberate the functions that the states will have to perform towards strengthening international amity. Emphasizing the duty of the state to its neighbouring states, he declared that a "truly independent free India was bound to run to the help of its neighbours in distress". And, this he believed would be done "not out of fear but as a matter of neighbourly duty".

He declared that the very first function of the national government in the field of international affairs would be to protect the rights and interests of its citizens abroad. Once, expressing his extreme dissatisfaction with the steps taken by the then Indian Government for the protection of the rights of Indians in South African Colonies, he observed: "The Government of India whose special obligation is to protect us, appears to raise its voice, a little at times out of fear but only a little." He recognized it to be the duty of the people, too, to protect, the interests of their brethren abroad. To quote him:

> "We very badly need a committee of active, prominent workers in India for our cause. The question affects not only South African Indians but Indians in all parts of the world outside India...I submit that our great men should without delay take up this question. Otherwise, within a very short time there will be an end to Indian enterprise outside India."[34]

He was also of the opinion that every state must have the ability and courage to subsist on what its soil can give to it and must neither depend on foreign charity, nor must it excite the greed of other countries. He also wanted the ideal state to give to the world a programme of moral rearmament in place of physical armament which he thought was suicidal.

A non-violent state of Gandhi's conception would offer full support to the peoples of all nations, clamouring for peace, freedom and democracy. Obversely, it would have nothing to do with those nations which are the enemies of democracy and justice, and who wage wars and commit aggressions. It would even participate in schemes of international economic sanctions against them.

He, however, permitted the use of men or money of one country for fighting the battle of another, if and to the extent treaty obligations exist between them. Further, when two countries are fighting with arms against one another, even a confirmed war-resister, like him, would lend moral help and blessings to the country whose cause he thinks is just. During such a state of hostility, he would also like the neutral states to effectively stop the invading army from crossing over to and devastating a neighbouring country. He would like them to present "a living wall of men...women and children", and invite the invaders to walk over their corpses, for he sincerely believed that "An army that dares to pass over the corpses of innocent men and women would not be able to repeat that experiment." From this account of international functions of the state, the following guiding principles of state's foreign policy may be deduced:

(1) Co-operation with, and strengthening of, the international associations and organizations with the object of the realization of the world political order;
(2) Promotion of international amity, co-operation, peace and security;
(3) Protection of the rights and interests of citizens abroad;
(4) Pursuit of the programme of moral rearmament and of 'physical disarmament'; and
(5) Non-participation in aggressive war and courageous non-violent resistance to, war-mongers, aggressors, invaders, including the imposition of international economic sanctions against them.

Gandhi would require the state to perform all these and similar functions, but would not recognize its monopolistic position, believing that there are many things which do not at all depend on it. In this connection, emphasizing the need of minimum state interference in the people's freedom, "I admit that there are certain things which cannot done without political power, but there are numerous other things which do not at all depend upon political power. That is why a thinker like Thoreau said that "that government is best which governs the least." This means that when people come into possession of political power, the interference with the freedom of people is reduced to a minimum. In other words, a nation that runs its affairs smoothly and effectively without such state interference is truly democratic.[36]

Elsewhere, he observed that "In nine-tenths of our activity we can manage our daily affairs without the aid of the Government... if only it will refrain from interfering with the people". And, in holding this view, he frankly acknowledged the inspiration he had derived from the writings of Henry David Thoreau.

He wanted that the state should not interfere with man's inner life, his thoughts and conscience. He, however, accepted the maxim that the state can neither force the people to become good nor can it force them to become bad. "There is and will always be the distinction between good men and bad men. But no law can lay down the dividing line between the good and the bad, or the high and the low, or the noble and the mean." The state, in other words, cannot prescribe morality. It can only enable its free spontaneous growth, by measures negative, as the maintenance of law and order, and positive, as the provision of the facilities for education and employment, for health and recreation.

Likewise self-respect and honour cannot be protected by others, much less by the state. In such cases, the state can "at best punish offenders after the offence has been committed. They cannot assure prevention except in so far as punishment acts as a deterrent". It can neither force the people to adopt any particular religion, nor can it interfere with the efforts and activities of the missionaries, for he rightly believed that religion is after all "a matter solely between my maker and myself".[37] It can be enforced only where a large majority of people are willing to submit to it. Moreover, custom, being tougher than the law itself, can be changed or "removed only by enlightened public opinion", and not by the letter of the law alone. These are virtual limitations of the law itself.

These, however, are only the instances of the many things that the state cannot, and should not do. At the same time, there are also the things which the state can, but for higher reasons, should not do; for instance, must not transgress the limits of its own law and must not imprison its best and wisest citizens or political leaders in order simply to harass them unnecessarily.

THE CONCEPT OF ENLIGHTENED ANARCHY

The final concept in Gandhian political thought is *Ramaraj* or the Kingdom of God on earth. *Ramarajya* embodied Gandhi's dream of the perfectibility of man and society. He gave to his ideal society the name *Ramarajya.* The term *Ramarajya* derives from the *Ramayana's* classic depiction of the victory of Rama, symbolizing the forces of good over Ravana; and symbolizing the forces of evil and the consequent establishment of a reign of righteousness and justice in the land. Gandhi's reference to *Ramarajya* aroused fear and suspicion in the minds of the Muslims and provoked a host of critics to aver that he wanted to go back to the mythical Golden Age. We have seen that as a medium of communication with the common people he employed traditional terms and gave them new meanings, as he himself admitted.

In his presidential address at the Third Kathiawad Political Conference held at Bhavnagar on January 8, 1925, Gandhi said:

> "Rama did justice even to a dog. By abandoning his kingdom and living in the forest for the sake of truth, Rama gave to all the kings of the world an object-lesson in noble conduct. By his strict monogamy he showed that a life of perfect self-restraint could be led by a royal householder. He lent splendour to his throne by popular administration and proved that *Ramarajya* was the acme of *Swaraj*. Rama did not need the very imperfect modern instrument of ascertaining public opinion by counting votes. He had captivated the hearts of the people. He knew public opinion by intuition as it were. The subjects of Rama were supremely happy. Such *Ramarajya* is possible even today. The race of Rama is not extinct. In modern times the first Caliphs may be said to have established *Ramarajya.* Abubaker and Hazrat Umar collected revenue running into crores and yet personally they were as good as *fakirs*."[38]

But later, Gandhi modified his position. In 1927 he said that "I assure you will find nothing there (in Gandhi's heart) but love for Rama whom I see face to face in the starving millions of India".[39] This is an instance of his utilising a mythical symbol in the interest of public service. He said in 1947, "Rama, Krishna etc. are called incarnations of God because we attribute divine qualities to them. In truth they are creations of men's imagination. Whether they actually lived or not does not affect the picture of them in men's minds. The Rama and Krishna of history often present difficulties which have to be overcome by all manner of arguments".[40] And "My Rama, the Rama of our prayers, is not the historical Rama, the son of Dasaratha, the king of Ayodhya. He is the eternal, the unborn, the one without a second".[41]

The picture of *Ramarajya* that Gandhi visualised was an expression of the yearning for a just and perfect society—the kingdom of righteousness on earth. *Ramarajya* meant more than *Swaraj* or political self-government. He said in 1929:

> "I warn my Mussalman friends against misunderstanding me in my use of the words 'Ramaraj'. By Ramaraj I do not mean Hindu Raj. I mean by Ramaraj Divine Raj, the kingdom of God. For me Rama and Rahim are one and the same deity. I acknowledge no other God but the one of truth and righteousness. Whether Rama of my imagination ever lived or not on this earth, the ancient ideal of Ramaraj is undoubtedly one of true democracy in which the meanest citizen could be sure of swift justice, without an elaborate and costly procedure."[42]

That he did not advocate Hindu Raj by the Kingdom of Righteousness may be illustrated from many of his statements made towards the close of his life.

Referring to the criticism of the employment of the term *Ramarajya* for his ideal society, he said: "It is a convenient and expressive phrase, the meaning of which alternative can so fully express to millions. When I visit the Frontier Province or address predominantly Muslim audiences I would express my meaning to them by calling it Khudai Raj, while to a Christian audience I would describe it as the Kingdom of God on earth."[43]

In 1937 Gandhi described *Ramarajya* as sovereignty of the people based on the pure moral authority, as distinguished from the British, Soviet or Nazi system of rule.

Later, Gandhi added a concrete meaning to the term. In an editorial on "Independence" *(The Harijan,* 5.5.46) he wrote:

> "Friends have repeatedly challenged me to define independence. At risk of repetition, I must say that independence of my dream is Ramarajya, *i.e.*, the Kingdom of God on earth. I do not know what it be like in Heaven. I have no desire to know the distant scene. If the present is attractive enough, the future cannot be very unlike.
>
> "In concrete terms, then, the independence should be political, economic and moral. 'Political' necessarily means the removal of

> the control of British arm in every shape and form. 'Economic' means entire freedom from British capitalists and capital, as also their Indian counterpart. In other words, the humblest must feel equal to the tallest. This can take place only by capital or capitalists sharing their skill and capital with the lowliest and the least. 'Moral' means freedom from armed defence forces. My conception of Ramarajya excludes replacement of the British army by a national army of occupation. A country that is governed by even its national army can never be morally free and, therefore, its so called weakest member can never rise to his full moral height."[44]

It can be religiously translated as Kingdom of God on Earth: politically translated it is perfect democracy in which inequalities based on possession and non-possession, colour, race or creed or sex vanish. In it, land and state belong to the people, justice is prompt, perfect and cheap and, therefore, there is freedom of worship, speech and the press—all this because of the reign of the self-imposed law of moral restraint.

Such a state must be based on Truth and Non-violence and must consist of prosperous, happy and self-contained villages and village communities. "It is a dream that may never be realized. I find happiness in living in that dreamland, ever trying to realise it in the quickest way."[45]

Gandhi held that "there can be no *Ramarajya* in the present state of iniquitous inequalities in which a few roll in riches and the masses do not get even enough to eat".[46] That is the reason why the political transfer of power in India did not enthuse him. In a prayer speech on December 2, 1947 he said, that "the independence of today stifled him. It was unreal and unstable."[47] He looked beyond the present for the state that would belong to the people. His pronouncements on the subject made during the last days of his life indicate that he improved upon his earlier abstract of concept.

To sum up, Ramarajya, notwithstanding its religious tenor and nostalgic reference, stands for an egalitarian non-violent democratic order, with moral values forming the base of such an order. Gandhi did not like the ancient myth to be transformed into a reality but at the same time he envisioned a future, which transcended the present to become a reality. Whether this 'utopia' is realizable through the method he advocated is a matter of sharp controversy, for it is a question as one's intellectual preference, but the urge behind this vision can hardly be ignored. It truly inspires.

Uniqueness of Gandhi's Anarchism

Gandhi used to quote Thoreau's statement that that government is the best which governs the least. He wrote: "That state is perfect non-violent where the people are governed the least. The nearest approach to purest anarchy would be a democracy based on non-violence."[48]

Max Stirner regarded the concepts of duty and sacred task as a superstition. Benjamin Tucker, like Max Stirner, was a gigantic egoist. Michael Bakunin had organised a secret brotherhood for promoting his anarchist ideas. His technics included activities of small secret groups, which were to inspire universal rebellion for the destruction of the state, which was to be substituted by a free federation of autonomous associations. Bakunin preached a war against God and the state. But, unlike him Gandhi was not an anarchist of the virulent type although he castigates the evils of modern industrial capitalist civilization. He did not teach the immediate neutralization of the state by violence. He stressed, to the contrary, the cultivation of moral strength and discipline. 'Gandhi's concept of truth, non-violence and purity, has no parallel in the thought of Max Stirner' or Bakunin or Tucker. Kropotkin was an advocate of communal, regional and national federations of production and consumption. Thus, it is clear that both in the matter of formulating an ideal and in the matter of specifying technics for the realization of that ideal, Gandhi's anarchism is radically different from its western counterpart.

In a letter to W.J. Wybergh, Gandhi in 1910 said, that he did not think Tolstoy ever believed that the entire world would be ever able to live in a state of "philosophical anarchy".[49] Like all world-teachers, Tolstoy also, in Gandhi's opinion, means to stress the loyalty to one's conscience. Everyone has to be "his own master", and seek, the kingdom of God within himself. Such a person is "superior to *all* government" and for him "there is no governmental power that can control him without his sanction." It is clear that even in 1910, Gandhi did not contemplate any large-scale organisation on the anarchical pattern but interpreted Tolstoy as a sixteenth-century French Monarchomach writer inculcating the superiority of religious (moral in the case of Tolstoy and Gandhi) authority to the organised political superior.

Because Gandhi preached resistance to unjustified law and advocated no-rent campaigns, hence the Indian conservatives and liberals regarded him as a political anarchist: Gandhi should be regarded as a religious anarchist, and not as a violent collectivist anarchist. Anarchism, to Gandhi, was never, a negative plan and formula. He felt that obedience to moral laws would slowly but certainly render unnecessary, and even useless, any reliance on the external mechanism of the public 'administration' of a sovereign state. Thus the primary emphasis in Gandhian thought is not on the deliberate and violent destruction of the state machine, as in some schools of western anarchism, but on truth and, non-violence which alone could be the basis of the enrichment and enhancement of the moral personality of man. Hence Gandhi wrote: "A society organised and run on the basis of complete non-violence would be the purest anarchy."

According to Gandhi, "...the weakest state can render itself immune from attack if it learns the art of non-violence. But a small state, no matter how powerfully armed it is, cannot exist in the midst of a powerful combination of well-armed states. It has to be absorbed by or be under the protection of one of the members of, such a combination."[50]

It may perhaps be long before any state can mould itself according to the principle of non-violence. Gandhiji prescribes non-violent resistance even to the states which have so far depended on violence as the means of defence. But a state can use the non-violent technique only if it cleanses its hands of all ill-gotten gains, territorial or otherwise.

His prescription to the Abyssinians, the Czechs, the Poles, the English and other victims of aggression was to refuse to fight and yet to refuse to yield to the usurper.[51] Refusal to yield means not to bow to the supremacy of the victor and not to help him to attain his object.[52] Thus concerning China he once remarked, "If the Chinese had non-violence of my conception, there would be no use left for the latest machinery of destruction which Japan possesses. The Chinese would say to Japan, bring all your machinery, we present half of our population to you. But the remaining two hundred millions won't bend their knee to you." If the Chinese did that, Japan would become China's slave.[53] It was essential to non-violent resistance, he wrote later, that the Chinese must develop love for the Japanese in their hearts, not by remembering their virtues, but in spite of their misdeeds.

When their country was at war, Gandhiji expected the pacifists to do nothing to weaken their own government so as to compel defeat. "But for fear of so doing they may not miss the only effective chance they have of demonstrating their undying faith in the futility of all war...This means that they put their conscience and truth before their country's so-called interest. For, regard for one's conscience, if it is really such, has never yet injured any legitimate cause or interest."[54] The pacifists should not wish success either to their own country or to the enemy but pray that the right should prevail. For, "It is very difficult to judge when both sides are employing weapons of violence which side deserves to succeed."[55] Whilst keeping themselves aloof from violence they should not shirk danger but serve friend and foe alike with a reckless disregard for their life.[56]

A non-violent neutral country should not allow an army to devastate a neighbouring country. It should refuse passage to the invading army by refusing all supplies. It should also present to the invader a living wall of men, women, and children and invite the invaders to walk over their corpses. The invading army, it may be said, would be brutal enough to walk over the non-violent resisters. But the latter shall have done their duty by allowing themselves to be annihilated. Besides, "An army that does pass over the corpses of innocent men and women would not be able to repeat the experiment." Gandhi also favours the economic boycott of the aggressor nation by neutral states.[57]

It is the duty of the neutral state to extend this moral sympathy and non-violent support to the victim of international aggression, even if the latter chooses to put up violent resistance. Gandhi distinguishes between aggressive and defensive violence and wishes the latter success, though he also wishes that resistance should have been non-violent.[58] If a victim is capable of uttermost bravery and selflessness and fights violently an unequal battle against an aggressor incomparably superior in strength, Gandhi would consider that violence almost as non-violence; for when there is no premeditated violence and when there is no capacity for proportionate violence, violent resistance means "refusal to bend before overwhelming might in the full knowledge that it means certain death." The Polish resistance of 1939 is an instance, of this kind.[59]

Undoubtedly, if all other states could unitedly offer against the aggressor, state moral resistance, war and aggression would be wiped out, but this can be possible only if the moral level of the average individual in the various states rises considerably. The victim of international aggression would welcome such moral support, but it should be prepared to rely on its own non-violent strength and to act alone.

War is a cultural rather than biological phenomenon[60] and never before was it so costly or so indiscriminate and universal in its destructiveness as it is today. War also necessitates the establishment of dictatorship. Besides being staggeringly destructive and expensive, war only deepens differences instead of settling them. In Satyagraha, on the other hand, the loss in men will be much smaller than in war, with absolutely no expenditure in armament and fortifications. In earlier pages we have shown how the hardest heart must melt before the suffering of non-violence and how there is no limit to the capacity of non-violence to suffer. The moral force created by genuine non-violent resistance of a state, though it may involve immense suffering, will produce incalculable moral effect and stagger the aggressor, the public opinion of the aggressor country will respond and the government of that country will find it hard to carry their own people with them.

Gandhi does not expect every citizen of a state, resorting to non-violent resistance for defence, to be a thorough-going *ahimsaist*, even as every citizen of a militarist country is not an expert in the military science. With a handful experts and with a disciplined non-violent army that may bear the same proportion to the total population as does the violent army a country would be able to defy any aggressor.

Thus as the technique of defence against international aggression the need of non-violent resistance is most pressing and its efficacy seems to be certain.

The principles we have discussed in this chapter indicate the broad outline of the social framework which is likely to form man's endeavour to reshape his life and environments according to the law of love. There is nothing final or fixed about these principles. In actual social adjustments these will be applied according to the urgencies of time and place in ways which cannot be foreseen today. Whether people will try to set up a non-violent state depends on whether they really desire liberty, peace and progress, *i.e.*, genuine democracy. The establishment of peace and the fulfilment of democracy are synonymous with the cultivation of non-violence. Non-violence alone can reconcile national existence with international co-operation, even as it alone can harmonize individual liberty and social life.

The non-violent state will be a genuine democracy because it will be based on the largest possible measure of liberty and equality of consideration. It will minimize exploitation and replace the master-servant and the capitalist-labour relationships by a new co-operative order based on rural culture. Equality of political rights will have a reality it lacks today, for it will be accompanied by decentralization and social and approximate economic equality. Functions will be related to capacities and the emphasis will be on service. Thus society will be simple enough to be within the grasp of the average man and yet rich in opportunity for a conscious life of freedom and individuality, service and constructive criticism.

NOTES

1. Paul F. Power, *Gandhi on World Affairs*, London, George Allen and Unwin, 1960, p. 36.
2. *Gandhian Outlook and Techniques*, New Delhi, Ministry of Education, Government of India, 1953, p. 210.
3. M.K. Gandhi, *Sarvodaya*, Ahmedabad, Navajivan Publishing House, 1962, p. 70.
4. *Young India*, 1919 to 1931 (Madras: Ganesen), 5-1-1922, p. 5.
5. M.K. Gandhi, *An Autobiography*, Ahmedabad, Navajivan Publishing House, 1962, p. 233.
6. *Young India*, 9-3-1922, p. 141.
7. *Ibid.*, 27-10-1921, p. 343.
8. H.T. Majumdar, *Mahatma Gandhi, Peaceful Revolutionary*, New York, Charles Scribner's Son, 1952, p. 106.
9. *Harijan*, 24-8-1947, p. 289.
10. C. Catlin, *In the Path of Mahatma Gandhi*, London, Macmillan & Co., 1948, pp. 322-23.
11. *Harijan*, 12-5-1946, p. 128.
12. *Ibid.*, 9-8-1942, p. 265.
13. M.K. Gandhi, *Satyagraha in South Africa*, Ahmedabad, Navajivan Publishing House, 1960, p. 35.
14. *Harijan*, 26-3-1938, p. 34.
15. *Ibid.*, 13-4-1940, p. 85.
16. D.G. Tendulkar, *Mahatma*, Delhi, The Publications Division, Ministry of Information and Broadcasting, Government of India, 1962, Vol. VII, p. 206.
17. *Harijan*, 30-9-1939, p. 285.
18. *Ibid.*, 9-6-1946, p. 169.
19. *Ibid.*, 1-9-1940, p. 265.
20. *Ibid.*, 12-10-1947, p. 366.
21. *Ibid.*, 13-12-1938, p. 360.
22. *Ibid.*, 18-6-1938, p. 152.
23. *Ibid.*, 15-9-1946, p. 310.
24. *Ibid.*, 4-1-1948, p. 497.
25. *Ibid.*, 11-1-1948, p. 507.
26. *Ibid.*, 8-9-1946, p. 293.

27. *Ibid.*, 25-3-1939, p. 65
28. M.K. Gandhi, *An Autobiography*, Ahmedabad, Navajivan Publishing House, 1960, p. 233.
29. *The Collected Works of Mahatma Gandhi*, Volumes I to 100, Delhi, The Publications Division, Ministry of Information and Broadcasting, Government of India, (thereafter *CWMG*), Vol. XXV, p. 520.
30. *Harijan*, A Journal of Applied Gandhism, 1933-1955 (in 19 Volumes) (New York and London, Garland Publishing, Inc., 1973), 21-9-1947, p. 334.
31. M.K. Gandhi, *Satyagraha in South Africa*, *op. cit.*, pp. 480-87.
32. *Young India*, 31-12-1931, p. 427.
33. *Harijan*, 14-6-1942, p. 188.
34. *CWMG*, Vol. XXV, p. 90.
35. *Young India*, 31-12-1931, p. 427.
36. *Harijan*, 11-1-1936, p. 380.
37. *Ibid.*, 9-8-1942, p. 261.
38. *CWMG*, Vol. XXV, pp. 558-59.
39. *Young India*, 24-3-1927, p. 93.
40. *Harijan*, 22-6-1947, p. 200.
41. *Ibid.*, 28-4-1946, p. 111.
42. *Young India*, 19-9-1929, p. 305.
43. *Harijan*, 18-8-1947, p. 266.
44. Quoted in T. Hingorani (ed.), *Towards Lasting Peace*, Bombay, Bharatiya Vidya Bhawan, 1956, pp. 216-17.
45. *Ibid.*
46. M.K. Gandhi, *Non-Violence in Peace and War*, Vol. II, Ahmedabad, Navajivan Publishing House, 1960, p. 248.
47. M.K. Gandhi, *Delhi Diary*, Ahmedabad, Navajivan Publishing House, 1962, p. 225.
48. *Harijan*, 21-7-1940, p. 209.
49. *CWMG*, Vol. X, p. 249.
50. *Harijan*, 7-10-1939, p. 293.
51. *Harijan*, 6-7-1940, pp. 185-841.
52. *Harijan*, 18-8-1940, p. 254.
53. *Harijan*, 24-12-1938, p. 394.
54. *Harijan*. 15-4-1939, pp. 89-90.
55. *Harijan*. 28-1-1939, p. 442.
56. *Ibid.*
57. *Harijan*, 28-1-1939, p. 441.
58. *Harijan*, 9-12-1939, p. 371.
59. *Harijan*, 23-9-1939, p. 281.
60. Quincy Wright, *A Study of War*, Vol. I, Chicago, Chicago University Press, 1942, p. 277.

3

Doctrine of Power

For a proper appreciation of the ideas of Mahatma on any subject, it is necessary to bear in mind two things. First, he was not a political philosopher in the conventional sense of the term. As J.B. Kripalani puts it, "If ever there was a planner without elaborate blue prints Gandhi was one."[1] Unlike other political scientists, he did not present his political thoughts in any systematic form and at one place; they have to be culled from innumerable articles, in his interviews, speeches, and answers to the questions etc. He did not assign himself the task of setting up an academic discipline. He was not a theorist; he was primarily an actionist—a *Karamyogi*. He himself admitted, "I am not built for academic writings. Action is my domain. What I understand, according to my lights, to be my duty and what comes my way I do."[2] He did not spin his theories in the cloistered atmosphere of his study, they grew and developed in the crucible of experience, in the course of his attempt to wrest freedom for his country and to solve the various practical problems as and when they emerged in the course of his long struggle against foreign domination. It could not have been otherwise in the situation he was placed in. The solutions he offered for the alleviation of the economic ills did not derive out of any rigid doctrinaire approach. His solutions were rooted in necessity. His political philosophy, was primarily a response, to use a Toynbee expression, to the challenge that poverty ridden India flung at a particular phase in the process of development of Indian history.[3] For a person in the position which Gandhi occupied it was incumbent that he took the most pressing political problems and issues into account and offered his own solutions and experiences, there emerged a definite political theory.

Second, his genius was more spiritual and moral than intellectual. His whole life was cast in the spiritual and moral mould of which truth and non-violence were the fundamental tenets. His politics has to be studied from the view-point of his own moral and spiritual principles and ideals. One must try to understand the language that Gandhi used. It was not the language used by specialists. It was the language of the market place which common man uses and understands.

In understanding any philosophy, we cannot ignore the conditions in which it evolved. Gandhi's political ideas, can, therefore be best understood in the light of physical and social conditions. Along with the objective background the ethos has to be taken into consideration. Failing this approach, pre-possessed feelings and subjective inclinations may blind our vision and lead us away from an intelligent appreciation of the subject.[4]

To understand what Gandhian Political system, one must, therefore, go back to Gandhi's writings and speeches in original. We must, however, keep in view, that there is no finality in the Gandhian concepts because they are relative. He himself kept on modifying, elaborating and enriching his own concepts on the basis of his experiences. "...I am not at all concerned with appearing to be consistent. In my search after Truth, I have discarded many ideas and learnt many new things. Old as I am in age, I have no feeling that I have ceased to grow inwardly, or that my growth will stop at the dissolution of flesh. What I am concerned with is my readiness to obey the call of Truth, my God, from moment to moment, and, therefore, when anybody finds any inconsistency between any two writings of mine, if he has still faith in my sanity, he would do well to choose the latter of the two on the same subject".[5]

At another place, he confessed that he grew 'from truth to truth'[6] in other words, his earlier utterances need to be understood in the light of his latter ones, not *vice versa*. Not having had the time and training for the systematic development of his thought Gandhi's ideas are in the main of an existential kind. They grew as he grew up.

He was not a man who embodied his ideas in a systematic treatise. Apart from his two well known works—the *Autobiography* or *The Story of My Experiments with Truth* and *Satyagraha in South Africa*—the only other considerable work which attempt to set forth his ideas in anything approaching a systematic manner is *Hind Swaraj*. All the rest of his truly voluminous writings are to be found scattered in his journalistic articles, his letters and memoranda and such of his speeches as have been recorded faithfully or of which the texts are available—are now available in the 100 volumes publication project *The Collected Works of Mahatma Gandhi*.

SOURCE OF POLITICAL POWER

Ahimsa

His whole life was cast in the spiritual and moral mould of which nonviolence was the operational tenet. Generally, nonviolence is understood as a body of "norms, inter-dictions or sanctions regarding avoidance or control of violence as well as the practice of good in day-to-day behaviour."[7] The meaning of non-violence can be divided into two types. The first type is where nonviolence connotes avoidance of certain types of actions, *e.g.* killing of animals, hurting the feelings of others, harbouring malice and avarice, etc. The second, connotation of the term 'nonviolence' is a positive norm of social action, or as a system of values to be cultivated by man. Here is not the withdrawal of certain temptations and self-denial of certain norms that connotes nonviolence but the cultivation and radiation of certain values in the behaviour of man. There should be a positive attitude in some form or the other, which requires of a man to add something to his personality by righteous actions and sublimation of self.

The term 'nonviolence' is not an exact equivalent for Sanskrit word *ahimsa*. The word *ahimsa* literally means non-injury, or, more narrowly, non-killing, and, more widely, harmlessness, the renunciation of the will to kill and of the intention to hurt any living thing, the absentation from hostile thought, word and act.[8] Gandhi extended the meaning of *ahimsa* and interpreted and applied it in his own manner. As early as 1916, he distinguished between the negative and positive meaning of *ahimsa*. "In its negative form, it means not injuring any living being, whether by body or mind...In its positive form, Ahimsa means the largest love, the greatest charity. If I am a follower of *Ahimsa*, I must love my enemy or a stranger to me as I would to my wrong doing father or son. This active *Ahimsa* necessarily includes truth and fearlessness."[9]

Thus he extended the meaning of *ahimsa* beyond non-killing or even non-injury. The principle of *ahimsa*, he held, is not "hurt by every evil thought, by undue haste, by lying, by hatred, by wishing ill to anybody...and by our holding on to what the world need."[10] The path of *ahimsa* is the path of non-attachment and entails continuous suffering and the cultivating of endless patience. In its relatively narrower sense, it means "not to hurt any living creature, by thought, word or deed for the supposed benefit of that creature."[11]

Gandhi's view of *ahimsa* is quite significant in the sphere of politics. Mainly, there are two views of nature of political power. The first is the Monolith Theory of Power, which assumes that the power of a government is a relatively fixed quantum (*i.e.*, 'a discrete unit quantity of energy'), a 'given', a strong, independent, durable (if not indestructible), self-reinforcing, and self-perpetuating force.[12] The theory assumes that the people are dependent upon the good will, the decisions and the support of their government. The power of the government is emitted from the few who stand at the pinnacle of command. Because of these assumed characteristics, it follows that in open conflict such power cannot in the last analysis be controlled or destroyed simply by the people but only by the threat or use of overwhelming physical force. The Monolith view would not allow for the possibility of other types of effective pressures and control. Conversely, according to the other view of nature of power, governments depend on people's goodwill, decision and support. Power is pluralistic. The supreme power is the state rests with the people. It is they alone who decide as to how the administrative machinery of a country has to be worked. The government of the country should be carried on according to the public opinion. The government exists not for its own good but for the good of the people. If the wishes of the people are ignored, they are always at the liberty to change the government.

In politics the use of *ahimsa* is based, in Gandhi's view, upon this second view that government is possible only as long as the people consent, either consciously or unconsciously to be governed, for *ahimsa* means absence of any kind of compulsion, imposition or oppression. Political power is fragile, always dependent for its strength and existence upon a replenishment of its sources by the co-operation of a multitude of institutions and people. This co-operation from the people may or may not continue. The government can function with the consent of the people and the people of the country are at liberty to withdraw that consent whenever they feel that the government is not functioning according to their desires. Gandhi regarded nonviolent struggle as a means of matching forces, one which have the greatest capacity for bringing real freedom and justice. In a passage addressed to the British rulers in *Hind Swaraj*, Gandhi wrote, "You have great military resources. Your naval power is matchless. If we wanted to fight with you on your own ground, we should be unable to do so, but if the above submissions be not acceptable to you, we cease to play the part of the ruled. You may, if you like, cut us to pieces. You may shatter us at the cannon's mouth. If you act contrary to our will, we shall not help you and without our help, we know that you cannot move one step forward."[13]

Consent of the Ruled

Thus Gandhi was of the firm view that the exercise of power depends on the consent of the ruled who, by withdrawing that consent, can control or even destroy the power of their opponent. A resolution drafted by Gandhi and approved by the working committee of the Indian National Congress, read and passed by public meeting on January 26, 1930, contained this statement on non-cooperation and the withdrawal of voluntary submission to the British Raj, "We hold it to be a crime against man and God to submit any longer to a rule that has caused this four-fold disaster to our country. We recognise, however, that the most effective way of gaining our freedom is not through violence. We will, therefore, prepare ourselves by withdrawing, so far as we can, all voluntary associations from the British Government, and will prepare for civil disobedience, including non-payment of taxes. We are convinced that if we can withdraw our voluntary help and stop payment of taxes, without doing violence, even under provocation, the end of the inhuman rule is assured."[14] All the movements that Gandhi launched were based upon the above theory. In other words, Gandhi used this technique to control, combat and destroy the opponent's power by nonviolent means of wielding power.

In his attempt to apply game theory to human conflicts Anatol Rapaport[15] divided conflicts in three categories: fights, games and debates. Fight is a game of pure opposition and strictly competitive in which the opponents try to eliminate and destroy each other by the use of threats and physical sanctions. Games is used by the opponents to outwit each other. The debate, is marked with the absence of threat and physical sanctions; the opponents try to convert each other by discussion and dialogue. It is generally assumed that each participant's strategy is predicted on the strategy selected by the opponent. Information about all possible strategies, rules and pay offs or the probabilities, enable each player to decide rationally to maximise benefits while minimizing losses. The last category is the only kind which could be productive and best possible for all. So the fights should be converted into games and the games into debates. Under Gandhi's conception of *ahimsa* its votary puts his refusal to hurt or injure his opponent despite the inconveniences of such an attitude to himself against those who desire to fight or outwit him; and he seeks to convert them to the use of non-coercive methods to gain their ends by finding an area of common interest, based upon common humanity, which would put the conflict of aims into a proper perspective.[16] Indulgence in *ahimsa* is a result of short-sightedness and can destroy both the parties. Gandhi did not deny the existence of conflicts in human society and admitted their existence in every walk of life but sought to make *ahimsa* the basis of a method of action.

Freedom of the Individual

From the use of *ahimsa* in politics flows the individual freedom. Gandhi was against all kinds of impositions, even against those imposed for the benefit of the person concerned. He upheld the dignity and authority of the individual throughout his life. In Champaran, where he conducted his first *satyagraha* in India, he was served with a notice to leave the district. But he refused to comply with the directive and a summon was served on Gandhi to appear before the court. He pleaded guilty and read a brief statement before the court wherein he said, "I have disregarded the order served upon me, not for want for respect for lawful authority, but in obedience to the higher law of our being, the voice of conscience."[17] Writing in 1939 in connection with the state's people movement. He observed, "Civil liberty consistent with the observance of nonviolence is the first step towards *swaraj*. It is breath of political and social life. It is foundation of freedom. There is no room there for dilution or compromise. It is the water of life. I have never heard of water being diluted."[18]

With the outbreak of Second World War, India was made a party to the War. Rigorous curbs were put on civil liberties of the Indian people. He strongly pleaded for freedom of speech as an inviolable fundamental right of the citizens even during the pendency of war. Explaining his mind at a greater length he observed, "But if they (the British) fight unto death for their freedom, and if they are at all reasonable, they must recognise our right. It is our duty to fight for that right.... This liberty is a concrete issue, which needs no defining. It is the foundation of freedom, especially when it has to be taken nonviolently. To surrender it, is to surrender the only means for attaining freedom."[19] He asked, "If the individual ceases to count, what is left of society? Individual freedom alone can make a man voluntarily surrender himself completely to the service of society. If it is wrested from him, he becomes an automation and the society is ruined."[20] He regarded the individual as the centre of power. He was categorical in his estimate of relation between individual and the state. He held that the state derived its existence and power from the individual.

The concept of ultimate authority of the individual logically paved the way for the enunciation of the theory of nonviolent non-cooperation with the state and the exploitative system that stand in the way of the all-round evolution of the individual. The emphasis on the moral power of the individual is the keynote of his philosophy. His anguish and indignation expressed in the pages of *Hind Swaraj* against modern civilization was based on this fundamental belief.

But he tried to reconcile individual freedom with social obligation. To Gandhi society was just like a family, and the relation between the individual and the society is one of the close interdependence. He rejected alike the unrestricted individualism that ignores social obligations as well as the individual as a mere cog in the social machine. He wrote, "I value individual freedom, but you must not forget that man is essentially a social being. He has risen to this present status by learning to adjust his individualism to the requirements of social progress. Unrestricted individualism is the law of the beast of the jungle. We have learnt to strike the mean between individual freedom and social restraint. Willing submission to social restraint for the sake of the well-being of the whole society, enriches both the individual and the society of which one is a member.[21] But between the individual and society, the individual comes first, though society is, by no means neglected. Ultimately it is the individual, which is the unit and in any scheme of social progress the first step always lies with him. Society must provide opportunities for the maximum growth of individual and individual in his turn must discharge his duties faithfully. In case, the either of the two goes wrong, the other should resist nonviolently. Thus nonviolence will reconcile individual freedom with social restraints. Nonviolence implies that mechanics of control which maintain social cohesion will consist of internal and non-coercive external sanction. The individual will use his opportunity to advance the greatest good of all while society will give to the individual maximum opportunity. The concept of ultimate authority of individual logically paved the way for the enunciation of the theory of nonviolent non-cooperation with the state and the exploitative system that stand in the way of the all-round evolution of the individual.

DECENTRALISATION OF POWER

For Gandhi violence was evil. Violence not only included physical coercion but also economic coercion. Economic coercion exists whenever there is a concentration of economic power in a few hands. Beginning with the position that the exploitation is at the root of all violence, he built his economic system in a manner suitable to non-exploitative society. His panacea was to do away with concentration of economic power by proposing economic decentralisation at the various levels of the power hierarchy of the Indian society. He frequently asserted that, "If India is to evolve along nonviolent lines, it will have to decentralise many things"[22] and economic decentralisation is one of them.

The concentration of economic power gave rise to a capitalist class, which exploited the natural and human resources of the society and created a fractured social order with a privileged few and under-privileged many. The concentration of economic power went hand in hand with that of political power, leading to the development of a dictatorial or authoritarian system. Taking into account all these Gandhi opted for decentralisation with village as the starting point. In his scheme of things, Gram Swaraj was co-equal with self-reliance in economic matters of each village. His was a sort of communitarian village that looked after food, clothing, shelter and educational needs of every individual living there.[23] He wanted the Indian village of his dream to be self-reliant not only in food but also in other basic needs. And since much of India lived in villages, it would bring the concept of *swadeshi* to the doorsteps of the whole country. His stress on Khadi emanated from his theory of decentralisation of economic power and self-reliance. Since Khadi was produced by the common man in the village, the economic power was distributed to every village and to every man. His theory of trusteeship when seen in this context becomes highly innovative and meaningful. Trusteeship would prevent the concentration of economic power both in the hands of state and individuals. It would also be an instrument to bring about a non-violent state and decentralisation of power.

POWER OF THE STATE

In the modern absolute state there is no limit to the power of physical coercion. This power, according to Gandhi, is a kind of organised violence. "The state represents violence in a concentrated and organised form. The individual has a soul, but as state is a soulless machine, it can never be weaned from violence to which it owes its very existence."[24] He, therefore, looked upon "an increase in the power of the state with the greatest fear because, although while apparently doing good by minimizing exploitation, it does the greatest harm to mankind by destroying individuality, which lies at the root of all progress."[25] As one who believed in the dignity of the individual and for whom the nonviolence was a fundamental creed, it was but natural for him to characterize the state in such a term. But creed and subjective faith apart, he drew enough lessons from the world he faced—a world where imperialist domination, economic exploitation and racial discrimination were inseparably tied up with political power. His encounters with the racist in South African regime and the British imperialist in India could only lead him to see the essential violent character of the state.

Gandhi thoroughly opposed the theory of the absolute power of the state according to which the laws of the state were the highest arbiters of the conduct of the citizens irrespective of the conformity of the laws to the general interests of the community. Obligation of the citizens to the state, according to this theory, is unlimited and unconditional. Gandhi resisted this absolute and non-responsible power of the state. The glorification of the sovereignty of the state was a challenge to the moral right of man to shape independently his own destiny. Hence, any concept of the exaltation of the absolute, uncontrolled and illimitable power of the state was, according to Gandhi, an attack on the moral fibre of civilization. He preached the right of inner conscience to oppose an unjustified law, statute, decree, ordinance or proclamation of the state. Both Western and Hindu political theorists give sanction for such resistance. "Our first duty" wrote Harold Laski, "is to be true to our conscience."[26] For Gandhi, "disobedience to the law of state becomes a peremptory duty when it comes in conflict with moral law."[27] As early as in 1909, he wrote in *Hind Swaraj*, "It is contrary to our manhood, if we obey laws repugnant to our conscience. So long as the superstition that men should obey unjust laws exists, so long will their slavery exist."[28]

Gandhi's main objection to the state sovereignty may be presumed to be based on following grounds: first, his metaphysical belief in the primacy of the spiritual authority over temporal authority of the political ruler. No ruler could claim to set himself up against God. Second, his faith in the inner moral conscience of the individual as superior to the organized might of the state. And third, against the organised power of the legal sovereign, Gandhi stood as the prophet of moral power of the people.

TOWARDS A STATELESS SOCIETY

He was convinced that stopgap arrangements would not bring perfection. The mere correction of institutional structure would not bring the desired result. The final concept in Gandhi's political thought is *Ramarajya* or the kingdom of God on earth. He stated that in this ideal society, there will be sovereignty of the moral authority of the people and the state as a structure of violence would be extinct. The real remedy for man's rampant maladies is to foster the inner moral strength of the people. By *Ramarajya*, he did not advocate Hindu Raj. I mean by "*Ramaraj* the Divine Raj, the kingdom of God. For me Rama or Rahim are one and the same deity. I know no other God but the one God of truth and righteousness."[29] He defined *Ramaraj* as "sovereignty of the people based on pure moral authority."[30] Later, Gandhi added a concrete meaning to the term. In an editorial on 'Independence' in the *Harijan* on 5-5-1946, he wrote, "At the risk of repetition, I must say that independence of my dreams means *Ramarajya*, *i.e.* the kingdom of God on Earth. In concrete terms, then, the independence should be political, economic and moral. 'Political necessary' means the removal of control of British army in every shape and form. 'Economic' means entire freedom from British capitalists and capital as also their Indian counterpart. In other words the humblest must feel equal to the tallest. This can take place only by capital or capitalists sharing their skill and capital with the lowliest and the least. 'Moral' means freedom from armed defence forces. My conception of *Ramarajya* excluded replacement of the British army by a national army of occupation."[31]

In terms of Western Political Science this ideal can be more concretely expressed as stateless society, the enlightened anarchy, where life has become so perfect as to be self-regulated. In this condition coercion will be replaced by pure goodwill. There will be no police, no law courts, heavy transport and centralised production. He visualised, "If national life becomes so perfect as to become self-regulated, no representation is necessary. There is then a state of enlightened anarchy. In such a state everyone is his own ruler. He rules himself in such a manner that he is never a hindrance to the neighbour. In the ideal state, therefore, there is no political power because there is no state." But his astute, sense of political realism led him to add, "But the ideal is never fully realized in life. Hence, the classical statement of Thoreau that, that government is best which governs the least."[32] Gandhi had a keen and solid sense of political realism. He himself was not sure about the realisability of this stateless society. He clearly stated, "I do not today conceive of such a golden age. But I do believe in the possibility of a predominantly nonviolent society. And I am working for it."[33] Thus, in spite of his opposition to the coercive state and its sovereignty, Gandhi did not contemplate the deliberate destruction of the state machine but believed in the final elimination of the coercive state by increasing observance of nonviolence in political action. This predominantly nonviolent state was Gandhi's second best ideal.

Gandhi being built of tremendous opposites, a unique combination of philosopher and politician sometimes spoke and wrote in terms of ultimate ideals and sometimes in terms of the immediate realizable objective. And there emerged two Gandhis—One the idealist philosopher and the other the realist politician. He dreamt of an enlightened anarchy and developed an ideal, which might serve as the eternal beacon light to the distracted humanity and in his role as the foremost leader of the national liberation movement the realist in him was sufficiently awake to the objective reality and he pressed forward for the establishment of a democratic political order. He took into consideration the limitations of human nature and of circumstances and conceded that the highest ideal may not be attained in the foreseeable future. His astute sense of realism impelled him to fight for the creation of a sovereign national state, which he knew would be far from perfect.

In 1916, on the occasion of the opening of the Benaras Hindu University, Gandhi called himself an anarchist, but of a different type.[34] (The reference was to the violent revolutionaries or terrorists as they were generally called.) One may not be sure that the distinction that he made between the two types of anarchism was a result of his acquaintance with the prevalent literature of anarchist political philosophy. But, as is generally known, he was influenced by Tolstoy's *The Kingdom of God is within You* to a considerable extent, who is generally described as the 'boldest heretic and revolutionary anarchist'.[35] Though Leo Tolstoy did not call himself an anarchist, because he applied the names to those who wished to change society by violent means yet his basic doctrines and particularly his categorical rejection of the state and of property fitted into general anarchist pattern. One may guess that Kropotkin also had influenced Gandhi. The biographer of Mahatma, D.G. Tendulkar, records, "Gandhi's three years' stay in England (1888-91) was eventful. Those were the years of great intellectual activity and unhindered freedom of thought and speech. The country as a whole had become a living university... Kropotkin's *Mutual Aid* was appearing serially in the Nineteenth century and Kropotkin himself was propagating his ideas in England."[36] It seems likely that Gandhi's young mind was exposed to the anarchist philosophy preached by Kropotkin.

His occasional reference to 'enlightened anarchy' as the ultimate ideal and his definition of *Ramarajya* as 'the sovereignty of the people based on pure moral authority' and other similar statements expressing abhorrence of the state as an institution, have lent the impression that he was a philosophical anarchist. Dr. Gopi Nath Dhawan and a host of other scholars subscribe to this view. To quote Dr. Dhawan, "To Gandhiji the end is 'the greatest good in all'. He is a philosophical anarchist because he believes that this end can be realized only in the classless and stateless democracy of autonomous village communities based on nonviolence instead of coercion, on service instead of acquisitiveness and on the largest measure of local and individual initiative instead of centralization."[37] Some scholars also described him as a religious anarchist or a pacific anarchist like Tolstoy.[38]

Like Anarchists Gandhi held that force tend to degrade those who possessed it and those on whom it was exercised. State, which is the embodiment of force, was considered by him something degrading and demoralising to the ruler as well as to the ruled, and repudiated the state in all its forms. Thus in terms of ultimate ideal of stateless society, his views are very akin to those of anarchist. Although some of the elements of Gandhian Philosophy bear resemblance to anarchist philosophy, he cannot be categorised as an anarchist thinker. The primary emphasis in Gandhian thought is not on the deliberate and violent destruction of the state machine, as it is found in some schools of Western anarchism, but on truth and nonviolence which alone can be the basis of the enrichment and enhancement of the moral personality of man. Gandhi, unlike some anarchists, did not contemplate dispensing with the machinery of state as long as it was necessary. Gandhi rebuked the government of the day for failing to do this or that for the masses, implying thereby that he had a functional and positive conception of state. Here his position is distinctly different from that of the anarchists who are out to abolish the state. Paul F. Power rightly commented, "Unlike Tolstoy, Gandhi did not endorse a stateless society for the temporal world. To do so would have precluded him from struggling for India's own national sovereignty...His approach to the ethical nature of the state agrees with Max Weber's view, that the state is a technical tool rather than something of intrinsic worth."[39] Further, *ahimsa* as a spiritual force has no parallel in the anarchist philosophy of Bakunin and Kropotkin. Again while the anarchists are apolitical or even anti-political,[40] Gandhi was intensely political. As a politician he knew that politics refers to the disposition of power. And so he moved for a shift of power from the hands of foreign imperialists to a democratic national state.

Gandhi's view about ideal state etc. also brought him close to the Marxian philosophy. The main objective of Gandhi and Marx was to improve the conditions and status of man in the society in which he lives. Both of them experienced that a transformation was necessary to improve the conditions of human beings in the society. So their main goal was the 'individual and society'. Both looked upon the state as an expression of force and visualized a stateless society or a state with minimum interference. Similarly, Gandhi like Marx, regarded private property as a source of evil and looked upon capitalism and landlordism as potent causes of human bondage. The points of contact between philosophy of Karl Marx and Gandhi appear to be very striking indeed. Yet, there are fundamental differences which are equally noteworthy.

Karl Marx enunciated the doctrine that economic systems are basic factors of history and that man and his institutions are but a reflex of the economic class-struggles which have regard throughout history. The attempt to establish a new social order characterized by freedom, according to Karl Marx, therefore, resolves into a struggle to establish a new economic order by the destruction of class domination. For Gandhi, revolution means, by and large, spiritual revolution. In order to achieve a stateless, classless society of Gandhi's ideal, what is needed above everything else is a transformation of the individual. Elimination of capitalism by any means, violent or nonviolent is the prerequisite for the Marxists for the establishment of a classless and stateless society. There is nothing essentially immoral in the employment of violence, when the goal aimed at is the establishment of a free society. End justifies the means to them. Marx and Lenin, however, rely heavily on violence as an unavoidable expedient and the only instrument of revolution since no other instrument is likely to succeed, violence has to be employed as a temporary expedient in overthrowing the class of exploiters. But for Gandhi violence is evil. Nonviolence is the root of all his philosophy. He wanted to conquer through love, affection, persuasion and not by the physical destruction. He made no distinction between the ends and means. He held that they were convertible terms. If the means neglect or violate the requirements of the moral law, the ends will not be what were intended and worked for. Further, Gandhi's programme is not the revolutionary 'seizure of power',[41] which Marxism holds to be very essential for the 'higher phase of communism', the stage of withering away of the state—but 'generation of power', from below which he hoped would avoid the incongruity of people's power with centralized state power. Gandhi never approved of centralization of state power even as a temporary expedient or as a transitional phase like the dictatorship of the proletariat. Many more differences can be pointed out between the philosophy of Gandhi and Marx, but the aim of the present study is not to compare and contrast the philosophy of Marx and Gandhi. Prof. Nirmal Kumar Bose succinctly summed up the position when he said, "Gandhi's conception of state is neither completely like that of Anarchists nor of the Communists. It approaches the former with regard to its aim of political and economic decentralisation, and that of the latter in that the interest of toiling millions will have a dictatorial position within the state."[42] It can be noticed that Gandhi did not ignore the demand or underrate the value of the immediate and the temporary for the sake of ultimate. Gandhi, in a rather exalted philosophical mood, could well share Shelley's anarchist vision of man in a world which still lies outside history and outside time, but the realist in him would wake up again to come to grip with the realities with a grim determination to reshape this timebound world.[43]

But he was very much suspicious of all the powers and rejected the normal notion of it. He was of the view that all political institutions were instruments for the pursuit of power, whether directly or indirectly. A few days before his assassination, he said at a prayer meeting, "I indeed wonder, if we can remain free from the fever of power politics or the bid for power, which afflicts the political world the East and the West."[44] As a politician, especially at the time of independence of India, Gandhi showed an extreme suspicion of political power as ordinarily understood—the power over the lives of the people that is vested in governments and is sought by legislatures. As a political thinker, however, Gandhi was really trying to challenge the very notion of power, which has acquired in the modern world the kind of importance and autonomous character that some medieval philosophers gave to the universal essence which they believed to constitute reality.[45]

Gandhi did not believe that it was possible for power to be organized as to ensure that those who seek it for its own sake nevertheless use it, to a considerable extent, for the public good. Even if one does not agree with Lord Acton that 'power tends to corrupt and absolute power corrupts absolutely',[46] there is no denying the fact that power has a strong tendency to corrupt its holder. Hunt for power is the root cause of competition among the individuals. Interests collide in the race to acquire more power and, for this sake the probability of corrupt practices cannot be ruled out. In his own words, "possession of power makes men blind and deaf, they cannot see things which are under their very eyes and cannot hear things which invades their ears. There is thus no knowing what power intoxicated government may not do."[47]

Gandhi divided power in two kinds: one is detained by the fear of punishment and other by act of love. Power based on love is a thousand times more effective and permanent than the one derived from fear of punishment.[48]

It is the coercive element of power which is the main target of Gandhi's criticism and suspicion. Coercion comprises the application or the threat of application of physical sanctions such as infliction of pain, deformity, or death; generation or frustration through restriction of movement; or controlling through force the satisfaction of needs such as those for food, sex, comfort and the like. Coercive element of political power has been highlighted by many authors of the subject. In his classic work *Politics among Nations*, Hans Morgenthau writes, "Political power may be exerted through orders, threats, persuasion, the authority of charishma of a man in an office, or a combination of any of these.[49] In this way political power is bound to admit sanctions for its execution. It revives the ancient question of force or violence in one form or the other.

ENNOBLING POWER POLITICS

To Gandhi, "the power that comes from service faithfully rendered ennobles. Power that is sought in the name of service and can only be obtained by a majority of votes is a delusion and a snare to be avoided."[50] In December 1947, Gandhi told his colleagues, the members of the Hindustani Talimi Sangh, "By abjuring power and by devoting ourselves to pure and selfless service of voters, we can guide and influence them. It would give us more real power than we shall have by going into the government. But a state may come, when people themselves may feel and say that they want us and no one else to wield the power. The question could then be considered.[51] He was of the considered view that it is natural for those in power to want to command and to use force, but those who obey commands are in a majority and can choose to express their will either by physical force or by soul force. If they prefer physical force, then the rulers and ruled alike become so many mad men, but if they choose to employ soul-force, they can honourably disregard unjust commands. He added, "Peasants have never been subdued by the swords, and never will be. They do not know the use of swords, and they are not frightened by the use of it by others.[52] What is more, coercion has temporary results while love-based conversion is everlasting. The use of coercion can further complicate the conflicts regarding its solution very difficult. "Soul force is matchless", he argued, "it is superior to the force of arms."[53] Soul force cannot be a weapon of the weak, it is not a cover for cowardice, but is the supreme virtue of the brave. Exercise of soul force requires greater bravery than that of swordsmanship. He admitted that "the strong will rob the weak and that it is sin to be weak. But this is said of the soul in man, not of the body. If it is said of the body, we could never be free from the sin of weakness. But the strength of soul can defy a whole world in arms against it. This strength is open to the weakest in body."[54] This soul force is the power of love and nonviolence and acquired through the conquest of passions. Time and again he stressed, "Nonviolence is a power which can be wielded equally by all, children, youngmen and women or grown up people, provided they have a living faith in the God of love and have, therefore, equal love for all mankind."[55] It is an active force of highest order. He acknowledged that with growing experience he could see with more and more clearness the immense power of *ahimsa*. Working under this law of soul power, "it is possible for a single individual to defy the whole might of an unjust empire to save his honour, his religion, his soul and lay the foundation for that empire's fall or its regeneration."[56] From the ruffian attempting to violate a woman to the foreign army of invasion, all according to Gandhi can be subdued by the moral power exercised by nonviolent individual or nation. Though he admitted that imperfect man cannot grasp the whole of that Essence—he would not be able to bear its full blaze—but even an infinitesimal fraction of it when it becomes active within us, can work wonders.[57]

Gandhi recognized that the pursuit of power is a basic human characteristic; he was also convinced that just as power creates its own normative rules, moral values also create power and enhance the possibility of individual effectiveness and collective survival. The interplay of power and moral values is at the centre of the problem of politics, but is usually understood in terms of moralizing the conduct of the state. Gandhi was, however, far more interested in challenging the conventional view of the nature and domain of politics, in widening the concept of power, and, above all, in destroying the dichotomies between private and public morals, religious values and political norms, ethical principles and political expediency.[58] In a materialistic civilization this requires nothing less than an assault on deeply rooted and widely held notions of realism and self-interest, narrowly defined, that flow from the segregation of true religion and power politics. In an acquisitive society the state is doomed to remain a sorely inadequate and not merely imperfect instrument, and its power a standing inducement to social corruption.

In the preface to his autobiography, Gandhi declared that his devotion to truth had drawn him into politics, that his power in the political field was derived from his spiritual experiments with himself, and those who say religion has nothing to do with politics, do not know what religion means.[59] He was concerned with spiritualization of political life and political institutions. He repeatedly insisted that politics could not be isolated from the deepest things of life. He said that when he found himself drawn into the political coil, he asked himself what was necessary to remain untouched by the immorality, untruth and political gains, and decided that a servant of the people must discard all wealth and private possessions." [60] Usually politics is understood as organized disputes about power and its use, involving choice among competing values, ideas, persons, interests and demands. Elaborating this view Michael Curtis wrote, "The study of politics is concerned with the description and analysis of manner in which power is obtained, exercised and controlled, the purpose for which it is used, the manner in which decisions are made, the factors which influence the making of those decisions, and the context in which these decisions take place."[61] To be more clear and precise, Harold Lasswell puts it, Politics! Who Gets What, When and How.[62]

By his attempt at purification of politics, Gandhi tried to wash out this idea of using politics for personal gains. Politics should not be used for sharing and exercising power. But political work must ever be looked upon in terms of social and moral progress. When he spoke disparagingly of politics, he referred to the politics of power and regarded it as an over estimated segment of politics as a whole.

To Gandhi, "Political power is not an end but one of the means of enabling people to better their conditions in every department of life. Political power means capacity to regulate national life through national representation. If national life becomes so perfect as to become self-regulated, no representation is necessary."[63] In Gandhi's view political power should be used for the benefit of the humanity. To gain, political power should not be an end but the means by which the lot of the masses is improved. Men are naturally unlike and, for this reason, distribution of power is bound to be unequal in any conceivable social and political system. As a practical course what may be desired is that the operation of the political system should be such, that no man's power to use his natural talents is diminished, rather it is increased to the extent that the elements of developmental and extractive power become consistent with each other. If at all one wants political power it should be for the reforms of the society and public welfare. Gandhi added, "when the energy to be spent in gaining that power means so much loss of energy required for the reforms, as threatens to be the case if the country is engaged in a duel with the Mussalmans and Sikhs, I would most decidedly advice the country to let the Mussalmans and Sikhs take all the power and I would go on developing the reforms."[64] Capacity to take political power should be in exact proportion to the ability to achieve success in the constructive efforts. He argued, "It is an illusion to think that MLAs are the guides of the voters. Voters do not send representatives to the Assemblies in order to be guided by them. On the contrary they are sent their loyally to carry out people's wishes. The people are, therefore, the guides, not the MLAs. The latter are servants, the former masters." Gandhi further stressed, "if we look around the world we shall find that the best guidance is given by those outside. If that were not so, a rot would set in all governments, because the field for guidance is vast and the Assembly is a very small thing. Parliaments are, after all, a mere drop in the ocean of national life.[65] Replying to a question of Dr. Zakir Hussain about the need of ideal men to run the ideal society, Gandhi replied, "We can send men of our choice, without going into the government ourselves. Today, everybody in the Congress is running after power. That presages grave danger. Let us not be in the same cry as power-seekers.... It is my firm view, that we should keep altogether aloof from power politics and its contagion."[66] When his attention was drawn to the need for acceptance of power, he categorically rejected its acceptance. Writing in *Young India* of May 7, 1931, he stated, "Office and power must be avoided. Either may be accepted when it is clearly for greater service."[67] He did not rule out the acceptance of office; if it was only meant for a greater pause, it would be then a conditional acceptance of power. He would not deny the very notion of power as such. Under certain circumstances it might be useful, but it would be qualified power capable of rendering good to the community.

When the Congress first decided to accept power in 1937. Gandhi's misgiving about this decision bordered on a controversy. It is clear that Gandhi's initial reaction was that Congress should accept office only if it was found to be in the larger interest of the nation. He was reluctant to advice the Congress to accept power as an end in itself. Gandhi also felt that once the Congress was in office, it might be tempted to abuse power. The record of the Congress governments was not wholly approved by Gandhi, particularly its resort to force. Gandhi's objection to political power was not minimized with the establishment of the National Government in 1947. He was even more sharply critical of the manipulation of power by the Congress. Gandhi was singularly alone in this respect of declining power even in a free state. Architects of other nations were absorbed in power soon after they were victorious. This was very true of those leaders who led a successful revolution and established powerful regimes in their country. But Gandhi was unique amongst all builders of nations. In his last testament on January 29, 1948, Gandhi warned the Congress about the dangers of the power politics and solemnly recommended its dissolution as a political party.[68]

Gandhi's rejection of power was not only negative, but quite positive also. He was not content merely with advising the Congress to decline power. His vision of a non-political society took a concrete form in the organization of constructive workers within the national fold of the Congress. He attached the greatest importance to the role of constructive workers. They were not to function merely as a subordinate and a secondary group to the predominantly political wing of the Congress. The constructive workers have to discharge a more important duty by remaining outside the politics in the Congress. Speaking in the meeting of Gandhi Seva Sangh he observed: "There shall be no politics in the Sangh. What after eschewing politics is constructive work."[69] Then only constructive workers could act as a corrective to the political in the Congress, and supplement its pre-eminent mission of independence of India. He emphatically made it clear that objective of the constructive work organisations, 'is to political power'[70] and not to capture it. His programme of generation of power, he hoped would invest the people with power to their own destiny. The plea for generation of power has rooted significance. This means that power is not to be imposed from above, it has to evolve upwards. And in his scheme, dissemination of power is only possible on a nonviolent basis.

State, to Gandhi, represented violence in an undiluted and organised form. Violence must be avoided but the state, to be realistic, cannot be done away with. So in order to eliminate the violence, the concentration of power must be avoided. He, therefore, advocated the decentralization of power of the state. He declared, the end to be sought is human happiness combined with full mental and moral development. I use the adjective moral as synonymous with spiritual. This end can be achieved under decentralization. Centralization as system is inconsistent with a nonviolent structure of society."[71] Centralization adds to the complexity of life which is a distraction in all creative moral endeavours. It damages initiative, resourcefulness, courage and creativeness and diminishes the opportunities of self-government. He further held, "Centralization cannot be sustained and defended without adequate force."[72] Centralization leads to the concentration of power in the hands of a few and that in its turn, robs the people of its supreme power in the matter of determination of publication not only this, in an over-centralized statesman loses his human dignity and becomes a cog in the wheel of the vast and impersonal state machine. Man becomes depersonalized. His programme of 'generation of power', he hoped would avoid the incongruity of people's power with centralized state power. That is why he laid much stress on Constructive Programme, the *modus oprandi* of nonviolent revolution. For him, democracy was "the art and science of mobilizing the entire physical, economic and spiritual resources of all the various sections of the people in the service of the common good of all."[73] In order to mobilize the total resources of the nation a sense of belongingness on the part of the people must be imparted and institutionally organized. Decentralization of power seemed to Gandhi to be the antidote to the alienation. He wanted to give a new direction to the politics and for that he went to the roots. He believed that power to be effective and genuine from the stand point of the masses, must lie with the people which could only be possible in small communities of villages. In a conversation with Louis Fischer, the American journalist, he explained, "The centre of power now is in New Delhi, or in Calcutta or Bombay, or in the big cities. I would have it distributed among the seven hundred thousand villages of India."[74]

He was of the considered view that under a free government the real power would be held by the people. He remarked that "there is no freedom for India as long as one man, no matter how highly placed he may be, holds in the hollow of his hands the life, property and honour of millions of human beings. It is an artificial, unequal and uncivilized institution. The end of it is an essential preliminary to *swaraj*."[75] He was also very much critical of the powers of the Cabinet or Council of Ministers. He argued, "True democracy could be worked by twenty men sitting at the centre. It had to be worked from below by the people of every village."[76] He further stressed that true democracy or real *swaraj* would come not by the acquisition of authority by a few but by the acquisition of the capacity by all to resist authority when it was abused. In other words, *swaraj* is to be attained by educating the masses to a sense of their capacity to regulate and control the authority.[77] The real seat of power is the people. They can exert pressure on the leadership. If the individuals recognise the power in their hands and use it constructively, to secure the social good (*sarvodaya*) or to engage in *satyagraha* against unjust laws and the repressive measures of the state, the monopolistic effectiveness of the state power would be reduced. The mightiest government will be rendered absolutely important if the people realizing their power use it in a disciplined manner for the common good. *Satyagraha* is the appropriate method for seeking correction of wrongs perpetuated or ignored by the political authority. It is the way, by which the law abiding citizens could adopt to exercise their power over the ruling elite.

Thus political power originally belonged to the people and should be transferred to them. When people come into the possession of political power, the interference with the freedom of the people is reduced to the minimum. In other words a nation that runs its affair smoothly and effectively without, such state interference is truly democratic.[78] Whilst power, superimposed, always needs the help of police and, military, power generated from within should have little or no use for them. So he gave the slogan 'Back to the Villages.'[79] His, most comprehensive statement in this respect reads as under, "Independence must begin at the bottom. Thus, every village will be a republic or panchayat having full powers. It follows, therefore, that every village has to be self-sustained and capable of managing its affairs even to the extent of defending itself against the whole world. It will be trained and prepared to perish in the attempt to defend itself against any onslaught from without. Thus, ultimately, it is the individual who is the unit. This does not exclude dependence on and willing help from neighbours or from the world. It will be free and voluntary play of mutual forces. Such a society is necessarily highly cultured in which every man and woman knows what he or she wants and, what is more know that no one should want anything that others cannot have with equal labour.... In this structure composed of innumerable villages, there will be ever-widening, never ascending circles. Life will not be a pyramid with the apex sustained by the bottom. But it will be an oceanic circle whose centre will be the individual always ready to perish for the village, the latter ready to perish for the circle of villages, till at last the whole becomes one life composed of individuals, never aggressive in their arrogance but ever humble, sharing the majesty of the oceanic circle of which they are integral units. Therefore, the outermost circumference will not wield power to crush the inner circle but will give strength to all within and derive its own strength from it. I may be taunted with the retort that this is all utopian and, therefore, not worth a single thought. If Euclid's point, though incapable to being drawn by any human agency, has an imperishable value, my picture has its own for mankind to live."[80] So far as possible every activity of these communities will be conducted on the cooperative basis. Such a village will be perfect democracy based upon individual freedom. The individual is the architect of his own government. The law of nonviolence rules him and his government. He and his villages are able to defy the might of the world. The village panchayat is to conduct the government of village and is to be the legislative, judiciary and executive combined in one. The panchayat can only work through the laws of their own making. Public opinion will be the most significant force in the Panchayati Raj. This deep attachment to the concept of decentralization indicates the radical and fundamental nature of Gandhi's view of political power.[81] He wanted to begin with the bottom. The common masses have to feel the thrill of participation in the exercise of political power. A small self-sufficient village community can certainly be an important force for the strengthening of the individual personality by the creation of a centre round which there can be the crystallization of the sentiments of organic density. In small communities, active and creative participation in self-government or *Swaraj* is possible because genuine civil and social participation is facilitated. If democracy is to be the institutional mechanism for the concrete expression of the sovereignty of the people and if the consent of the governed has to be the justification of the exercise of the political power, decentralization is bound to be a necessary element of democracy. The local authorities are to be not mere branches of the central government exercising delegated power but in the Gandhian scheme they are to be almost autonomous republics.

NOTES

1. J.B. Kripalani, *Gandhi: His Life and Thought*, Calcutta, Orient Longmans, 1961, p. 252.
2. *Harijan* – A Journal of Applied Gandhism 1933-1955, New York, Garland Publishing Inc., 1973, 3-1-1946, p. 28.
3. Buddhadeva Bhattacharya, *Evolution of the Political Philosophy of Mahatma Gandhi*, Calcutta, Calcutta Book House, 1969, p. 167.

4. Jai Narain Sharma, *Alternative Economics*, New Delhi, Deep and Deep, 2003, p. 2.
5. *Harijan*, 29-4-1933, p. 2.
6. *Ibid.*, 28-9-1934, p. 260.
7. T.K.N. Unnithan and Yogendra Singh, *Traditions of Nonviolence*, New Delhi, Arnold Heinemann, India, 1973, pp. 11-12.
8. Monier-Williams, *Sanskrit English Dictionary*.
9. *CWMG*, Volume 13, p. 295.
10. M.K. Gandhi, *From Yervada Mandir*, Ahmedabad, Navajivan Publishing House, 1932, (translated by V.G. Desai), p. 7.
11. M.K. Gandhi, *Ashram Observations in Action* (translated by V.G. Desai), Ahmedabad, Navajivan Publishing House, 1973, p. 9.
12. Gene Sharp, *The Politics of Nonviolent Action Power and Struggle*, Part-I, Boston, Poter Sargent Publishers, 1973, p. 9.
13. M.K., Gandhi, *Hind Swaraj*, Ahmedabad, Navajivan Publishing House, 1982, p. 100.
14. Gene Sharp, *Gandhi Wields the Weapon of Moral Power*, Ahmedabad, Navajivan Publishing House, 1960, p. 54.
15. Anatol Rapaport, *Fights, Games and Debates*, Ann Arbor, University of Michigan Press, 1960.
16. Raghavan N. Iyer, *The Moral and Political Thought of Mahatma Gandhi*, Delhi, Oxford University Press, 1973, p. 188.
17. *The CWMG*, Volume XIII, p. 375.
18. *Ibid.*, Volume LXIX, p. 356.
19. *Harijan*, 22-9-1940, p. 293.
20. *Ibid.*, 1-2-1942, p. 27.
21. *Ibid.*, 27-5-1939, p. 144.
22. *Ibid.*, 30-12-1939, p. 391.
23. *Ibid.*, July 26, 1942, p. 238.
24. *Modern Review: A Monthly Review and Miscellany*, Calcutta, The Modern Review Office, October, 1935, p. 412.
25. *Ibid.*
26. Harold Laski, *Grammar of Politics*, London, George Allen & Unwin, 1948, p. 289.
27. M.K. Gandhi, *Ethical Religion*, Ahmedabad, Navajivan Publishing House, 1968, p. 16.
28. M.K. Gandhi, *Hind Swaraj*, *op. cit.*, pp. 80-81.
29. *Young India*, 19-9-1929, p. 305.
30. *Harijan*, 2-1-1937, p. 374.
31. *Ibid.*, 5-5-1946, p. 116.
32. *CWMG*, Volume XLVII, p. 91.
33. *Harijan*, 9-3-1940, p. 31.
34. *CWMG*, Volume XIII, p. 214.

35. Stefan Zweig, *Adepts Self-Portraiture* (translated by Eden and Cedar Paul), London, Lassell & Co. Ltd., 1952, pp. 280-281.
36. D.G. Tendulkar, *op. cit.,* Volume 1, pp. 32-33.
37. Gopi Nath Dhawan, *The Political Philosophy of Mahatma Gandhi*, Ahmedabad, Navajivan Publishing House, 1962, p. 5.
38. Oscar Jaszi, "Anarchism", in Seligman, Edwin, R.A. (ed.), *Encyclopaedia of the Social Sciences*, New York, The Macmillan Company, 1957, p. 50.
39. Paul F. Power, *Gandhi on World Affairs*, London, George Allen & Unwin Ltd., 1961, pp. 46-47.
40. George Woodcock, *Anarchism*, London Penguin Books, 1963, p. 27.
41. *Harijan*, 17-2-1946, p. 14.
42. Nirmal Kumar Bose, *Studies in Gandhism*, Calcutta, Indian Associated Publishing Co. Ltd., 1940, pp. 85-86.
43. Buddhadeb Bhattacharyya, Article, "Gandhi's Attitude Towards Political Power", in Biswas, S.C. (ed.), *Gandhi: Theory and Practice, Social Impact and Contemporary Relevance*, Simla, Indian Institute of Advanced Study, 1969, p. 272.
44. D.A. Tendulkar, *op. cit.*, Volume VIII, p. 280.
45. Raghavan N. Iyer, *op. cit.*, p. 54.
46. Lord Acton wrote this maxim in a letter to Bishop Mandell of London on April 5, 1887. Quoted in Acton, John Emerich Edward Dalberg, *Essays on Freedom and Power*, London, Thomas and Hudson, 1956, p. 335.
47. *Young India*, 13-10-1921, p. 327.
48. *CWMG*, Volume XXV, p. 563.
49. Hans Morgenthau, *Politics among Nations*, *op. cit.*, p. 28.
50. *CWMG*, Volume XXV, pp. 124-25.
51. Tendulkar, D.G., *op. cit.,* Volume VIII, p. 228.
52. Gandhi, M.K., *Hind Swaraj*, *op. cit.*, p. 83.
53. *Ibid.*, p. 81.
54. *CWMG*, Volume XXX, p. 414.
55. *Harijan,* 5-9-1936. pp. 236-37.
56. *CWMG*, Volume XVIII, p. 133.
57. *Harijan*, 12-11-1938, p. 326.
58. Raghavan Iyer, *op. cit.*, p. 40.
59. M.K. Gandhi, *An Autobiography*, p. x (Preface).
60. *CWMG*, Volume XLVIII, p. 51.
61. Michael Curtis, *Comparative Government and Politics: An Introductory Essay in Political Science*, New York, Harper & Row, 1968, p. 1.
62. Harold D. Lasswell, *Politics: Who Gets What, When and How*, New York, McGraw Hill Book Co., Inc., 1936.
63. *CWMG*, Volume XLVII, p. 91.
64. *Ibid.*, pp. 91-92.
65. *Harijan*, 28-4-1946, p. 112.
66. Tendulkar, D.G., *op. cit.*, Volume VIII, p. 229.

67. *CWMG*, Volume XLVI, p. 108.
68. M.K. Gandhi, *Nonviolence in Peace and War*, Ahmedabad, Navajivan Publishing House, 1960, Volume 11, pp. 379-81.
69. *CWMG*, Volume LXXI, p. 244.
70. Tendulkar, D.G., *op. cit.*, Volume VIII, p. 230.
71. *Harijan*, 18-1-1942, p. 5.
72. *Ibid.*, 30-12-1939, p. 391.
73. *Ibid.*, 27-5-1939, p. 143.
74. *Tendulkar*, D.G., Volume VI, p. 96.
75. *CWMG*, Volume XXV, p. 315.
76. *Harijan*, 18-1-1948, p. 519.
77. *Young India*, 29-1-1925, pp. 40-41.
78. *Harijan*, 11-1-1936, p. 380.
79. *Ibid.*, 18-1-1942, p. 4.
80. *Ibid.*, 28-7-1946, p. 236.
81. Jai Narain Sharma, *Gandhi's View of Political Power*, New Delhi, Deep and Deep, 1987, p. 81.

4

Concept of Politics

Between men and animals, there are various differences: some intellectual and some emotional. One of the chief emotional differences is that some human desires, unlike those of animals, are essentially boundless and incapable of complete satisfaction.[1] Usually animals are satisfied with existence and reproduction, men cherish unlimited desires. Of the infinite desires of man, the chief are desires for power and glory. It is often observed that even when man's material needs have been satisfied, his pursuit of power does not end. Thomas Hobbes considered desire for power the well-spring of human behaviour. In his own words: "I put for general inclination of all mankind, a perpetual and restless desire of power that ceaseth only in death."[2] And for this urge there is indeed no rest but proceedings.

The question of power has assumed particular importance both in the realm of theory and practical politics. Political theorists in recent times have articulated the universal impulse to power to an extent that is unprecedented. The meaning of political science has changed from one of being a study of state and government to that of being a study of power. As Michael Curtis puts it: "Politics is organised dispute about power and its use involving choice among competing values, ideas, persons, interests and demands. The study of politics is concerned with the description analysis of the manner in which power is obtained, exercised, and controlled, the purpose for which it is used, the manner in which decisions made, and factors which influence the making of those decisions, a context in which those decisions take place."[3] Power remains the axis around which the social common weal spins. "All politics," says Hans Morgenthau, "is a struggle for power".[4] Whatever may ultimate aims of politics, power is always the immediate aim. Statesman and the people alike may ultimately seek freedom, security, or progress. They may define their goals in terms of religious, philosophic, economic or social ideals. But whenever they strive to realize their goal by means of politics, they do so by striving for power.

George Catlin evolved a systematic theory of a conceptual framework for political science in which power is placed at the centre. Politics is regarded as "the study of Government," if Government meant control. Catlin adopts Max Weber's definition of politics as "the struggle of or the influencing of those in power". The field of political science, according to him, "is the field of study of social control, or more specific the central relationship of human, and even animal, wills".[5] 'Politicisation' by which he means "the extension of the approach by study of distinctive political function of control in areas other than civil dominion" and the use of power hypotheses are regarded by Catlin as "perhaps the two revolutionary changes in political science in recent years which have seriously affected the nature of political science."[6]

We had to wait for Harold Lasswell and Abraham Kaplan to find the most detailed analysis of this subject. "The concept of power", they write, "is perhaps the most fundamental in the whole of political science: the political process is the shaping, distribution and exercise of power".[7] Lasswell quotes with approval the views of Catlin that "politics as a theoretical study is concerned with the relations of men, in association and competition, submission and control, in so far as they seek not the violent production and consumption of some articles but to have their way with their fellows...What men seek in their political negotiation is power."[8]

The attempt to study and explain politics by analysing relations of power is not only modern, but ancient too. Aristotle explained political systems according to their internal distribution of power. The difference in the location of power, authority, or rule among the citizens of a political society served as one criterion for differentiating among actual constitutions, and it entered into his distribution between good constitutions and bad ones. Kautilya, in his *Arthashastra* gives a vivid account of what a king should also to acquire, increase and retain political power. Machiavelli instructed his prince how to seize and secure power. Hobbes considered the desire for power the well-spring of human behaviour. Marx argued that political power inevitably accrues to the economically dominant class. But with few exceptions political theorists did not press their investigations very far into certain aspects of power that have seemed important to political scientists in the twentieth century.

One thing becomes absolutely clear from the above discussion that politics has become a game of acquiring power. All those who enter politics, work for more and more power. Harold Lasswell has rightly titled his book as *Politics: Who Gets What, When, and How*?[9]

One fundamental fact about the nature of power is that it "tends to corrupt and absolute power tends to corrupt absolutely"—Lord John Emerich Edward Dalberg Acton wrote this maxim about power in a letter to Bishop Mandell Creigton of London on 5 April 1887. He further wrote: "Great men are almost bad men, even when they exercise influence and not authority: still more when you super add the tendency of the certainty of corruption by authority. There is no worse heresy than that the office sanctifies the holder of it."[10] It would be easy to say simply that power itself does not corrupt, although it may be used for corrupt or immoral ends. Few would deny that where power is used to limit or to enslave the human spirit, it does, in fact, corrupt both: those who exercise it as well as their victims. One thinks of the long recital of such abuses in the Old Testament, one thinks of the seizure of Troy and slaughter of its inhabitants and the atrocities committed by Mahmud Ghazani and so on. There are other innumerable examples of this type in human history which is full of countless wars among nations, creeds, classes which have brought death and desolation to millions in nearly every country and continent in the world.

Even if this is considered as the extreme, there is no doubt that power has a strong tendency to corrupt its holder. Hunt for power is the root cause of competition among the individuals. Interests collide in the race to acquire more and more power and, for this sake, the probability of corrupt practices cannot be ruled out. Gandhi himself was suspicious of all the power and rejected the normal notion of it. He was of the view that all political institutions were instrument for the pursuit of power, whether directly or indirectly. A few days before his assassination he said at a prayer meeting: "I indeed wonder, if we can remain free from the fever of politics or bid for power, which afflicts the political world, the East and the West."[11]

Two conclusions can be safely drawn from the above discussion. One, that politics is the game to acquire more and more power, and the other, that power usually corrupts its holder.

BEYOND POWER FOR POWER'S SAKE

Though power has always been what matters most in politics, it does not follow that there is some immutable law of nature which says that power is always the ultimate aim of politics. The assertions that all politics is struggle for power or that politics is the game of power that do not hold good in every case. A microscopic study can show that there are countless persons in the human history who remained in politics but their aim was not to acquire power. Rather power can be used for the good of the society. Power does not enslave but liberates also. One thinks of uses of power in ancient times to create the glorious cultures of Maurya and Gupta regimes and the grandeur that was India. One thinks of public schools, highways, hospitals, playgrounds and all types of public services made possible only by the use of political power.

Coming to Gandhi, as a political thinker and politician he challenged this very notion of power politics which has acquired in the modern world the kind or importance and autonomous character that some medieval philosophers gave to the universal essences which they believe to constitute reality.

Gandhi was not a career politician. He did not enter politics to gain political power. He was prepared to opt in and out of political arena. Such an unconventional political ambition and lack of commitment to constant political involvement implied a challenge to the basic assumptions of power politics.

The political experience in *satyagraha* that Gandhi conducted in South Africa and later on in India constituted a total challenge to the conventional power politics. If his techniques repudiated anything very clearly, it was the need for a conventional power criterion in the political struggle. The traditional patterns of political behaviour are altered in his politics. His technique of *satyagraha*, since the beginning of its evolution in South Africa during 1906-1914, has had valuable evidence on this matter. When Gandhi found that General Smuts did not implement the agreement in 1913, he planned a protest march of the *satyagrahis* from Durban on 1 January, 1914. The plan was in preparation, and all efforts were being made to make it a success. In the meanwhile, Gandhi went to Pretoria with C.F. Andrews. But the Union Railways made the position of the government extremely delicate. Gandhi was faced with a potential dilemma. It was open for him to bargain with his opponent, when he was in difficulty by exploiting his weakness as was usually done in the conventional power politics. Here was an excellent opportunity waiting for him. In fact, Gandhi admitted in his *satyagraha* in South Africa that some of his colleagues urged him to take advantage of the situation. But he was guided by the ethics of his nonviolent technique alone which required that he should not press his demands at a time when the government was confronting a genuine difficulty. He resisted all types of pressures from his colleagues and decided to postpone the contemplated march. He wrote about this decision: "But I declared that Indians could not thus assist the railway strikers, as they were not out to harass the Government, their struggle being entirely different and differently conceived. Even if we undertook the march we would begin it at some other time when the railway trouble had ended." This is the difference between Gandhi's techniques based on nonviolence and the other techniques based on power politics. The working of the nonviolent technique is not affected by the consideration of power. This decision, was greatly appreciated by the Britishers.

This gesture of cordiality amidst an acute conflict evoked a natural response from the adversaries. "This decision of ours", Gandhi added, "created a deep impression, and was cabled to England by Reuter." Lord Ampthill cabled his congratulations from England...One of the secretaries of General Smuts jocularly said: "I do not like your people, and do not care to assist them at all. But what am I to do? You help us in our days of need. How can we lay hauls upon you? I often wish you took to violence like the English strikers, then we would know how to dispose of you. But you will not injure even the enemy. You desire victory by self-suffering alone and never transgress your self-imposed limits or courtesy and chivalry. And that is what reduces us to sheer helplessness."[12] Here is a testimony from the enemy about the impact of the nonviolent technique. The adversary was not humbled or outwitted but converted the idea behind it is not to destroy or harass the opponent, but to convert him or win him over by sympathy, patience and self-suffering. Even when the Smuts-Gandhi agreement embodying the substantial acceptance of the demands of the Indian settlers in South Africa was signed on 30 January, 1914, Gandhi was urged by his associates to press for more demands. But he declined this plea as it would be contrary to the spirit of *satyagraha*. Referring to this question Gandhi wrote in the *Indian Opinion* of 11 February, 1914: "It needs to be understood, once and for all, that the path of truth is not meant for ends not consistent with truth. It is our belief that raising our demands will amount to untruthfulness."[13] And this rare spirit is usually uncommon to power politics.

During the Ahmedabad Mill strike in 1917, when certain workers suggested to increase the demands beyond 35 per cent hike in wages, he refused to do so, saying: "I say you can demand even a 100 per cent increase. But it would be unjust if you do so. Be content in the present circumstances, with what you have demanded, if you ask for more it will pain me. We cannot demand anything unreasonable from anybody."[14]

He reminded the workers of their own shortcomings. When he noticed the signs of their weakening in the face of hardships, he undertook an indefinite fast to demonstrate his readiness to die for their cause. Later on, when the employers yielded, he refused to take full advantage of the situation and press for a complete acceptance of the workers' 'demand'. His stand possibly antagonized a section of the workers for a while, but he pacified them. The conclusion of the struggle embodied the true spirit of *satyagraha* where no advantage was taken from the difficulties of the opponent.

The Gandhian technique, as operated by the Indian National Congress, was marked by a positive rejection of power. When the Congress demonstrated its faith in the nonviolent movement by implementing its programme with unprcedented enthusiasm in 1919-21, the whole seemed to vindicate Gandhi's leadership. Romain Rolland wrote in his biography of Gandhi: "In 1921 Gandhi's power was at its apogee. His authority as a moral leader was vast, and without having sought it, almost unlimited political authority has been placed in his hands."[15] The nonviolent cooperation movement was thoroughly shaken by the tragedy of Chauri Chaura in February 1922, when mob violence claimed many lives. The technique of Gandhi was again on the horns of a dilemma. If Gandhi was keen on attaining power, he could have continued the movement despite the happenings in Chauri Chaura. In view of the mounting popular participation, he might not have been deterred by usual norms, from the course he took, as an unquestioned leader of his people. But Gandhi immediately suspended the non-cooperation movement after the Chauri Chaura incident, and made a public confession of his mistake. Writing in *Young India* of 16 February, 1922, he explained his unexpected move: "Suspension of mass civil disobedience and subsidence of excitement are necessary for further progress, indeed indispensable to prevent further retrogression. I hope, therefore, that by suspension every Congressman or woman will not feel disappointed but he or she will feel relieved of the burden of unreality and of national sin."[16] The nonviolent movement of 1930 was also withdrawn in 1932-34. The withdrawal of a political movement when it was deviating from the main principle was basic to Gandhi's notion of politics without power. And this notion brought for him more and more power. Time and again he went on rejecting the conventional notion of power politics and political power went on concentrating around him.

Gandhi took over the control of the Congress in Nagpur in December 1920 and he maintained it as a well oiled political machine with varying degree of success right till the end of his life in January 1948. Right from 1920 onwards, the Congress began to preach its doctrines and a large number of Congressmen accepted Gandhi not merely as apolitical leader but also as a religious preceptor.

His position did not depend on holding any office in any organization, not even in the Congress. To be the President of the Congress was no great achievement for him. He had virtually controlled the organizational structure of the Congress long before its session at Belgaum in December 1924, when he formally accepted the role of President. Repeatedly he refused to become the President of the Congress and gave this to some of his colleagues and lieutenants. He even resigned from the primary membership of the Congress in 1934 and, thereafter, wielded no formal authority on it except that was delegated to him for specific purposes.

As stated earlier, Gandhi was not a career politician, anxious for continuing power. He was prepared to opt in and out of the political activity as conditions and circumstances changed. His retirement from the Congress in 1934 was an emphatic assertion that he would lead only when he felt he could do so on his own terms. Such unconventional political ambitions and lack of commitment to constant political involvement is a challenge to the modern concept of power politics. To take part in politics is not always for gaining power. His conduct in the decision making processes of the Congress, his career in the national movement; and his efforts to control the political forces of the country for the good of the masses amply reveal his view of power. He acquired political power not because this was his aim for participation in politics. But he realised that taking part in politics is an effective means for the service to his people. It was acquired through service, by identifying himself with the lowliest in the country and by rising above his own self-interest. In December 1947, he told his colleagues, the members of the Hindustani Talimi Sangh: "By abjuring power and by devoting ourselves to pure and selfless service of voters, we can guide and influence them. It would give us more real power than we shall have by going into the government."[17]

RELIGIOUS BASIS OF POLITICS

Gopal Krishna Gokhale (1866-1915), the Moderate leader from Maharashtra, who is sometimes regarded by his admirers as the Indian Gladstone, although only three years senior to Mahatma Gandhi, was venerated by the latter as his political Guru. Gandhi wanted, like Gokhale, a spiritualization of politics. Gokhale stressed the incorporation of moral value in politics and this principle was incorporated in the constitution of the Servants of Indian Society. Gandhi also wished to be guided by that message. Like Gokhale, Gandhi was opposed to considering politics as a pastime. For him politics was the pathway to the service of God. But Gandhi's attachment to the concept of non-violence was far deeper and more extensive than that of Gokhale.

Gandhi pointed out that the lives of Buddha and Christ were inspired by the synthesis of active work and deep love. It is not correct to interpret Buddha and Christ as immersed solely in contemplation and illumination because they had great interest in society. He wrote in an article entitled "Neither a Saint nor a Politician":

> "What was the larger 'symbiosis' that Buddha and Christ preached ? Gentleness and love. Buddha fearlessly carried the war into the enemy's camp and brought down on its knees an arrogant priesthood. Christ drove out the moneychangers from the temple of Jerusalem and drew down curses from heaven upon the hypocrites and the Pharisees. Both were for intensely direct action. But even as Buddha and Christ chastized, they showed unmistakable gentleness and love behind every act of theirs."[18]

Gandhi claimed to adopt a religious attitude to political problems. He wrote:

> "But though by disclaiming sainthood I disappoint the critic's expectations, I would have him give up his regrets by answering him that the politician in me has never dominated, a single decision

> of mine, and if I seem to take part in politics, it is only because politics encircle us today like the coil of a snake from which one cannot get out, no matter how much one tries. I wish, therefore, to wrestle with the snake, as I have been doing with more or less success consciously since 1894, unconsciously, as I have now discovered, ever since, reaching years of discretion. Quite selfishly, as I wish to live in peace in, the midst of a bellowing storm howling round me, I have been experimenting with myself and friends by introducing religion into politics. Let me explain what I mean by religion. It is not the Hindu religion which I certainly prize above all other religions, but the religion which transcends Hinduism, which changes one's very nature, which binds one indissolubly to the truth within and which ever purifies. It is the permanent element in human nature which counts no cost too great in order to find expression and which leaves the soul utterly restless, until it has found itself, known its Maker and appreciated the true correspondence between the Maker and itself."[19]

A religious life, thus, means a purified and chastened life and such a life is bound to have immense social and political impact. Religions are meant to tame our savage nature. They aim to suppress the beastly in man and to enshrine his spiritual and moral will. The victory of Rama over Ravana is a symbol of the conquest of physical power by spiritual strength. Thus Gandhi wanted the religious spirit to flourish which means a recovery of divine faith and the consequent purification of motives and conduct. It implies the cooperative adherence to the moral laws of God by the members of society.

Gandhi categorically said that he wanted to bring religion into politics:

> "For me the road to salvation lies through incessant toil in the service of my country and of humanity. I want to identify myself with everything that lives. In the language of the *Gita*, I want to live at peace with both friends and foe. So my patriotism is for me a stage on my journey to the land of eternal freedom and peace. Thus it will be seen that for me there are no politics devoid of religion. They subserve religion. Politics bereft of religion are a death-trap because they kill the soul."[20]

Religion is based on the recognition of the superiority of moral vows. A religious life signifies the dedicated pursuit of these vows.

Hence, corporation of religion in politics means a progressive movement towards the continued and faithful practice of moral vows and love. The central principle of Gandhian political philosophy is that the fundamental religious ethics common to all the religions has to be made concrete in individual, social and political life. It is, hence, opposed to regarding political action as the sphere of the "non-moral". Summarizing his reflections upon life in the last chapter of his Autobiography he wrote:

> "To see the universal and all-pervading spirit of Truth face to face one must be able to love the meanest of creation as oneself. And a man who aspires after that cannot afford to keep out of any field of life. That is why my devotion to Truth has drawn me into the field of politics; and I can say without the slightest hesitation and yet in all humility, that those who say that religion has nothing to do with politics do not know what religion means."[21]

Gandhi also said: "Most religious men I have met are politicians in disguise: I, however, who wear the guise of a politician, am at heart a religious man." Gandhi as a religious soul constantly stressed the sanctity of the purified, truth-oriented inner light which should prevent men from doing in collective life what they would not do to themselves or their family. By the religious basis of politics Gandhi would, hence, mean the supremacy of the concept of the moral right of conscience in place of the divine right of rulers, princes and other ascendant groups. He would never sanction the supremacy of the ecclesiastical pontifs, or the priests or the magicians. Thus his political theory is thoroughly different from that of Gregory VII or Boniface VIII. He is a prophet of the sanctification of the criteria of our action and is not a champion of any Church or a Sangha or a religious tribe.

It is this concept of religion as sanctified dynamic altruism, or *Karmayogi*, that he wanted to make the basis for the transformation of social and political action because he felt that no stable good could be rendered to society unless man purified his own conduct. Religion provided the dynamic impetus to Gandhi's actions as a *Karmayogi*. His political actions and technics followed from his religious world-view. In his letter to Prime Minister Ramsay Macdonald indicating his determination to "fast unto death". If separate electorate was provided for the *Harijans*, Mahatma Gandhi stated "... as a man, of religion that I hold myself to be, I have no other course left open to me." He stated that his proposed fast would be undertaken in fulfilment of a definite philosophy of life that he had been following."

That the religious ethics of piety, forgiveness, meekness, humility and, universal tolerance should influence human action in view of Gandhi. His views, thus, are a challenge to the arrogance of power politicians, some of whom claim infallibility for views and actions. His aim is not to exalt the existing political structures and powers as being ordained and sanctified by God but to them raise them to higher moral planes and thus to correct social and political inadequacies. He is not a champion of the divine right of the holders of political authority but stands for purifying even the structure of politics. Thus it is clear that by emphasizing the religious basis of individual social and political action Gandhi is not teaching any dogmatic, conservative or reactionary gospel.

Thus we see that when Gandhi talked of the religious basis of politics he was not preaching a going back to primitivism or Graeco Roman paganism or Vedic antiquity. He emphasized a life of strenuous dynamic morally-oriented activity in quest of the good of one's soul and mankind and the eradication of wrong and injustice. Gandhi treated political activity as a means of humanitarian service which, in its turn, was a technic of God-realization. Hence politics had to be seriously treated by being rooted in religious vows. He said:

> "Religion is a thing not alien to us it has to be evolved out of us. It is always within us; with some, consciously so, with others quite unconsciously. But it is always there. And whether we wake up this religious instinct in us through outside assistance or by inward growth, no matter how it is done, it has got to be done, if we want to do anything in the right manner, or to achieve anything that is going to persist."

Gandhi had taken to *satyagraha* in South Africa as a matter of religious duty. He was championing resistance to wrong on religious grounds. In his first letter to Tolstoy, Gandhi had stated: "... a law which I and many other considered to be degrading and calculated to unman those to whom it was applicable. I felt that submission to law of this nature was inconsistent with the spirit of true religion."

Furthermore, Gandhi said: "Politics divorced from religion, has absolutely no meaning...Politics are a part of our being; we understand our national institutions. We may do this from our infancy... But we want also the steady light, the infallible light of religious faith."[22]

It is essential to repeat, however, that when Gandhi is referring to the religious bases of politics he is not preaching theocratic dogmatism. He does not have in his mind the possibility of a scholastic crusading politics because too often in the name of religion bloody battles have been fought. By his religious basis of politics one must not understand any replica of the regime of Solomon or of his father David or any system like that of the theocracy of Tibet or the empire of the Incas. In the Hebrew Theocracy, God was regarded as the king of the Jews, the civil and religious authority were one and the same and the enemies of the Jews were regarded as the enemies of God. This theocratic pattern is absolutely different from the Gandhian scheme according to which no state religion is to be tolerated. Gandhi is not referring to the alliance between the temporal and the secular powers. Nor is he advocating the mingling of the sphere of Caesar and the sphere of Christ as was indicated in the doctrine of Caesaro-Papalism held by Justinian and Charlemagne. His theory is also different from Rousseau's Civil Religion.

Gandhi would never sanction any political exploitation of religion because he was not concerned with the growth of organized churches or narrow-minded sects. His sole emphasis was on the, development of loyalty to moral-vows in a serious and dedicated sense. He had supported the Khilafat movement in 1920-22 out of humanitarian and not out of considerations of political bargaining. Gandhi can in no sense be accused of communalism or revivalism. Therefore, some of the critics who would like to level the charge of archaism or revivalism on Gandhi are doing him an injustice. Sometimes it is said that Gandhi, through the non-cooperation movement fought to bolster the medieval and archaic institution of the Caliphate in Turkey. In so doing he provided support to the religious passions of the Indian Muslims. To be fair to Gandhi it must be stated that he supported the Khilafat movement because he felt that Britain had failed to redeem its pledges to the Turks.

Religion is not to be identified with any credal dogmatic theology. Gandhi never wanted the abdication of the rights of conscience at the altar of superstitions. Hence, he never refrained from condemning the weaknesses of organized religions. He denounced untouchability in categorical terms although according to the Sanatanist pandits it is in organic part of Hinduism. He pleads for a cleansing of the structure of society which will result in the elimination of those "gross superstitions and customs which have usurped the place of true religion."

According to Gandhi, the social and political plans for the future India should be constructed on the solid and substantial foundations of true religious consciousness, because religion, being synonymous with personal purification was also an immensely powerful social bond. "Religion binds man to God and man to man."[23] "Religions are not for separating men from one another; they are meant to bind them."[24] The non-violent society of the future which is almost the same as Panchayati Raj or *Ramaraj* will be based on religions. This means that it will be based not merely on territorial loyalty, constitutional allegiance and political attachment but will have the foundation of spiritual consensus. Religion in the sense of philanthropy, forbearances, justice, fraternity, peace and all embracing love can alone be the basis of the continued existence of the world. No social structure can subsist on the basis of force, power or legal obligation alone. It must be rooted in the moral will of the people. Hence Gandhi said: "To try to root out religion itself from society is a wild goose chase. And were such an attempt to succeed, it would mean the destruction of society." The quest of the religious consciousness in this socio-moral sense is the basis of a stable social and political structure.

The religious basis of politics as enunciated by Gandhi signifies the stress on moral values for political action. He aimed to free politics from its Machiavellian implications and like St. Augustine, wanted to base the commonwealth on justice. He wrote:

> "My motive has been purely religious… I could not be leading a religious life unless I identified myself with the whole of mankind; and this I could not do unless I took part in politics. The whole gamut of man's activities today constitutes an indivisible whole. You cannot divide social, political and purely religious work into watertight compartments. I do not know any religion apart from human activity. It provides a moral basis to all other activities which they would otherwise lack, reducing life to a thing of sound and fury, signifying nothing."

While in the political thought of Marsiglio and Hobbes, religion is subordinated to politics, in Gandhian political thought, religious considerations have priority over political considerations. Thus like Plato, Cicero, Kant and Croce, Gandhi championed the priority of moral values in social and political life.

SUPERIORITY OF LOYALTY TO GOD TO POLITICAL LOYALTY

Gandhi believed in the superiority of spiritual authority. He definitely considered the eternal and divine laws of God to be superior to the positive laws of the commonwealth and the state. If a choice had to be made between loyalty to the commands of God as revealed through the intimations of the "inner voice" and loyalty, to the laws of the state, Gandhi would unhesitatingly recommend obedience to the laws of God. The overwhelming majesty of the divine power has pre-eminence in Gandhi's thinking. He emphatically declared in the speech at the inauguration of Benaras Hindu University: "If we trust and fear God, we shall have to fear no one, not Maharaja, not Viceroys, not the detectives, not even King George."[25]

He urged that men should obey God rather than an aggressive imperialism. Loyalty to God whose commands are revealed in the promptings of conscience has a higher obligatory character than loyalty to the political superior. Like Seneca and St. Augustine, he taught the priority of obedience to God to political obedience.

The man who wants to follow a genuinely religious code will be ready to lay down his life for the vindication of the moral laws of God. He will never tolerate any kind of untruth, oppression and exploitation. The religious attitude demands struggle for the vindication of truth and divine laws and not acquiescence in the policy of the holders of authority. Gandhi states that to submit to an unjust law would be "sin". It is also a sin to transgress the divine law. Explaining the divine law he says that it means that (a) one has to suffer pain before he can enjoy pleasure; and (b) one's true self-interest consists in the realization of good of all. Thus obedience to divine law involves the readiness for utter self-sacrifice.[26] Hence Gandhi was deadly opposed to the conservative use of religion for the support of obsolete social customs and irrational political authority. Religion is never to be made an adjunct of social and political power. Hence Gandhi wrote: "It was a sign of religious atrophy to sustain an unjust government that supported an injustice by resorting to untruth and camouflage." Thus Gandhi championed the concept of absolute allegiance to the laws of God which implies the subordination of the political and social loyalties to loyalty to God.[27] His concept of loyalty to God reminds one of the Christian theory of "divided allegiance". The concept of undivided allegiance to the political superior, the omnipotent sovereign, is thoroughly unknown to Gandhism.

The theory of divided allegiance[28] implying the superiority of the obligation to obey God and the intimations of inner conscience, or political obedience, is a monumental contribution of Gandhi to political philosophy. He regarded fearlessness as the key to *swaraj* and stated that a man who realizes his humanity is not afraid of any law except the laws of God. His stress on the religious concept of resistance to unjustified coercive political authority which is a logical corollary to the concept of divided loyalty can act as a great deterrent to the emergence of any totalitarian system because *satyagraha* upon the autonomy of moral will is bound to be an antidote to all types of political tyranny.

There is a far greater element of radicalism in Gandhi than in the old Hindu political writers like Bhisma, Kautilya and Manu. In Gandhi's political thought loyalty to the supreme moral laws of God takes precedence over loyalty to any unjustified imperialistic system. In the political thought of Manu and Sukracharya, on the other hand, an attempt was made to invest the holders of political authority with a religious halo. They pleaded for the deification of the king. But the political thought of Gandhi makes a radical departure from their standpoint because it never ascribes a theological foundation to political governance.

It is absolutely wrong to say that this concept of two-fold loyalty as implied in Gandhi's views would apply only when India had been under British imperialism and is inapplicable in a democratic set-up. To say so is a vulgarization of Gandhism. To Gandhi, truth was perennially uppermost, regardless of the external structure of the state where it had to have its social or political application.

SECULARISM AND POLITICS

Gandhi was a man of profound religious convictions and wanted to incorporate moral values, which are the essence of religion, into politics. But although he wanted to strengthen the religious bases of politics it was in a strictly moral sense. He would not tolerate any privilege to any particular religious group or sect, neither would he discriminate against any group. He would also certainly disfavour an attempt by the state to make men religious in the sense of forcing them to give loyalty to certain creeds and dogmas. He rejected the concept of coercion in the field of religion and earnestly pleaded, for "leaving every individual to follow that form of religion which best appealed to him without any interference from the state." He categorically wanted that "the state should undoubtedly be secular." Neither did he accept the concept of state religion. He wrote:

"I do not believe in state religion even though the whole community had one religion. The state interference would, probably always be unwelcome. Religion was purely a personal matter. There were in reality as many religions as minds. Each mind had a different conception of God from that of the other." He was also opposed to state aid partly or wholly to religious bodies. For he knew that an institution or group, which did not manage to finance its own religious teachings, was a stranger to true religion. "This did not mean that the state schools would not give ethical teachings. The fundamental ethics were common to all religions."[29]

Gandhi accepted the imparting of the teaching of the fundamental moral norms and ideals common to all religions, in educational establishments run or subsidized by the state. He had sponsored such a programme for the Gujarat Vidyapitha which, however, was a private institution. But certainly, he was opposed to the inculcation of denominational and sectarian religious teachings in state institutions. He wrote:

> "I do not believe that the state can concern itself or cope with religious education. I believe that religious education must be the sole concern of religious associations. Do not mix up religion and ethics. I believe that fundamental ethics is common to all religions. Teaching of fundamental ethics is undoubtedly a function of the state. By religion, I do not have in mind fundamental ethics but what goes by the name of denominationalism. We have suffered enough from state-aided religion and a state Church. A society or a group, which depends partly or wholly on state aid for the existence of its religion, does not deserve or, better still, does not have religion worth the name. I do not need, to give any illustrations in support of this truth obvious as it is to me."[30]

Thus it is clear that Gandhi regarded religion as a matter of private judgement. The organized agencies of the state were not to meddle with religious affairs of the people. Hence, he would not agree to the inculcation of religious dogmas by the state. He stressed the necessity of holiness of living and did not relish conversion and proselytism. It is evident that he condemned conversion if impelled by political considerations. He felt that all religions were true but all contained some inadequacies because the religious truths were promulgated by teachers, who, being human beings, were imperfect.

GANDHIAN POLITICS

The interplay of power and moral values is at the centre of the problem of politics, but is usually understood in terms of moralising the conduct of the state. Gandhi was, however, far more interested in challenging the conventional view about the nature and domain of politics in widening the concept of power, and, above all, in destroying the dichotomies between private and public morals, religious values and political norms, ethical principles and political expediency. In the preface to his autobiography, he wrote that his devotion to truth had drawn him into politics, that his power in the political field was derived from his spiritual experiment with himself, and those who say religion has nothing to do with politics, do not know what religion means.[31] He repeatedly insisted that politics could not be isolated from the deepest things of life. He said that when he found himself drawn into the political coil, he asked himself what was necessary to remain untouched by the immorality, untruth and political gains, and decided that a servant of the people must discard all wealth and private possessions.

By this attempt at purification of politics, Gandhi tried to wash out the idea of using politics for personal gains and sharing and exercising power. Political work must ever be looked upon in terms of social and moral progress. When he spoke disparagingly of politics, he referred to the politics of power and regarded it as an overestimated segment of politics as a whole. To him: "Political power is not an end but one of the means of enabling people to better their conditions in every department of life. Political power means capacity to regulate national life through national representation."[32] In his view power should be used for the benefit of humanity. To gain political power should not be an end but the means by which the lot of masses is improved. He added: "When the energy to be spent in gaining that power means so much loss of energy required for the reforms, as threatens to be the case if the country is to engage in a duel with the Mussalmans and Sikhs, I would most decidedly advice the country to let the Mussalmans and Sikhs take all the power and I would go on developing the reforms."[33] Capacity to take political power should be in exact proportion to the ability to achieve success in the constructive efforts. He argued: "It is an illusion to think that MLAs are guides of the voters. Voters do not send representatives to the Assemblies in order to be guided by them. On the contrary, they are sent there loyally to carry out people's wishes. The people are, therefore, the guides not the MLAs. The latter are servants, the former masters". He further stressed: "If we look around the world, we shall find that the best guidance is given by those outside. If that were not so, a rot would set in all governments because the field for the guidance is vast and the Assembly is a very small thing. Parliaments are, after all, a mere drop in the ocean of the national life."[34] Replying to a question of Dr. Zakir Hussain about the need of ideal men to run the ideal society, he said: "We can send men of our choice, without going into the government ourselves. Today, everybody in the Congress is running after power. That presages grave danger. Let us not be in the same cry as power seekers. It is my firm view that we should keep all together aloof from power political and its contagion."[35] When his attention was drawn to the need for acceptance of power, he categorically rejected its acceptance. Writing in *Young India* of 7 May, 1931, he stated: "Office and power must be avoided. Either may be accepted when it is clearly for greater service."[36] He did not rule out the acceptance of office; if it was only meant for a greater cause. It would be then a conditional acceptance of the power. He would not deny the very notion of power as such. Under certain circumstances it might be useful, but it would be a qualified power capable of rendering good to the community.

Gandhi's rejection of power was not only negative, but quite positive also. He was not content merely with advising the Congress to decline power. His vision of a non-political society took a concrete form in the organization of the constructive workers within the national fold of the Congress. He attached the greatest importance to the role of constructive workers. They were not to function merely as subordinates and a secondary group to the predominantly political wing of the Congress. The constructive workers have to discharge a more important duty by remaining outside politics in the Congress. "There shall be no politics in the Sangh", he said, "what is left after eschewing politics is constructive work".[37] Then only the constructive workers could act as a corrective to the political workers in the Congress, and supplement its pre-eminent mission of the independence of India.

When the Congress first decided to accept power in 1937, Gandhi misgivings about this decision bordered on a controversy. It is clear that Gandhi's initial reaction was that Congress should accept office only if it was found to be in the larger interest of the nation. He was reluctant. I advise the Congress to accept power as an end in itself. Gandhi also felt that once the Congress was in office, it might be tempted to abuse power. The record of the Congress governments was not wholly approved by him particularly its resort to force. His objection to political power was not minimized with the establishment of the national government in 1947. He was even more sharply critical of the manipulation of power by the Congress. In his last Testament on 29 January, 1948, Gandhi warned the Congress about the dangers of power politics and solemnly recommended its dissolution as a political party.[38]

Power has a tendency to corrupt its holder. This maxim of Lord Acton need not hold good in every case. Gandhi was himself suspicious of the corrupting aspect of power and wielded immense political power during his lifetime, but not even single critic of him could level any charge that he used that power for his personal benefit. The Indian National Congress was largely his creation, but he never hankered after any official post in its organisation. He became its President only once and never accepted this office again even when it was offered to him. Had he wished to become the President or the Prime Minister of the country after independence in 1947, it would have been a cakewalk for him. His was the most legitimate claim. There was nothing unusual in making such claim. Architects of all great nations accepted the highest office soon after they were victorious. This is very true of those leaders who led a successful revolution and established powerful regimes in their country. George Washington struggled for the independence of America and became its President soon after it got freedom. Same is true about Lenin of the USSR, Mao of China, and Jinnah of Pakistan. But Gandhi was unique amongst all builders of nations. He never thought of accepting any office anywhere.[39]

Thus, it is evident from the above discussion that power is not always the ultimate aim of politics and that power does not always corrupt. We have analysed only one case of Gandhi in support of our conclusion. But this is not the only example. There are many more cases of this nature in human history.

NOTES

1. Bertrand Russell, *Power: A New Social Analysis,* London, George Allen and Unwin, 1957, p. 7.
2. Thomas Hobbes, *Leviathan,* New York, Penguin, 1977, p. 161.
3. Michael Curtis, *Comparative Government and Politics: An Introductory Essay in Political Science,* New York, Harper and Row, 1968, p. 1.
4. Hans J. Morganthau, *Politics among Nations: The Struggle for Power and Peace,* Calcutta, Scientific Book Agency, 1966, p. 27.
5. George, E.G. Catlin, "Political Theory: What in it", in James A. Gould and Vincent V. Thusby (eds.), *Contemporary Political Thought: Issues in Scope, Value and Direction,* Holt, Richard and Winston, 1969, p. 28
6. *Ibid.*, p. 29.
7. Harold D. Lasswell and Abraham Kaplan, *Power and Society: A Framework for Political Inquiry,* New Haven, Yale University Press, 1950, p. 74.
8. George E.G. Catlin, *The Science and Methods of Politics,* New York, Alfred A. Kropt, 1927, pp. 210-11.
9. Harold Lasswell, *Politics: Who Gets What When and How,* New York, McGraw Hill Book Co., 1936.
10. John Emerich, Edward Dulberg Acton, *Essays on Freedom and Power,* London, Thames and Hubon, 1956, pp. 335-36.
11. D.G. Tendulkar, *Mahatma, op. cit.*, Vol. VIII, p. 280.
12. *Ibid.*, p. 295.
13. *CWMG*, Vol. XII, p. 350.
14. *Ibid.*, Vol. XIV, p. 217.
15. Romain Rolland, *Mahatma Gandhi*, Agra, Shiva Lal Aggarwal & Co., 1953.
16. *CWMG*, Vol. XXI, p. 418.
17. D.G. Tendulkar, *Mahatma, op. cit.*, Vol. VIII, p. 228.
18. *Young India*, 12-5-1920, p. 2.
19. *Ibid.*
20. *Ibid.*, 3-4-1924, p. 112.
21. M.K. Gandhi, *An Autobiography, op. cit.*, pp. 377-80.
22. M.K. Gandhi, *Speeches and Writings*, Madras, G.A. Natesan, 3rd ed., p. 162.
23. *Harijan*, 4-5-1940, p. 117.
24. *Ibid.*, 8-6-1940, p. 156.
25. Hingorani (ed.), *op. cit.*, pp. 43-44.
26. *CWMG*, Vol. VII, pp. 121-23.

27. M.K. Gandhi, *Speeches and Writings*, *op. cit.*, p. 380.
28. *CWMG*, Vol. VII, p. 470.
29. *Harijan*, 16-3-1947, p. 62.
30. *Ibid.*, 23-3-1947, p. 76.
31. M.K. Gandhi, *An Autobiography*, *op. cit.*, pp. 377-80.
32. *CWMG*, Vol. XL, p. 91.
33. *Ibid.*, pp. 91-92.
34. *Harijan*, 28-4-1946, p.112.
35. D.G. Tendulkar, *Mahatma*, *op. cit.*, Vol. VIII, p. 229.
36. *CWMG*, Vol. XL, p. 108.
37. *Ibid.*, Vol. XL, p. 244.
38. M.K. Gandhi, *Non-Violence in Peace and War*, Vol. II, *op. cit.*, pp. 392-94.
39. Jai Narain Sharma, 'Power Politics: A Gandhian Alternative', *Gandhi Marg*, A Journal of Gandhi Peace Foundation, New Delhi, September 1986, p. 378.

5

On Democracy

In a somewhat paradoxical vein one can define democracy as something which exists as an ideal but not reality "If we examine not the verbal definitions, that most people, including dictionary makers, give for democracy, but the way in which they use the word in practical application to affairs of our time, we will discover that it does not have anything to do with self-government".[1]

Literally, democracy means 'power of the people' exercised freely. It is, however, just a dictionary meaning.[2] The terms we use stand for something that exists in reality. And when we try to define democracy in reality, we find little resemblance between the facts and the label. So although 'democracy' has precise literal meaning this does not really help us to understand what it actually is.

Demos in the fifth century B.C. of Greece meant the Athenian community gathered in the Ekklesia. The meaning of the term 'demos' has, however, changed drastically across different languages, cultures and nations.[3]

The Italian term *popolo*, as well as its French and German equivalents (*peouple, Volk*) convey the idea of a singular entity, whereas the English word people indicates a plural. In the former case we are easily led to think that *popolo* denoted an organic whole which may be expressed by an indivisible general will, whereas in the latter case it means policracy, a separable multiplicity. Similarly people may mean an approximate plurality, (a great many); an integral plurality, (everybody); an entity or an organic whole; a plurality expressed by an absolute majority; principle; or a plurality expressed by a limited majority principle.[4]

"We can dismiss the first interpretation", writes Giovanni Sartori, "the people understood as the many, because it cannot be used as a criterion, and each case would require separate examination. "We may also dismiss the second, the people understood as everybody, because by this strict standard, no democracy ever has or ever will exist. From the people understood as an organic whole we can infer that each individual counts for nothing; from the idea that the people equals an 'absolute majority' we can conclude that only the majority counts; whereas the limited majority principle comes to mean that even the minority counts."[5]

If the people is understood in the way the romantics suggest, as an organic whole or as a kind of over soul, it is not difficult to see that this approach can justify the most tyrannical rule. In the name of the whole each and all can be crushed one at a time. In fact, no democracy properly called takes the people in organismic, romantic meaning of the term. In practice, democracies break up that compact entity, resort to counting, and are concerned with majorities. A people, understood as the absolute right of the majority to impose its will on the minorities seems, therefore, to be the first and acceptable meaning of the term. Yet it is not quite so assuming that the victorious 51 per cent count for everybody and the losing 49 per cent do not count at all, the winners are in a position to prevent the losers return to power. One can come to the conclusion that only the last meaning of 'people'—while recognising majority rule nevertheless protects minority right—can be regarded as correct interpretation and a working solution. Thus the notion of people fits in a democratic system only if understood in its most elusive technical meaning of requiring majority rule to be limited by minority rights.

The analysis of the meaning of 'people' implies also a problem of historical referents. When the term demokratis was coined, the people concerned were the demos of a Greek polis, a small tightly knit community, operating on the spot as a collective deciding body. Now, when the etymological theory of democracy, so to speak attempts to illustrate tangibly "Who are the people"? What it recalls is the Greek demos, whereas little if any attention is paid to the fact that the larger a polity becomes the less does the concept of people designate real community, and the more does it tend to denote a logical construction, or a logical fiction.

The western world no longer living in polis, and it is living in metropolises and megalopolises. Much of Asia, Africa and to some extent even Latin America, however, still lives in rural communities—the villages. In the West, the loss of rural communities gave rise to the term the 'masses' wherein the identity of the individual and his dignity was lost tomorrow. The term 'masses' became popular in

France during the years between the revolutions of 1830 and 1848, to refer to that part of people which remained absent and external to the political orders. Even Karl Marx in his early writings upto 1844 spoke about masses: it was only through his contacts with French Socialism, that he recasted the concept of both masses and classes into the notion, of proletariat.[6]

The present day world moves at such a great speed that in the brief span of a life one has difficulty in his old age in recognising the world he knew as child. Man has neither the time nor the means to adjust himself to it. It is more so in megalopolises where the pace of change is really astounding. As the European colonial influences enveloped the rest of the world, the community bonds based on natural connective tissues weakened and the society was divided into classes: elites and masses, rich and poor, developed and undeveloped, black and white etc. As the primary group structures became loose, intermediate relations of neighbourhood, occupations, and association got in to unsuccessfully fill in the great emptiness brought by our brave new world. The individual feels lonely, alienated and self-estranged in the west and east alike. In a word, he is rootless that is why there is a need for social integration and socialisation of man and the proper label for the present day society is 'mass society'.[7]

It must be emphasized that a mass man and a mass people are at the antipodes of balanced and orderly society required for government of the people. Kornhauser, among others, has made the point very forcibly. "The psychological type characteristics of mass society provides little support for liberal democratic institutions. The individual seeks to overcome the anxiety accompanying self-alienation by apathy or activism...Thus the mass man is vulnerable to the appeal of mass movements, which offer him a way of overcoming the pain of self alienation."[8] An atomized society can be easily mobilised and manipulated. The mass man is isolated, exposed, and hence available. His behaviour tends to be extreme behaviour, in which activist modes of response and intervention in the political process are the only alternative to apathy. All in all, a mass society is open to charismatic domination and to total mobilization.

The Western theorists of democracy like de Tocqueville, Dicey and Bryce have been concerned with its organisational and juridical aspects. Gandhi, on the other hand, emphasised three basic factors in the democratic theory, which have not received the attention they deserve. The mathematics of Western democracy has been satisfied with the triumph of the fifty-one per cent, but Gandhi was extremely solicitous for the rights of the minority or that matter even an individual. A decision by a majority need not be right. It is the minority which triggered off healthy changes in society in the past. Without going into the details of the procedures and processes of distinguishing right from wrong, he would resort to the criteria of truth and non-violence for judging what is right and wrong rather than what is a arithmetic majority.

Another significant factor in the Gandhian theory of democracy is the emphasis on grassroots institutions. Gandhi did not focus on local autonomy, home rule, financial devolution, etc. But Gandhi was trenchant in his view that democracy essentially meant the conversion of Indian villages into autonomous rural republics with the capacity to satisfy their basic requirements almost independently of any outside agency. He was opposed to the concentration of power in the hands of higher level governments and institutions even if created democratically.

A third element in the Gandhian theory of democracy emanates from the fact that he was very demanding in the pursuit of the moral principles. He would be concerned not merely with the legal aspects of legitimacy but also and more importantly with honest adherence in words as well as spirit. Thus, in his political vocabulary, clever manipulation, hypocritical profession and diplomatic manoeuvres dictated solely by considerations of egoistic self-interest would not have any place. He would condemn all partisanship and would stand for a moral alertness for the vindication of democratic values.

Gandhi was concerned with violence in three contexts: (1) As a subjective norm of inner purification, as the sole antidote to all types of deviant and untruthful duct, and as the only way for the realisation of Truth, which is God. (2) As a means of Indian freedom struggle against the military might of the British empire. Historians and political scientists agreed that non-violent technics were primarily responsible for mobilising that strength in the country, which eventually resulted in the withdrawal of the British power. (3) As group non-violence in the context of communal conflicts. The carnage enacted in Noakhali and Bihar at the time of the partition of the country evoked his deepest anguish and grief. He did regretfully acknowledge that India's non-violence had been that of the weak. The feelings of revenge, jealousy, malice and hatred that were accumulating for the years and decades were manifested in irrational acts of mad communal violence. In this field, Gandhi did acknowledge that his nonviolence had not been a great success although he did refer to the bright examples of some illustrious martyrs who had sacrificed themselves in the fire of communal violence. Yet another (fourth) sector in which nonviolence could have been used on a mass scale but was not experimented with the settlement of the economic problems of the country: landlessness, poverty, inequality, etc. If Gandhi were alive, he would have possibly resorted to *satyagraha* to set these right, as Vinoba Bhave did to secure land for the landless.

The true test of democracy, according to Gandhi, is that it attempts to replace force by social will: "In democracy the individual will was governed and limited by the social will which was the state governed by and for democracy."[9] Democracy and violence cannot be reconciled. Nonviolence as positive love implies the thorough elimination of distrust and suspicion of the political opponents. Gandhi stressed that nonviolence alone could lead to true democracy. He even went to the extent of defining democracy as the rule of unadulterated nonviolence and insisted on recognising nonviolence as a living political bond. The true democrat defends his personal freedom, the national freedom and the freedom of mankind through the means of nonviolence.[10]

In Gandhi's scheme of things, military and police force was a dangerous antithesis to the free growth of the soul and hence it will "be a poor democracy that depends for its existence on military assistance." There is a radical incompatibility between the evolution of democracy and the dependence upon the police and the army. That did not mean that India of the future would necessarily do away with the army and accept complete nonviolence. Nonetheless he stood for progressive approximation to the true democracy without violence.

CRITIQUE OF WESTERN PARLIAMENTARY DEMOCRACY

Hind Swaraj contains Gandhi's indictment of the British parliamentary practices and procedures. To quote him:

> "That which you consider to be the Mother of Parliaments is like a sterile woman and a prostitute. Both these are harsh and unparliamentary words which he later expressed his desire to withdraw but exactly fit the case. Since the Parliament had not of its own accord, done a single good thing, he compared it to a

> sterile woman. It is like a prostitute because it is under the control of ministers who change from time to time.
>
> "...as a matter of fact, it is generally acknowledged that the members are hypocritical and selfish. Each thinks of his own little interest. It is fear that is the guiding motive.... When the greatest questions are debated, its members have been seen to stretch themselves and to doze. Sometimes the members talk away until the listeners are disgusted. Carlyle has called it the 'talking shop of the world'. Members vote for their party without a thought. Their so-called discipline binds them to it....Parliament is simply a costly toy of the nation.
>
> "...they (the Prime Ministers) cannot be considered really patriotic....I do not hesitate to say that they have neither real honesty nor a living conscience.
>
> "If India copies England, it is my firm conviction that she will be ruined."[11]

Unfortunately India chose to copy England. Only the spirit of Gandhi can now to take to the genuine path of democracy.

Gandhi wrote to Maganlal Gandhi on April 2, 1910:

> "It is very difficult to get rid of our fondness for Parliament. It was no doubt barbarous when people tore off the skin, burned persons alive and cut off their ears or nose; but the tyranny of Parliament is much greater than that of Chengiz Khan, Tamerlane and others... Modern tyranny is a trap of temptation and, therefore, does greater mischief. One can withstand the atrocities committed by one individual as such; but it is difficult to cope with the tyranny perpetrated upon a people in the name of the people....The common man in India at last believes that the Parliament is a hoax."[12]

These views on British Parliament apart, Gandhi being a practical idealist devoted his whole life to the attainment of Parliamentary Swaraj in India (*Young India*, 26 January, 1921). The compulsion of the given stage of the nationalist struggle dictated him to take up this position. Without being unmindful of the basic malady of parliamentary democracy. In 1925, he wrote: "The peoples of Europe have no doubt political power but no *swaraj*. Asian and African races are exploited for their partial benefit, and they, on their part, are being exploited by the ruling class or caste under the sacred name of democracy."[13]

Again he wrote in 1938, "Democracy of the West is, in my opinion, only so-called. It has germs in it, certainly of the true type. But it can only come when all violence is eschewed and malpractices disappear. The two go hand in hand. Indeed malpractice is a species of violence. If India is to evolve the true type, there should be no compromise with violence or untruth."[14] Stressing on nonviolence as the soul of democracy, he wrote: "Democracy and violence cannot go together. The states that are today nominally democratic have either to become frankly totalitarian or, if they are to become truly democratic, they must become courageously non-violent."[15] While writing these, Gandhi had western democracies in views.

"The democracies, therefore, that we see at work in England, America and France are only so-called, because they are no less based on violence than Nazi Germany, Fascist Italy or even Soviet Russia. The only difference is that the violence of the last three is much better organized than that of the three democratic powers. Nevertheless we see today a mad race for outdoing one another in the matter of armaments. And if, when the clash comes, as it is bound to come one day, the democracies win, they will do so only because they have the backing of their peoples who imagine that they have a voice in their own government, whereas in the other three cases the peoples might rebel against their own dictatorships."[16]

An American journalist trekked to Sevagram in April 1940 for an interview with Gandhi which was in the form of questions and answers.

Q. "Why do you say that democracy can only be saved through non-violence?"

A. "Because democracy, so long as it is sustained by violence, cannot provide for or protect the weak. My notion of democracy is that under it the weakest should have the same opportunity as the strongest. That can never happen except through nonviolence. No country in the world today shows any but patronizing regard for the weak. The weakest, you say, go to the wall. Take your own case. Your *lama* is owned by a few capitalist owners. The same is true of South Africa. These large holdings cannot be sustained except by violence, veiled if not open. Western democracy, as it functions today, is diluted Nazism or Fascism. At best it is merely a cloak to hide the

Nazi and the Fascist tendencies of imperialism. Why is there the war today if it is not for the satisfaction of the desire to share the spoils? It was not through democratic methods that Britain bagged India, What is the meaning of South African democracy? Its very constitution has been drawn to protect the white man against the coloured man, the natural occupant. Your own history is perhaps blacker still, in spite of what the Northern States did for the abolition of slavery. The way you have treated the Negro presents a discreditable record. And it is to save such democracies that the war is being fought ! There is something very hypocritical about it."[17]

We make no apology for reproducing a rather longish excerpt, for this statement of Gandhi is a document of much significance since it contains the basic grounds of his opposition to the so-called Democracies.

Gandhi told Louis Fischer when he visited him in June 1942:

> "I see no difference between the Fascist or Nazi powers and the Allies. All are exploiters, all resort to ruthlessness to the extent required to compass their end. America and Britain are very great nations but their greatness will count as dust before the bar of dumb humanity, whether African or Asiatic....They have no right to talk of human liberty and all else unless they have washed their hands clean of the pollution.... Then but not till then, will they be fighting for a new order."[18]

In a conversation held in 1940 (Mahadev Desai's report) he unequivocally stated: "The European Democracies are to my mind a negation of democracy."

Gandhi's indictment of Western democracies was based on three fundamental counts: (a) exploitation of the weak 'by a few capitalist owners'; (b) expansion of capitalism resulting in the exploitation of the weaker peoples; (c) white racialism.

To Gandhi exploitation and violence are indistinguishable. He could very well comprehend the fundamental contradictions of modern age. It was indeed his genius that was needed, to pierce the outer shells of Western democracies and expose violence in its nakedness. We use the word 'genius' deliberately because his was the lone voice of political prudence and maturity in an otherwise highly confused scenario. While the pronouncedly progressive forces in and outside the country, the, official Congress leadership not excluded, were busy rationalizing the distinction between the fascia or Axis powers and democratic or Allied powers, he was the only political leader who could expose the basic coercive character of capitalist democracy. It may not be irrelevant here to refer to the formulation made round about that time by the professedly most advanced and radical force of the world, viz. the Communist International. According to Manuilsky, one of the top leaders of the Communist Party of Soviet Union as well as of the Communist International:

> "The growing menace of world imperialist war is causing all ciass, national and state forces to separate into two camps: the camp of war and the camp of peace. The centre of forces which are operating to bring about war, to accelerate its outbreak is FASCISM; in Europe the most reactionary and aggressive form of Fascism exists in Hitlerite Germany. In Asia, it is in military-fascist Japan....Italy stands fully armed..."[19]

This logic led the official world communist movement to brand fascism as the 'greater enemy' and imperialism as the 'lesser enemy' which culminated in a broad peace front composed of Communists and the 'democratic' imperialists. The history of transformation of 'peace front to people's war' and then to 'People's Age' is the history of unabashed betrayal of the fundamental interests of the colonial peoples and the working men of capitalist countries wearing the label of democracy. Incidentally, this appraisal of the world situation in characterizing imperialist powers as 'democratic' violates the fundamentals of international socialism as propounded by Marx, Engels and Lenin. The military-diplomatic alliance between the Soviet Union and the capitalist democracies of Britain, France and America was presented as the camp of peace. In the words of Stalin:

> "It may now be considered indisputable that in the course of war imposed upon the United Nations by Hitlerite Germany a radical demarcation of forces and the formation of two opposite camps has taken place—the camp of the Italo-German coalition and the camp of the Anglo-Soviet-American coalition."[20]

So there appeared to the world Communist movement and all the units owing allegiance to the Communist International a radical or qualitative change in the character of 'democratic' imperialism. Objective analysis of the basic character of imperialism-capitalism was tabooed; independent judgement was declared a heresy. The fundamental characteristics of the imperialist democracies, allegedly turned 'prisoners in the people's camp', were ignored and the injunction was issued that in order to defeat fascism, criticism of 'democratic' powers was to be suspended not to speak of organized action of the peoples against them. In such a situation, Gandhi, while remaining indifferent to the theoretical niceties of social dynamics, could, by his incisive political insight, easily get at the root of the problem. Therein lay the superiority of his political acumen. Unlike the 'progressives' who branded him a 'social reactionary' and 'an agent of the Indian capitalists', Gandhi was uninhibited in his outlook and thinking. That dogma-free attitude enabled him to look at world affairs in a clear perspective while the 'vanguards' sang to the tunes set by the bandmaster at 'the citadel of world revolution'.

VIEWS ON INSTITUTIONAL BASIS OF DEMOCRACY

The fundamental institution on which the parliamentary system of government is based is that of periodic elections. In fact, elections have become the linchpin on which the entire constitutional apparatus of parliamentary government hangs. The enormous importance given to elections tends to equate democracy with the majority rule. In effect, this so-called, majority rule is only the rule of a minority. Under a system of franchise as we have in India or in Great Britain, it is possible for a government to command a majority in the Parliament on the basis of minority votes. It is an unavoidable adjunct of the present system. Even taking for granted that a genuine majority rule, *i.e.*, the rule of 51 per cent, of the electorate is established, can it be equated with genuine democracy? Gandhi's concept of democracy was not limited to formal adherence to the external mechanism of the parliamentary type of government. His approach was essentially moral. He did not believe in the priority of political mechanism to one's own conscience.

In 1920, he wrote: "...in matters of conscience the Law of Majority has no place."[21]

The next year he commented: "Let us not push the mandate theory to ridiculous extremes and become slaves to resolutions of majorities. That would be a revival of brute force in a more virulent form. If rights of minorities are to be respected, the majority must tolerate and respect their opinion and action... It will be the duty of the majority to see to it that minorities receive a proper training and are not otherwise exposed to insults, *swaraj* will be an absurdity if individuals have to surrender their judgment to majority."[22]

Individual freedom, according to Gandhi, is the essence of democracy.

> "The rule of majority has a narrow application, *i.e.*, one should yield to the majority in matters of detail. But it is slavery to be amenable to the majority no matter what its decisions are....Democracy is not a state in which people act like sheep. Under democracy, individual liberty of opinion and action is jealously guarded. I, therefore, believe that the minority has a perfect right to act differently from the majority..."[23]. (*Young India*, 2.3.22)

Gandhi's democratic government was not based on the coercion of even a minority but on the conversion of it. In his opinion, the rule of majority, when it becomes coercive, is as intolerable as that of a bureaucratic minority.[24] Further elaborating his views he said in 1944:

> "The way of approaching a question is not to examine the numerical strength of those behind the opinion, but to examine the soundness of opinion on merits, or also we will never reach a solution, and if we reach one, it will be a blind solution, simply because it is the wish of the largest body. If the largest body goes wrong, it is up to me to say you are wrong and not to submit."
> "The rule of majority does not mean that it should suppress the opinion of even an individual, if it is sound. Opinion of an individual should have greater weight than the opinion of many, if that opinion is sound on merits. That is my view of real democracy."[25]

It is clear that Gandhi did not have a high regard for the quantitative principle of democracy. On the other hand, he attached the highest importance to quality irrespective almost of quantity. As a believer in the first principle of moral rectitude of the individual, he asked "not to be cowed down by the thought of a small minority."[26] For to be in a minority is sometimes a privilege and he would rather love to be in the minority of one. Gandhi's life shows that he literally lived the life of 'a minority of one' and ploughed a lonely furrow for the vindication of the principle he thought to be true.

Hind Swaraj records that elections as the mechanism of determining the will of the people did not appeal to Gandhi. He moderated his views later. Voicing the demands of the Indian people for the inauguration of a democratic political system, he wrote in *Young India*[27] that by *swaraj* he meant "the government of India by the consent of the people as ascertained by the largest number of the adult population". A democrat in the true sense of the term, he wanted the elementary political right for the people.

In 1931, he declared: "I am wedded to adult suffrage.... I cannot possibly bear the idea that a man who has got wealth should have the vote but that a man who has got character but no wealth" or "literacy should have no vote, or that a man who works honestly by the sweat of his brow day in and day out should not have the vote for the crime of being a poor man."[28]

In 1940, he wrote: "If independence is born nonviolently all the component parts will be, voluntarily interdependent working in perfect harmony under a representative central authority which will derive its sanction from the confidence reposed in it by the component parts." The central power, he added, would be based on "universal suffrage exercised by a disciplined and politically intelligent electorate."[29]

Again in 1947: "As to the franchise, he swore by the franchise of all adults, male and female, above the age of twenty-one or even eighteen. He would bar old men like himself. They were of no use as voters....Thus he would have a bar against persons beyond a certain age, say fifty, as he would against youngsters below eighteen."[30]

Along with adult franchise, or even before that, he would have universal education, not necessarily literary, except perhaps as an aid. We have seen above that in *Hind Swaraj* Gandhi was not favourably disposed towards the party system. He maintained this point of view during the rest of his life. A question may be raised: Why did he then associate himself with the Indian National Congress? It should be noted here that the Indian National Congress, in the pre-independence days, was not a political party in the sense a party is understood to function. A heterogeneous organization like the Congress was more of a broad political anti-imperialist platform rather than an agency of coming to power through normal constitutional channels. It was more of a movement than a party-political machine. As we have observed earlier, Gandhi did not struggle for power as an end in itself; it was for him a means of rendering service to the people of investing them with authority. A few days before the meeting of the All India Congress Committee in November 1947, Gandhi mooted the idea that the political goal of the Congress having been achieved with the attainment of independence, the Congress ought to liquidate itself voluntarily.[31] Because of the changed character of the Congress, turned a party of the ruling capitalist class of India since independence, Gandhi could carry nobody with him in that direction. The day before he was assassinated, he outlined his ideas on the reconstitution of the Congress in a draft plan, which subsequently came to be known as his 'Last Will and Testament'. The preamble of the draft ran: "Though split into two, India having attained political independence through means devised by the Indian National Congress, the Congress in its present shape and form, as a propaganda vehicle and a parliamentary machine, has outlived its use. India has still to attain social, moral and economic independence in terms of its seven hundred thousand villages as distinguished from its cities and towns....For these and similar reasons, the A.I.C.C. resolves to disband the existing Congress organization and flower into a Lok Sevak Sangh." The idea conveyed here suggests that he wanted power as a means of service, and not as an end in itself.

Since Gandhi had to operate within a given concrete historical situation, his corporate or political activities were directed towards which ultimately paved the way for the creation of a national democratic state order. He was alive to this development. But so far as his theoretical concept was concerned, he did not move from his original position. The following excerpt from a conversation with Louis Fischer will bear this out:

"I realize that despite my views there will be a central government administration. However, I do not believe in the accepted Western form of democracy with its universal voting for parliamentary representatives."

"What would you have India do?" Fischer asked.

"There are seven hundred thousand villages in India. Each would be organized according to the will of its citizens, all of them voting. Then there would be seven hundred thousand votes and not four hundred million. Each village, in other words, would have one vote. The villages would elect their district administrations, and the district administrations would elect the provincial administrations, and these in turn would elect a president who would be the national chief executive."

"That is very much like the Soviet system," Fischer said.

"I did not know that," Gandhi admitted. "I don't mind."[32]

Pursuing the discussion further Gandhi reminded Fischer, "Parliamentary democracy is not immune to corruption."[33]

It may be pointed out here that at the Round Table Conference, Gandhi suggested indirect election through the Panchayats.

Gandhi had his own concept of representative democracy backed by a non-violent sanction. In an interview with Gandhi a few days before his death, Mr. Vincent Sheen asked: "If those who believe in the ideal of nonviolence keep away from government, government will continue to be carried on by the use of force. How is then the transformation of the existing government to be brought about?"

Gandhi admitted that ordinarily government was impossible without the use of force. "I have, therefore, said that a man who wants to be good and do good in all circumstances must not hold power."

"Is all government to come to a standstill then?" Mr. Sheen asked, "No," Gandhi replied. "The man of nonviolence can send those to the government who represent his will. If he goes there himself he exposes himself to a corrupting influence of power. But my representative holds power of attorney only during my pleasure. If he falls prey to temptation, he can be recalled. I cannot recall myself. All this requires a high degree of intelligence on the part of electorate. There are about half a dozen constructive work organizations. I do not send them to the parliament. I want them to keep parliament in check by educating and guiding the voters."

"You mean to say that power always corrupts."

"Yes," said Gandhi "emphatically."[34]

Gandhi wanted to evolve political system suited to the genius of the Indian people. He told Fischer: "I do not think that a free India will function like the other countries of the world. We have our own forms to contribute. And that form was Village Swaraj or Panchayati Raj or in plain English, democracy from the below. True democracy cannot be worked by twenty men sitting at the centre. It has to be worked from below by the people of every village."[35] Before outlining his concept of Village Swaraj let us proceed to consider the Gandhian concept of the foundations of democracy.

FOUNDATIONS OF DEMOCRACY

In a foregoing section on *swaraj*, we have seen that Gandhi believed in the "sovereignty of the people based on pure moral authority". Institutional framework of democracy does not guarantee power to the people. So, that is not enough. "Democracy is an impossible thing until the power is shared by all... Even a pariah, a labourer... will have his share in self-government."[36]

But how to achieve such a democracy? The essence of democracy lies in nonviolence, Gandhi reminds us. In our earlier discussion on his criticism of Western democracies we have seen that his fundamental objection rested on the ground that these nominal democracies were founded on violence. For Gandhi the *swaraj* of the masses, was integrally related to a nonviolent structure of society.

Gandhi held the view that "without the recognition of nonviolence on a national scale there is no such thing as a constitutional or democratic government." It was his conviction that "Science of nonviolence alone can lead one to pure democracy."[37] He stated his belief in no uncertain terms: "True democracy or *swaraj* of the masses can never come through untruthful and violent means, for the simple reason that the natural corollary to their use would be to remove all opposition through the suppression or extermination of the antagonists. That does not make for individual freedom. Individual freedom can have the fullest play only under a regime of an unadulterated *ahimsa*." Addressing the historic August (1942) session of All India Congress Committee, Gandhi reiterated his faith once again that violent means led to the concentration of power in the hands of a few and frustrated the ends of popular revolutions. "I read Carlyle's French Revolution while I was in prison, and Pandit Jawaharlal has told me something about the Russian revolution. But it is my conviction that inasmuch as these struggles were fought with the weapon of violence, they failed to realize the democratic ideal. In the democracy established by nonviolence, there will be equal freedom for all. Everybody will be his own master."[38] And, "...true democracy can only be the outcome of nonviolence. The structure of a world federation can be raised only on a foundation of nonviolence, and violence will have to be totally abjured from world affairs."[39]

Gandhi said in the same speech: "Ours is not a drive for power." So far as Gandhi himself was concerned the statement was more than proven. But for others, namely the leadership of the Congress, it was a different case. He told Dr. Zakir Hussain in December 1947: "Today everybody in the Congress is running after power. Let us not be in the same cry as the power-seekers...but keep altogether aloof from power politics and its contagion. The objective of the constructive work organisations is to generate political power, not to capture it."[40]

This is a key point of Gandhian Political Philosophy. Gandhi had undoubtedly an ethical attitude towards politics, but to dismiss this essential point as moralistic would be to miss the essence of Gandhi. The plea for generating political power has deep-rooted sociological and political significance. This means that power is not to be imposed from above, it has to evolve upwards. And in the Gandhian scheme, dissemination of power is only possible on a nonviolent basis.

For Gandhi democracy was not merely a matter of power-form, he laid much stress on the cultivation of democratic spirit. "I hold that democracy cannot be evolved by forcible methods. The spirit of democracy cannot be imposed from without. It has to come from within."[41] Thus the democracy of Gandhi's, conception: does not demand dead uniformity; toleration is one of the essential basis of such a concept. He wrote in *Harijan*:

> "Evolution of democracy is not possible if we are not prepared to hear the other side. We shut the doors of reason when we refuse to listen to our opponents, or having listened, make fun of them. If intolerance becomes a habit, we run the risk of missing the truth. Whilst, with the limits that nature has put upon our understanding, we must act fearlessly according to the light vouchsafed to us, we must always keep an open mind and be ever ready to find that what we believed to be truth was, after all, untruth. This openness of mind strengthens the truth in us."[42]

Democracy presupposes freedom of thought of the fundamental rights of the individual, the right to freedom of thought and expression, in an ultimate as well as in an instrumental sense. Gandhi accepted this liberal (in its original sense) view of democracy and fostered real freedom of thought in all his activities. But that was not the distinctive note of Gandhi in the history of political theory and action. What marked him off from, other political theorists was his insistence on the means of arriving at Truth, that is to say, on the application of the satyagraha method. Self-suffering, he used to say, is the law of man as violence is the law of the brute. Civilization, he held, consists in the substitution of intoleration and violence by methods of toleration and persuasion wherever conflicts occur in human relations. This attitude of toleration in human relations flows from his philosophical belief of Truth appearing in fragments. "The golden rule of conduct, therefore, is mutual toleration, seeing that we will never all think alike and we see Truth in fragment and from different angles of vision. Conscience is not the same thing for all. Whilst, therefore, it is a good guide for individual conduct, imposition of that conduct upon all will be an insufferable interference with everybody's freedom of conscience."[43] The method of persuasion and conversion, that is, the nonviolent way, is the best way, so argued Gandhi, of attaining democracy.

Democracy to be genuine needs an appropriate mental climate of the citizens. Toleration of and respect for others' opinions help in the growth of such a climate. Gandhi pointed to that direction. As Prof. Nirmal Kumar Bose reminds us: "One of Gandhiji's greatest contributions to India has been this insistence upon the philosophical foundation of democracy."[44]

This philosophical approach holds the key to an understanding of his concept of state being a secular one. In his opinion, "The state should undoubtedly be secular. Everyone living in it should be entitled to profess his religion without let or hindrance, so long as the citizen obeyed the common law of the land." "If I were a dictator", he said in 1946, "religion and state would be separate. I swear by my religion. I will die for it. But it is my personal affair. The state has nothing to do with it...That is everybody's personal concern." He did not believe in state religion even though the whole community had only one religion. He was opposed to state aid, partly or wholly, to religious bodies. This does not mean, Gandhi explained, that the state schools would not give ethical teaching. In his opinion, teaching of fundamental ethics is common to all religions. But the state cannot concern itself or cope with religious instructions. It is superfluous to add that by religion he meant denominational religion and not fundamental ethics which, in his opinion, "is common to all religions".

Secularism as a concept is integrally related to democracy. Gandhi underlined the kernel of democracy by stressing on this aspect. This apparently bears little significance. But a close examination will lead to a different conclusion. First, because of the obvious historic limitations imposed on India, the pattern of the development of modern Indian history did not resemble the classical democratic type; secondly, as a corollary to the same, the forces of obscurantism, social orthodoxy and communal reaction were firmly rooted in the body politic. They had social bases to stand upon. Sociologically speaking, the pre-capitalist values (in the classical sense) held sway over a large mass of the Indian people. Gandhi preached secularism at a period when the forces of social reaction tried to thwart the course of national development on a democratic basis. His emphasis on the secular character of the state reflected the opinion of the advanced section of the nation. His advocacy of the idea helped in accelerating the pace of national democratic development. Therein lies its significance.

Gandhi broadly accepted the categories of modern governments, namely dictatorships, monarchies and democracies. Though he conceded the fact that democracy is not always good that autocracy is not always bad, he was of the definite view that the rule of one man over many is intolerable. He rejected the theory of the divine right of the kings to rule and the humble duty of the ryots to pay respectful obedience their masters on the ground that it promotes inequality, which is injurious to the well-being of society." He said: "The liberty of the people should not depend upon the will of an individual, however noble and ancient may be his descent."[45] He believed that man, being by nature "consciously-divine", rational and sociable, has an inborn capacity to govern himself. *Swaraj* must, therefore, mean government by the consent and participation of the people. It must actually be a "government by the many". He, thus, espoused the cause of democracy. In *Harijan,* he observed: "if the reality faces me, my choice will be death or the rule of the people by the people for the people."[46]

His awareness of the merits and demerits of direct and indirect democracies led him to prefer the latter. He was averse to the former for, he thought, it rested on the institution of mass meetings which, at best, accorded emotional support to the popular movements. In these meetings, the uninformed and the unintelligent masses are called upon to vote on questions whose implications and subtleties they do not understand. Very often, people have no opinion to express, may be because they know practically nothing about the proposed measures. Moreover, they have the option only to say "yes" or "no" to them. There is no scope for the partial approval or rejection of the actual proposals. Some people may like some provisions of a Bill but have to vote against it because they do not like the other provisions. Gandhi thought that the system of direct or "plebicitary" democracy with all these inevitable drawbacks would not be in keeping with his ideal state.

He was practical enough to espouse the cause of representative or "parliamentary" democracy instead. The very implication of his notion of *swaraj* is that the government should be based on the consent of the people ascertained by the vote of the largest number of voters. He often used the analogy of an umbrella to illustrate his point. He compared the government with an umbrella which is of the choice of the person who pays for it and which is sustained and made use of by its owner so long as it serves the purpose for which it was selected and bought. In *Young India,* for instance, he observed that "every citizen silently but nonetheless certainly sustains the government of the day".[47] He, thus, subscribed to the notion of the ultimate "popular sovereignty" of the people who are called upon, periodically, to elect the representatives of their choice to exercise the functions of the government. His very notion of "political power" was characteristic of his belief in the institution of parliamentary democracy. He maintained that "political power means capacity to regulate national life through national representatives."

He wanted the institutions of parliamentary democracy to be organized for the welfare of the people in all the spheres of human activity. To him, democracy was nothing but the art and science of mobilizing the entire physical, economic and spiritual resources for the common good of all. He desired the democratic institutions to harmonise the interests of the individual and the state, and to secure "equal freedom" and prompt, perfect and inexpensive justice to the former. He championed the cause of democracy also because he thought it can better protect the weak, and respect the "individuality" of man, which lies at the root of all progress. In *Harijan,* he observed:

> "If the individual ceases to count, what is left of society? Individual freedom alone can make a man voluntarily surrender himself completely to the service of society. If it is wrested from him, he becomes an automation and society is ruined. No society can possibly be built on a denial of individual freedom."[48]

The individual, however, is not merely a beneficiary, he is also a participant. Gandhi reiterated the fact that in democracy "power is shared by all" in some way at some stage of political development.

Hence, greater the opportunities for people's participation, nobler is the institution of democracy. But, he cautioned that the range of people's participation must never "degenerate democracy" into mobocracy. Gandhi was against mob-rule not because, like John Stuart Mill, he thought "public" to be just a "miscellaneous collection of a few wise and many foolish individuals". On the contrary, he declared that people "have a heart of gold", they "feel for the country" and "want to be taught and led." Mobocracy is to be disowned for the simple reason that mobs "have no mind, no premeditation", and consequently they "act in a frenzy", though they also "repent quickly". It is popular terrorism which is "antagonistic to the growth of the democratic spirit". Mob-rule kills the very spirit of democracy and amounts either to "unorganized violence of the people" or to the rule of the unscrupulous and thick-skinned capitalists who resort to bribery and corruption. This is even worse than the organized violence of the government and, thus, Gandhi had nothing to do with either. He thought that a band of intelligent and sincere workers is all that is needed to organize the whole nation to act intelligently, *i.e.* to evolve democracy "out of mobocracy."

STRUCTURE OF THE DEMOCRATIC GOVERNMENT

In this section, we propose to examine Gandhi's views on (1) Constitution; (2) Head of the State; (3) Legislature; (4) Parliamentary Executive; (5) Judiciary; (6) Provincial Administration; (7) Village Administration; and (8) the Holders of Authority.

CONSTITUTION FOR DEMOCRATIC GOVERNANCE

A democratic government has, in terms of its functions, three branches namely, legislative, executive, and judicial, whose structure and functions are the major contents of any constitution. Once expressing his views about the type of constitution a free government ought to have, he observed: "Free *Indian Government* would set up a Constitution suited to Indian genius, evolved without dictation from outside… The dictating factor will not be an outside one, but wisdom". On an earlier occasion, he emphasized the suitability of the Constitution by declaring that "Constitutionalism, legality and such other things are good enough within their respective spheres, but they become a drag upon human progress immediately the human mind has broken these bonds and flies higher." This shows that he never had a liking for the rigidities and complexities of constitutionalism, though had clearly realized the necessity of some suitable constitution for every democratic government. In this connection, once commenting on the draft of the Government of India Act of 1935 he wrote that the "rigid and cramped constitution of today has of course no place in this picture",[49] that is, in his picture of the democratic government that governs the least.

HEAD OF THE STATE

In his scheme of the democratic government, Gandhi wanted an humble, or as he put it, a rustic President as the ceremonial head of the Indian state, so that even the humblest and the lowliest could feel that *swaraj* had come to them. Commenting on the Indian Independence Bill of 1947, he indicated his choice as follows:

> "If I have my way I would put a suitable *Harijan* girl in the presidential chair. In a free India knowledge of English won't be necessary for the President. She need not have knowledge of high politics. All the learned statesmen of the country would help her to carry on the Government... *I would rejoice to think that we had a Mehtar girl of stout heart, incorruptible and of crystal like purity to be our first President.* It is no vain dream. There are such *Harijan* girls, if we would but set our hearts on having rustic Presidents. Did I not choose little Gulnar, the daughter of the late Maulana Mahomad Ali, as my successor?[50]

The head of the state of his conception would, thus, be symbol of the neglected sections of society, including the untouchables, the minority religionists and the women.

RESPONSIBLE UNICAMERAL LEGISLATURE

Gandhi believed in the supremacy of legislatures, for he thought that a body of elected representatives alone can have a fully representative status. "Being responsible to the voters they should not merely play the negative role of exposing the misdeeds of the executive." Their role should essentially be constructive. They should, for instance, redress peoples' genuine grievances and pass welfare legislation without waiting for representations and petitions. The laws passed by them should be in consonance with the wishes of the people. Then alone would the statute be of people's own making, *i.e.* legislation "imposed by people upon themselves".

The actual working of legislatures in the European countries was, however, to his mind a farce of democracy, "a negation of democracy". *Hind Swaraj* contains his indictment of the western parliaments which he thought had a democratic form without substance. He was pained to find that the very institutions of democracy were being misused for the expansion of capitalism, imperialism and racialism. He criticized them for their apathy, inertia, inconclusiveness and selfishness. He found that their procedures and practices resulted in the wastage of national money and time. These were virtually the "emblems of slavery", for they perpetuated tyranny "upon the people in the name of the people.

To measure the worth of the Western legislatures, he took the example of the British Parliament which is considered to be the Mother of Parliaments. He found that the British Parliament had not done "a single good thing" of its own accord, and thus, he equated it with a sterile woman who "can do nothing" without external pressure. He also likened it to a "prostitute", for he thought it helplessly surrenders itself into the hands of the prime ministers who, often, lack honesty and purity of feeling. In the actual functioning of the British Parliament, he, thus found a glaring example of the abuse of legislative practices and procedures. The remedy, however, is not the avoidance of legislatures, "but reduction of possibility of abuse to a minimum."

There is also evidence to show that Gandhi was inclined to prefer unicameral to the bicameral legislatures. His main argument was that in comparison to the former, the latter are complicated and expensive. In his speech at the Round Table Conference, he observed:

> "I am certainly not enamoured of, nor do I swear by, two legislatures. I have no fear of a popular legislature running away with itself and hastily passing some laws of which afterwards it will have to repent... I think that a popular legislature can take care of itself, and, since we are dealing with the poorest country in the world, the less expenses we have to bear the better it is for us."[51]

PARLIAMENTARY EXECUTIVE

Parliamentary Executive is that executive which is an integral part of and directly and collectively responsible to the legislature. Gandhi preferred the parliamentary form of executive, to the Presidential one, for the latter is neither an integral part of, nor accountable to the legislature. Expressing his personal opinion on this matter he once declared that the "executive should be...a responsible one chosen from the elected members of the central legislature". In *Harijan,* he observed that "A popular ministry is responsible to the legislature and cannot do anything without their consent." He, moreover, wanted that this executive should consist of the elected members of the legislature belonging to the majority party alone, and not to all the parties in the legislature. He had realized that the want of "team work and team-spirit...demoralizes the government and imperils the integrity of the services". This realization enabled him to declare that "an all-party government...will be no government of the people for the people. It will be the government of a caucus for its own ends".

Gandhi, however, did not limit the responsibility of the parliamentary executive merely to the legislature from amongst whose elected members it was to be constituted, but also extended it to cover the voters and the provincial, as well as the national, organization of the political party to which the members of that executive belonged. This four-fold responsibility of the parliamentary executive was once explained by him as follows:

> "Congress ministers have a four-fold responsibility. As an individual a minister is primarily responsible to his constituents. If he is satisfied that he no longer enjoys their confidence or that he has changed the views for which he was elected, he resigns. Collectively the ministers are responsible to the majority of legislators who, by a non-confidence vote or similar means, may any moment drive them out of office. But a Congress minister owes his position and responsibility to his Provincial Congress Committee and the A.I.C.C. also. So long as all these four bodies act in co-ordination, ministers have smooth sailing in the discharge of their duty."[52]

Finally, he wanted the acts of Parliamentary executive to be subject to review not only by their legislature, but also "by their courts", so that an overall attitude of impartiality and fairness be maintained.

INDEPENDENT AND IMPARTIAL JUDICIARY

Though Gandhi believed in the essential harmony between the legislature and the executive, he wanted to separate judiciary. From these two branches of the government, for he questioned the prudence of the person who strove to administer justice without having an impartial tribunal to advise him, or the one who had risen to the rank of a judge from being a Government official. This belief enabled him to declare that the judiciary will have to be above board and, therefore, independent of them. Contrariwise, he observed that "no minister had the right to interfere with the course of justice even for his dearest."[53]

Besides permitting the courts to perform their normal function of deciding cases and disputes according to law, he wanted them specifically to protect the rights and liberties of the people to enforce the division of powers between the centre and the states and amongst the states *interse*, and to review and interpret the decisions of the legislative and executive organs of the government. In the exercise of these functions he wanted the courts to adopt an attitude of strict impartiality so that they may be able to treat everyone as an innocent person before they actually find him to be guilty. Though he emphasised the necessity of law courts for the due performance of these multifarious functions, he was against the cumbersome procedure and unnecessary legal complications usually involved in the administration of justice. He wanted the whole judicial be simple, prompt and inexpensive.

PROVINCIAL ADMINISTRATION

Subscribing to the view that in a federal form of state ever community should be entitled to organize as a self-determining entity, and maintaining that "Responsible government in the states is a goal by itself", Gandhi pleaded for the "linguistic political redistribution of provinces". He wanted every province to draw "by an overwhelming majority" its own Constitution in conformity with that of the Centre. The securing of this right to every province, he thought, would not only avoid internal conflict but shall also enable it to retain its culture and language. He also desired that the form and organization of the provincial government should be the same as that of the Centre, excepting that in case of a province, the formal and the actual executive heads were to be styled as the Governor and the Chief Minister respectively. Emphasizing the necessity and importance of the Governor's office he said:

> "...it would be bad economy to do away with the provincial Governors and regard Chief Ministers as a perfect equivalent. Whilst I would resent much power of interference to be given to Governors, I do not think that they should be mere figureheads. They should have enough power enabling them to influence ministerial policy for the better. In their detached position they would be able to see things in their proper perspective and thus prevent mistakes by their cabinets. Theirs must be an all-pervasive moral influence in their provinces."

He not only assigned this important role to the Governors, but also prescribed for them the following qualifications: (a) they must be teetotalers; (b) they must represent hand-spinning; (c) they must dwell in the cottages accessible to all; (d) they must not practise untouchability in any form; (e) they must represent the best of all religions; and (f) they must spéak both the national and the provincial languages.

VILLAGE ADMINISTRATION

In order to underline the principle of the decentralization of public power and economy, Gandhi gave the slogan of "Back to the villages". Under Plato's inspiration, he maintained that every village should eventually become "a self-sufficient republic" and that, therefore, its ideal population should not exceed 1,000. He wanted it to be "a complete republic, independent of its neighbours for its own vital wants, and yet interdependent for many others in which dependence is 'a necessity'".

He was also desirous of arranging political power in ever-widening concentric circles whose centre would be the individual and in which village panchayat as a primary unit of political power shall play a dominant role. His most comprehensive statement in this respect reads as follows:

> "Independence must begin at the bottom. Thus every village will be a republic or *Panchayat* having full powers...In this structure composed of innumerable villages there will be ever-widening, never ascending circles. Life will not be a pyramid with the apex sustained by bottom. But it will be an oceanic circle, whose centre will be the individual always ready to perish for the village, the

latter ready to perish for the circle of villages till at last the whole becomes one, life composed of individuals never aggressive in their arrogance but ever humble, sharing the majesty of the oceanic circle of which they are integral units."[54]

In view of such a categorical statement of Gandhi, Shriman Narayan Agarwal's submission that the administrative system envisaged by Gandhi was that of "a pyramid whose broad base is composed of numberless village communities of the country" cannot be sustained.

HOLDERS OF AUTHORITY

Gandhi, thus preferred the federal form of state whose democratic government would have directly elected unicameral legislatures, parliamentary executives and independent and impartial judiciary. In order to bring home to the people the real he wanted that these various governmental agencies be composed of the best available public-men, for he knew that the authority blurs the vision of its possessor."[55] He, prescribed the following qualifications for the public-men who would occupy various political offices:

(1) They must be votaries of Truth and *Ahimsa*;
(2) They must like a life of utter simplicity;
(3) They must be "easily approachable";
(4) They must be eager to know the true condition of their subjects;
(5) They must belong to the common people, live like them and think like them;
(6) They must be the genuine servants of the people;
(7) They, must read the signs of the times and march with them;
(8) They must be watchful of their own personal and public conduct;
(9) They must take from the revenue the honest minimum necessary to support themselves as a commission for their labours on behalf of the ryots;
(10) They must not break their promises;
(11) They must not indulge in moral turpitude;
(12) They must not pass most of their time outside their States;
(13) They must not be the members of any communal organization; and
(14) They must not receive for their own personal use "addresses of value or costly floral tributes."

He wanted the services also to be "manned by the most qualified men and women", for he thought that the administration to be efficient must always be in the hands of the fittest. His objective was to make the people feel that the officials were not the masters but the servants and that there was no trace of communalism among them.

NOTES

1. James Bentham, *The Machiavellians: Defenders of Freedom*, New York, Pioneers, 1943, p. 243.
2. Richard Robbinson, *Definition*, Oxford, Clarendon Press, 1954, p. 17.
3. Jai Narain Sharma, "Etymology of Power" in R.C. Saini and R.K. Gupta (eds.), *Peoples Power: Indian Reality*, New Delhi, Commonwealth, 1994, p. 34.
4. Giovanni Sartari, *Democratic Theory*, Calcutta, Oxford, 1965, p. 18.
5. *Ibid.*
6. Karl Marx, *Early Writings*, London, C.A. Watts & Co., 1963.
7. William Kornhavur, *The Politics of Mass Society*, Glencoe, Routledge and Kegan Paul, 1959, pp. 234-49.
8. *Ibid.*
9. *Harijan*, 28-9-1947, p. 350.
10. *Ibid.*, 5-1-1947, p. 473.
11. M.K. Gandhi, *Hind Swaraj*, *op. cit.*, pp. 22-24.
12. *CWMG*, Vol. X, 204.
13. *Young India*, 3-9-1925, p. 304.
14. *Harijan*, 3-9-1938, p. 242.
15. *Ibid.*, 12-11-1938, p. 328.
16. *Ibid.*, 11-2-1939, p. 8.
17. *Ibid.*, 18-5-1940, p. 129.
18. Louis Fischer, *A Week with Gandhi*, Bombay, International Book House, 1944, p. 51.
19. G. Adhikari (ed.) *From Peace: Front to People's War*, Bombay, People's Publishing House, 1960, p. 3.
20. *Ibid.*, p. 387.
21. *Young India*, 4-8-1920, p. 3.
22. *Ibid.*, 8-12-1921, p. 401.
23. *Ibid.*
24. *Ibid.*, 26-1-1922, p. 52.
25. D.G. Tendulkar, *Mahatma*, *op. cit.*, Vol. VI, pp. 283-84.
26. *Young India*, 13-8-1925, p. 279.
27. *Ibid.*, 29-1-1925, p. 40.
28. *Ibid.*, 8-10-1931, p. 297.
29. *Harijan*, 13-10-1940, p. 320.

30. *Ibid.*, 2-3-1947, p. 45.
31. Pyarelal, *Mahatma Gandhi: The Last Phase*, Vol. II, Ahmedabad, Navajivan Publishing House, 1956, p. 675.
32. Louis Fischer, *op. cit.*, p. 44 .
33. *Ibid.*, p. 45.
34. D.G. Tendulkar, *Mahatma*, *op. cit.*, Vol. VIII, p. 283.
35. *Harijan*, 18-1-1948, p. 519.
36. *Young India*, 1-12-1927, p. 204.
37. *Harijan*, 15-10-1938, p. 290.
38. D.G. Tendulkar, *Mahatma*, *op. cit.*, Vol. VI, p. 153.
39. *Ibid.*, p. 158.
40. *Ibid.*, Vol. VIII, pp. 229-30.
41. *Ibid.*, Vol. VIII, p. 301.
42. *Harijan*, 31-5-1942, p. 172.
43. *Young India*, 23-9-1926, p. 334.
44. N.K. Bose, "Gandhism and Gandhi" in K. Roy (ed.), *Gandhi Memorial Peace Number, The Viswa Bharati Quarterly*, Shantiniketan, 1949, p. 25.
45. M.K. Gandhi, *Wither His Highness*, (ed.) by Dewan Ram Prakash, Lahore, Gandhi Publications League, 1948, p. 26.
46. *Harijan*, 13-10-1940, p. 320.
47. *Ibid.*
48. *Harijan*, 1-2-1942, p. 27.
49. *Harijan*, 1-9-1940, p. 266.
50. *Harijan*, 15-6-1947, pp. 191-93.
51. M.K. Gandhi, *Nation's Voice*, (ed.) by C. Rajagopalachari and J.C. Kumarappa, Ahmedabad, Navajivan Publishing House, 1947, p. 19.
52. *Harijan*, 13-11-1937, p. 332.
53. *Harijan*, 3-11-1946, p. 382.
54. *Harijan*, 21-12-1947, p. 473.
55. *Harijan*, 28-7-1946, p. 236.

6

Human Rights

Like a towering lighthouse guiding sailors towards the coast, 'development' stood as the idea which oriented emerging nations in their journey through post-war history. No matter whether democracies or dictatorships, the countries of the South proclaimed development as their primary aspiration, after they had been freed from colonial subordination. Four decades later, governments and citizens alike still have their eyes fixed on this light flashing just as far away as ever; every effort and every sacrifice is justified in reaching it, but the light keeps on receding into the dark horizon.

The lighthouse of development was erected right after the Second World War. Following the breakdown of the European colonial power, the United States found an opportunity to give worldwide dimensions to the mission of their founding fathers had bequeathed to them: to be the 'beacon on the hill'. They launched the idea of development with a call to every nation to follow in their footsteps. Since then, the relations between North and South have been cast in this mould: 'development' provided the fundamental frame of reference for that mixture of generosity, bribery and oppression which has characterized the policies towards the South. For almost half a century, good neighbourliness on the planet was conceived in the light of 'development'.

Today, the lighthouse shows cracks and is starting to crumble. The idea of development stands like a ruin in the intellectual landscape. Delusion and disappointment, failures and crimes have been the steady companions of development and they tell a common story: it did not work. Moreover, the historical conditions which catapulted the idea into prominence have vanished: development has become outdated. But above all, the hopes and desires which made the idea fly, are now exhausted: development has grown obsolete.

Nevertheless, the ruin stands there and still dominates the scenery like a landmark. Though doubts are mounting and uneasiness is widely felt, development talk still pervades not only official declarations but even the language of grassroots movements. It is time to dismantle this mental structure.

THE AGE OF DEVELOPMENT

The age of development began on 20 January, 1949, when Harry S. Truman for the first time declared, in his inauguration speech, the Southern Hemisphere as 'underdeveloped areas'. The label struck and subsequently provided the cognitive base for both arrogant interventionism's from the North and pathetic self-pity in the South. However, what is born at a certain point in time 'can die again at a later point; the age of development is on the decline because its four founding premises.'

First of all, it was a matter of course for Truman that the United States along with other industrialized nations—were at the top of the social evolutionary scale. Today, this premise of superiority has been fully and finally shattered by the poverty and ecological predicaments. Granted the US may still feel it is running ahead of the other countries, but it is clear now that the race is leading towards an abyss. For more than a century, technology carried the promise of redeeming the human conditions from sweat, toil and tears. Today, especially in the rich countries, it is everybody's best kept secret that this hope is nothing other than a flight of fancy.

After all, with the fruits of industrialism still scarcely distributed, we now consume in one year what it took the earth a million years to store up. Furthermore, much of the glorious productivity is fed by the gigantic throughput of fossil energy; on the one side, the earth is being excavated and permanently scarred, while on the other a continuous rain of harmful substances drizzles down or filters up into the atmosphere. If all countries 'successfully' followed the industrial example, five or six planets would be needed to serve as mines and waste dumps. It is thus obvious that the 'advanced' societies are no model; rather they are most likely to be seen in the end as an aberration in the course of history. The arrow of progress is broken and future has lost its brightness: what it holds in store are more threats than promises. How can one believe in development, if the sense of orientation has withered away?

Secondly, Truman launched the idea of development in order to provide a comforting vision of a world order where the US would naturally rank first. The rising influence of the Soviet Union—the first country which had industrialized outside of capitalism—forced him to come up with a vision that would engage the loyalty of the decolonising countries in order to sustain his struggle against communism. For over several decades, development has been a weapon in the competing between political systems. Now that the East-West confrontation has come to a halt. Truman's project of global development is bound to lose ideological steam and to remain without political fuel. And as the world becomes polycentric, the scrapyard of history now awaits the category 'Third World' to be dumped, a category invented by the French in the early 1950s in order to designate the embattled territory between the two superpowers.

Nevertheless, new, albeit belated, calls for development may multiply, as the East-West division gets absorbed into the rich poor division. In this light, however, the entire project fundamentally changes its character: prevention replaces progress as the objective of development; the redistribution of risk rather than the redistribution of wealth now dominate the international agenda. Development specialists shrug their shoulders about the long promised industrial paradise, but rush to ward off the flood of immigrants, to contain regional wars, to undercut illicit trade, and to contain environmental disasters. They are still busy identifying deficits and filling gaps, but Truman's promise of development has been turned upside down.

Thirdly, development has changed the face of the earth, but not in the way it had intended. Truman's project now appears as a blunder of planetary proportions. In 1960, the northern countries were twenty times richer than the Southern countries stepped on the gas, but the North outpaced them by far. The reason is simple: in this kind of race, the rich countries will always move faster than the rest, for they agreed towards a continuous degradation of what they have to put forth: the most advanced technology. They are world champions in competitive obsolescence.

Social polarization prevails within counties as well; the stories about falling real income misery and desperation are all too familiar. The campaign to turn additional man into modern man has failed. The old ways have been smashed, the new ways are not viable. People are caught in the deadlock of development: the peasant, who had made it in the city, but is now laid off as a result of cost-cutting measures. They are all like refugees who have been rejected and have no place to go. Shunned by the 'advanced' sector and cut off from the old ways, they are expatriates in their own country; they are forced to get by in the noman's land between tradition and modernity.

Fourthly, suspicion grows that development was a misconceived enterprise from the beginning. Indeed, it is not the failure of development which has to be feared, but its success. What would a completely developed world look like? We don't know, but most certainly it would be both boring and fraught with danger. For development cannot be separated from the idea that all peoples of the planet are moving along single track towards some state of maturity, exemplified by the nation's 'running in front'. In this view, Tuaregs, Zapotecos or Rajasthanis are not seen as living diverse and non-comparable ways of human existence, but as somehow lacking in terms of what has been achieved by the advanced countries. Consequently, catching up was declared to be their historical task. From the start, development's hidden agenda was nothing else than the westernization of the world.

Decades after Truman's invention of underdevelopment, the historical conditions which had been given rise to the developmental perspective have largely disappeared. By now development has become an amoeba-like concept, shapeless but ineradicable. Its contours are so blurred that it denotes nothing while it spreads everywhere because it connotes the best of intentions. The term is hailed by the IMF and Vatican alike, by revolutionaries carrying their guns as well as field experts carrying their Samsonites. Though development has no content, it does possess one function: it allows any intervention to be sanctified in the name of a higher goal. Therefore, even enemies feel united under the same banner. The term creates a common ground—a ground on which right and left, elites and grassroots fight their battles.

IDEOLOGY OF DEVELOPMENT AND RIGHTS OF THE PEOPLE

As a principle 'robbing Peter to pay Paul' (especially when Peter is rich and Paul poor) tends to draw sympathy even from the liberals, since Robin Hoods are accepted as heroes. But the point at which the liberals bring down their axe most forcefully is precisely the point at which Marxists despair of applying their principles of dialectical materialism to the conception of dictatorship of the proletariat. Although recent discussions, such as that between Althuser and R. Thompson, attempt to marginalize this despair the final political and conceptual consequences of dialectical materialism cannot be evaded. Dictatorship of any form, say the liberals, is bad. Man must be free to decide his own destiny; people must have the rights to self-determination even against the state, they say. But how far do the liberals themselves succeed in protecting people from the tyranny of the exploitative forces?

'Liberty is a fine thing,' said J.S. Mill after writing 'On Liberty', but he added that the Indians in the colony are not competent to have this. Aristotle had similarly proclaimed the freedom of all people in Athens; but the slaves, he went on to add, are not people. This will not do, reacted Jeremy Bentham, and he championed another principle of liberalism: the 'greatest happiness,' couched now in terms of 'welfare' and 'development'. But the 'greatest number' has been lost sight of. In fact Bentham himself lost sight of it when he wrote the penal code for India. He lost sight of the fact that another parallel penal code was being worked out at the same time in India—for the forest dwellers and tribals—in addition to the one that this is parallel code took away, for he was propounding the tribals numerous rights and liberties which were available to other Indians. The tribals in India number more than million people—not a small number by any standard of greatness. If the happiness of millions of people being ignored, surely one is far from achieving the 'greatest happiness for the greatest number' not by accident but by design.

What is upshot of this? The fact that it is not enough to champion the rights and liberties of people as liberal. The central question for liberalism is: Whose rights and liberties are being championed? This, as we shall see, is not always easy to decipher; nor is it always possible to assure that the beneficiaries of the rights and liberties will be those who are most in need of it.

However, the problems of class inclusion and exclusion is not the problem that liberalism is riddled with sound as it is otherwise, in its advocacy for a just and free society. The major problem concerns the means that are to be adopted to this end. Liberalism propounds the social rules of egalitarianism as its goals; but as means to attain them, it asserts mostly the utilitarian rules of the jungle, such as free competition, and *laissez faire.* The liberals trend to believe that action in accordance with these rules of the jungle would lead to the emergence of the best in society. There would be a true Darwinian selection of the fittest—a goal which a particular metaphysics of the society would approve as desirable. This is how things would in fact be if society were truly a jungle. But the social realm is not like the natural realm. Here there is very little 'free' competition in the true sense of the word. It is manoeuvred by vested interests. There is little deserving by merit, for what counts as merit and what does not is also a matter of variety of interests. There cannot be *laissez faire* (leave them to develop by themselves), for the social and economic opportunities are skewed in favour of some. To argue for *laissez faire* in such situation is to argue for *status quo*. This made sense when Adam Smith wanted the exploiting East India Company and the British mercantile class to be left alone to do what they were doing; but it did not make sense as a liberal principle even then.

It is not as if the liberals do not realize that free competition is a sham. Their insistence on the utilitarian principles of the jungle—such as: 'it is rational to maximize your self-interest, therefore, cannot be taken to the hypocrisy or self-deception. It seems to emerge from a deeper confusion about the theology and metaphysics of community. They seem to labour under hope that the utilitarian principles will somehow yield the best in society in the end, since they do achieve this in nature. Thus, for example, John Rawls labours with a basic concept of the 'veil of ignorance' on which he bases his principles of fairness. The 'veil of ignorance' is the situation in which the participants do not know what goals they may want to achieve later, and what is in their immediate interest.

Now such an epistemological assumption makes good sense when applied to the community of bees or ants or of elephants. Here members may not know what goals they would want to achieve in the near future, if not ultimately. Rawls, of course, has an ideal or a hypothetical society in mind; but if this artificial society does not share essential features with real societies the analogy, and hence the justification for fairness, holds little ground. In a real society, information and opportunities are unevenly distributed. This is what makes some classes of people advantaged or privileged. An unrealistic, epistemological assumption cannot provide a philosophy of action for real societies.

The general distinction between social realm, which governed by the social rules woven around the notions of equality, freedom, dignity, etc., and the natural realm, which is governed by the rules of the jungle woven around the notions of competition, free-play, self-interest etc. invoked so far in this discussion, would need a more detailed explication than provided here. Such an exercise would take us away from the central theme. The distinction, however, even in its bare sketch, is necessary for understanding the difficulties in these ideologies. In the absence of a detailed exposition with an example before making further points about liberalism.

The development discourse is made up of key concepts. It is impossible to talk about development without referring to concepts such as poverty, production, the notion of the state, or equality. These concepts first rose to prominence during modern Western history and only then have they been projected on the rest of the world. Each of them crystallizes a set of tacit assumptions which reinforce the occidental worldview. Development has to pervasively spread these assumptions that people everywhere have been caught up in a Western perception of reality. Knowledge, however, wields power by directing people's attention; it carves out and highlights a certain reality, casting reality, casting into oblivion other ways of relating to the world around us. At a time when development has evidently failed as a socio-economic endeavour, it has become of paramount importance to liberate ourselves from its dominion over our minds.

But the problem is that new forms of dependency and the onset of the age of technology has increased the gap between the development standards of the rich and poor countries. The global restructuring of eighties' and the nineties' has structurally foisted newer and sinister forms of exploitation and further marginalisation of Third World countries from the world economy with progressive decomposition of social and economic structures. India has not been left untouched by this process. Not only has been Indian economy depredated by this process, its development paradigm under a great deal of strain but we are also witnessing the growing ecological and environmental malaise that is its byproduct. A natural and logical corollary of this process is that communities are losing their inalienable human rights to live and subsist the way they have done for centuries together. By implication, it is also denying individuals their personal rights to a safe livelihood and right to make sanguine and personal choices of liberties and entitlements. Thus globalisation has rendered the traditional relationship between the state and the communities outdated, as if it were. The state, being subjected to the forces of neo-imperialism is being forced by the logic of development to impose "anti-people" policies and exploitative politics on the community. National sovereignty has been replaced by new concepts of 'intellectual property rights', based on the interests of corporations (MNCs and TNCs) and the reality of social, economic and political organization of industrialized western countries.

INDIA'S DEVELOPMENT PATH AND HUMAN RIGHTS

At the time of independence India borrowed a colonial model of economic development. Modernization was identified with industrialization. The mega industries established in collaboration with foreign finance were presented as models. The Iron and Steel Company in Durgapur was with British collaboration, in Rourkela with German and the Bokaro plant was with Russian assistance. Besides there were other mega projects with foreign collaborations. Though the country loudly made pronouncement for a socialistic pattern of economic development, the model was capitalistic. With the process of globalization, the country has adopted the capitalist model both in words and deeds.

Human Right activists, concerned citizens and several NGOs are of the opinion that the country is for sale with the opening of the economy for Multinational Companies, Transnational Corporations and Business Houses. Laws have been introduced making it easy for foreign nationals to acquire land, property and carry on business. While the foreigners easily become citizens in the name of capital and markets, citizens are ousted from their houses and evicted from their colonies and slums, all in the name of development. The biggest human rights violations in India today are in the name of development. The globalized model of development is causing untold misery and hardships to the average citizens in the country.

The word 'develop' is a twelfth or thirteenth century word. The Italian form according to Oxford English Dictionary is '*velupare*', which means significantly 'to unrap', 'to disentangle', and 'to rid free of'. The opposite of 'develop' is 'envelop' which means 'to hide', 'to cover up', 'to put constraints upon'—which is what we do when we envelop something. When we develop we do the reverse. We remove constraints whatever they may be. The word develop maintains its original definition in photography. When we develop a film we reveal what is already latent in that film. We cannot put new things into the film and call it developed. Development is thus a process of revealing as we continue with the dictionary definition, it says to unfold, as a tale or as a story develops to lay open by removal of that what enfolds. That is to say, something more comes out of that which already exists. Rural development should proceed on the basis rather than blindly following the theories of development propounded by the western authors. This is what the Mahatma preached.

How are developments—induced displacements, human rights violations? Let me provide you three examples from three states of recent so-called development projects.

Sardar Sarovar Project: The project is intended to bring drinking water to Kutch and other drought prone regions of Gujarat and to irrigate a vast area of that state as well as two districts of Rajasthan. But the dam will submerge 37,000 hectares of land in three states—Gujarat, Maharashtra and Madhya Pradesh. It will require approximately another 80,000 hectares of land, more than twice as much land as the submergence area. The project when completed will be one of the largest water resource projects. The impact of the project will affect a large number of people specially tribals. Majority of the oustees is tribal. Over a lakh of people who live in 245 villages in the area will be affected by submergence. Another one lakh forty thousand farmers will be adversely affected by the irrigation system. The Department of Environment and Forests estimates the timber loss in the forest to be of Rs. 40,000 crore.

The *Rengali Dam Project* in Orissa has submerged 265 villages and displaced 10,847 families in two districts, three subdivisions and nine blocks. The Upper Indravati hydroelectric project located in southern Orissa has affected 97 villages with 67 villages fully submerged, 34 villages from Kalahandi, 18 from Nawrangpur and 13 from Koraput districts. Only 5,448 families have been assisted with rehabilitation. Majority of the affected are tribals.[7]

The two 1000 MW nuclear plants established in 1980 at Koodankulam in Tamil Nadu resulted in the immediate eviction of the people of the Koodankulam village itself, barely 3 kilometres from the reactor site and villages of Panjal and Perumanal, very close to the site. Over 25,000 people were evicted. The setting up of the nuclear plants has curtailed fishing activities in a belt of nearly 75 km. This has posed a threat to the livelihood of nearly 3 lakh fisherfolk. Once unclear radiation leak from the nuclear plants contaminate the sea, there will by no way by which the fisherfolk will be able to sustain their life. Besides, fishing activities around 10 km have severely affected. One lakh people were expected to be evicted and the livelihood of 5 lakh persons was threatened. Most of the people around are SCs and the poors. These are stray examples. The list can be multiplied.

Though development projects are not meant to induce poverty, displacement in India specially affects the already impoverished, SCs/STs and other marginalised groups. They hardly benefit from the projects. Tribals of Sardar Sarovar have not even been provided with any rehabilitation. According to the government, these tribals are "encroachers" on government land although they had been cultivating the land for generations in accordance with their customary usage though without formal title.

Then there are the Project affected people. According to the Tribunal Award 1979, they were to be given land to replace land they were losing, house sites and short term financial protection. There are no example in India where the government has done this in any project. Land at times has been provided as an exchange. Very often compensation is given for house sites and land. In some places one job per family is provided to some families. Beyond that there are no example of any other assistance.

Besides the Project affected there are those project dependent. There are primarily who work as labourers, milkmen, tillers, harvesters, cow and sheep rearers and flower and vegetable vendors. As a result of the sale of land their lives are affected. They are not at all a category in the rehabilitation package. When the government or any other business company acquires large land for development purposes, these people who are dependent on the lands lose their livelihood and thus their very life or existence.

Unfortunately, the human rights movements in our country have confined itself to a legal positivist view of rights. A comprehensive understanding of development has never been its agenda. This has happened because a definition of rights has not emerged from the notion of rights of the people in collective. The new Indian middle class has borrowed the concept of human rights from the practices and experiments of the West. There have been attempts to have an Indian agenda, especially related to incidents of state violation of constitutional and other codified rights. So far, the natural rights of the people to livelihood and self-reliance have not come under its purview. This is one reason why the human rights movement has not gone below the first-two layers of the Indian society. This inherent limitation persists because human rights discussions in India have continued to exist as an urban phenomenon. A vast rural hinterland of the country is left outside its domain.

The urban culture is basically individual centred. The middle class is more concerned with individual rights and interests. This is one reason why human rights activists have responded primarily on the issue of police atrocities on individuals. In reality, the Indian state has been continuously violating the collective rights of the people using ways and means, which are, at times, diabolical. The development policies of the state, in fact, are the greatest violators of people's right to livelihood and human dignity, and more importantly to life. The development policies have uprooted people from their traditional life system based on values, collective growth and sustainable development. They have dissociated people from their self-propelling growth pattern, based on indigenously evolved science and technology. Majorities of them are then placed in an alien economic life where their very human dignity carries no meaning. That is why human rights is a community issue and a collective concern. Debates on human rights, therefore, should have been on democratic rights of communities and various other collectivities of the marginalised people. This is again necessary because the violation of human rights is a continuous occurrence against the poor and the marginalised sections.

A limited understanding of human rights, however, has restrained the issue to become an integral part of the collective rights of the people. People assert their rights through resistance and protests against state actions. Continuous dialogue between human rights groups of the country, environment experts and the grassroots activists is necessary to make human rights more meaningful and effective.

This interaction can become successful if human rights debates go beyond the domain of codified rights. Because by codifying laws state intends to safeguard the narrow interests of its political system and sovereignty of its territorial boundary. People's interests, in fact, are much wider than those of the state. Therefore, different dimensions of deprivation of humans, including the lack of political freedom to individuals and absence of personal security must be incorporated in the understanding of human rights. Rights carry a meaning when an individual is free from stress and tensions and when there is space for him to enjoy life. An interface between growth of the country and the notion of life and liberty of human communities is, therefore, necessary.

This linkage is again called for in view of the fast inroad of globalisation in our society. Globalisation denotes to unchallenged capacity of the transnational companies to determine the production process and consumption pattern of a nation and its people. This is colonialism no doubt, but different from that which we had experienced earlier. Capturing a nation-state physically, perhaps, is not the agenda of globalisation. 'Free' economic and cultural systems of a nation, however, are made to be regulated by the global marketing framework of the TNCs, the MNCs and the international financial institutions. This regulation, in the process, takes away the capacity of independent growth of a nation and its people. Independent nations are vulnerable to the global power dictates. Globalisation is thus not an administrative invasion. Rather, it is an economic penetration and a cultural subjugation. India is one of those countries, which are becoming increasingly victims of the stratagem of change and modernisation fabricated by the global economic powers.

Globalisation negates plurality of culture and their origin, and destroys the life systems sustained around different cultural milieu. Plurality is replaced by a monolithic and homogenised culture. Many of our value-based, people-centred cultural heritage, which is the main strength of our societal bonds, are fast disappearing under the pressure of a global economy.

Human rights debates, therefore, need reflections on globalisation as an urgent agenda for concern. Because multinational companies have been making all-out efforts to establish harmful chemical factories, to experiment hazardous bio-scientific projects in our country.

However, massive ecological disasters and crises of life have compelled us to rethink about the feasibility of large industries, big projects and rapid growth of consumerism in Indian society. Even though rejection of the present model of development is necessary, it does not mean turning back to growth and prosperity. It also does not argue for going back to a primitive life system. Rather, it pleads for an indigenous development process. In fact, it emphasises on continuous innovation of science and technology without compromising on the need for exchanging knowledge and skills between different societies on equal terms. What it intends to refuse is a blind adoption of the model of growth of 'developed countries' as the solution to the backwardness or underdevelopment of India.

The Indian politico-economic system, unfortunately has failed to look into the basic needs of the people from this perspective. Instead it has defined basic needs of the people from a limited notion which includes only shelter, clothing, food, education and health. Such an understanding is devoid of an environmental consideration because it does not assure pure oxygen, pure water and fertile topsoil as essential for human society.

Over the centuries, human communities in India have evidently proved their tremendous power and capacity to advance in science and technology. Yet, people have enabled themselves to grow along with preservation of natural resources and society. Due to this reason, an increasing number of people at the grassroots have started resisting India's present development model. True, they do not have many success stories so far. But, through each of their attempts to prevent this growth model they have renewed their strength and power to protect their right to life and livelihood. More importantly, they have understood the problems not from any specific ideology. It is their own experiences that have given them the theory for sustenance and human rights.

Human rights, therefore, can become instrumental in changing society if it integrates itself with the people's way of transforming individual rights into new collective and community rights. This will not only strengthen an indigenous development into practice and will thus safeguard human rights in its true spirit.

Perhaps the most important challenge to mankind today is not that all people should be aware of the various "rights" which we have because we are "all born free and equal in dignity and rights", are "endowed with reason and conscience and should act towards one another in a spirit of brotherhood", as stated in the first Article of the Declaration, but that we should realize, "this earth is one country and mankind its citizens".

The United Nations' Universal Declaration of Human Rights was "adopted and proclaimed" without a single dissenting vote in Paris on 10th December, 1948 (the six members of the Soviet Bloc and Saudi Arabia and the Union of South Africa abstained)[8]. Following this historic act, the General Assembly of the United Nations called upon all member-countries to publicise the text of the Declaration and "to cause it to be disseminated, displayed, read and expounded, principally in schools and other educational institutions..." Many efforts have been made and are continuing to carry out the request of the General Assembly. In India a National Human Rights Commission was established by an act of Parliament in 1991 and since then a number of State Human Rights Commissions have also been established.

The questions that human rights address are perennial. What does it mean to be a human being? What is the purpose of life on this earth? What should our intellectual and emotional attitude towards one another be? Asks Dr. Jai Narain Sharma.[9]

FROM HUMAN RIGHTS TO HUMAN DIGNITY

So much has been said about human rights lately that the term defies a precise definition. Defining human rights may be both simple and complex. Simple in the sense that one can argue that human rights implies a universal ethic which claims that certain rights ought to be believed and observed everywhere by everyone. They are possessed by human beings simply as being human *per se*. And complex, because when an attempt is made to list those rights, geographical diversities, cultural variances and differences in social values make the attempt a near impossibility to agree upon a universally accepted list of rights.[10]

Therefore, for the present purpose I have chosen the concept of 'Human Dignity' as the cornerstone of human rights. Any action, which would affect, distort or violate the inherent dignity of a human being, would amount to violation of his/her human rights. Keeping this aspect in mind one may conclude that human rights are the basic rights of a person which are essential for the realization of his/her personality, as an individual as well as a member of the society in which he/she lives. They are based upon the belief that all persons are born free and with equal dignity and natural rights.[11]

Moreover, the concept of human rights is closely associated with the worth and dignity of the individual, and accords highest respect to human personality without any discrimination on grounds of caste, religion, creed, race, colour, sex, or place of birth. It is self-evident that human rights primarily aim to protect the human dignity of an individual. Human rights provide the necessary and vital protection to an individual so that he/she may continue his/her life and contribution to the society in a dignified manner. Hence, if this be the case then the rights which protect the individual's freedom and inherent human dignity may thus be termed as inalienable and inviolable human rights.

India is an ancient society, but a modern state. The Indian has largely been a tolerant society embracing and respecting the dignity of its friends and foes alike. India has always welcomed and accommodated foreigners from alien societies. The very fact that Indian culture could withstand and flourish amidst 'foreign' ideologies, both social and religious, speaks volumes of its eclecticism. In a way Indian culture has emphasised some of the fundamental principles of modern day philosophy of human rights from time past, which can be evidenced in the declarations, made in the *Rig Veda*:

> No one is superior or inferior. All are brothers. All should strive for the interest of all and should progress collectively.[12]

It may be recalled that from time immemorial Indians have called their culture by the name of 'human culture' [*manav dharam/manav sanskriti*]. No gainsaying the fact that human dignity had universal appeal and Indian culture had tried to be so comprehensive as to suit the needs of every human being, irrespective of age, sex, colour or caste.

But human dignity is very much associated with human wants. The right to be human is, of course, the leitmotif of all human rights thought and action. All the same, the human being who is the bearer of these rights may not have her basic material needs fulfilled; no right to use physical force is conceded to her, even in order to fulfil basic needs; and threats to the right to be human arising from civil society are not a part of the problematic of human rights. In the circumstances, human rights thought and action becomes a programschrift, a blueprint, for a just society; but a blueprint with vacant spaces, disallowing at the outset the preconditions for exercising the right to be human.

It is characteristic of classical and contemporary western liberal thought to ignore the entire problematic of basic human needs. The whole tradition of discourse from John Stuart Mill to John Rawls illustrates this tendency massively. Thus, Mill's famous Essay on Liberty excluded the backward nations, women and children from the right to liberty[13]. John Rawls, at the end of a spectacularly cogent and massive analysis in *A Theory of Justice* is able to say, without a frown on his face, on page 543 of his well-acclaimed work, that the lexical priority of liberty, after all, may not apply to societies where basic wants of the individual are not fulfilled !

In his own words, "To be sure, it is not the case that when the priority of liberty holds, all material wants are satisfied. Rather these desires are not so compelling as to make it rational for the persons in the original position to agree to satisfy them by accepting a less than equal freedom. The account of the good enables the parties to work out a hierarchy among their several interests and to note which kinds of ends should be regulative in their rational plans of life. Until the basic wants to individuals can be fulfilled, the relative urgency of their interest in liberty cannot be firmly decided in advance. It will depend on the claims of the least favoured as seen from the constitutional and legislative stages. But under favourable circumstances the fundamental interest in determining our plan of life eventually assumes a prior place."[14]

Now the basis for the priority of liberty is roughly as follows: as the conditions of civilization improve, the marginal significance for our good of further economic and social advantages diminishes relative to the interests of liberty, which become stronger as the conditions for the exercise of the equal freedoms are more fully realized. Beyond some point it becomes and then remains irrational from the standpoint of the original position to acknowledge a lesser liberty for the sake of greater material means and amenities of office. Let us note why this should be so. First of all, as the general level of well-being rises (as indicated by the index of primary goods the less favoured can expect) only the less urgent wants remain to be satisfied by further advances, at least in so far as men's wants not largely created by institutions and social forms. At the same time the obstacles to the exercise of the equal liberties decline and a growing insistence upon the right to pursue our spiritual and cultural interests asserts itself. Increasingly it becomes more important to secure the free internal life of the various communities of interests in which persons and groups seek to achieve, in modes of social union consistent with equal liberty, the ends and excellence to which they are drawn. In addition men come to aspire to some control over the laws and rules that regulate their association, either by directly taking part themselves in its affairs or indirectly through representatives with whom they are affiliated by ties of culture and social situation.

It might seem that even though the desire for an absolute increase in economic advantages declines, men's concern for their relative place in the distribution of wealth will persist. In fact, if we suppose that everyone wishes a greater proportionate share, the result could be a growing desire for material abundance all the same. Since each strives for an end cannot be collectively attained, society might conceivably become more and more preoccupied with raising productivity and improving economic efficiency. And these objectives might become so dominant as to undermine the precedence of liberty. Some have objected to the tendency to equality on precisely this ground, that it is thought to arouse in individuals an obsession with their relative share of social wealth. But while it is true that in a well-ordered society there is most likely a trend to greater equality, its members take little interest in their relative position as such. As we have seen, they are not much affected by envy and jealousy, and for the most part they do what seems best to them as judged by their own plan of life without being dismayed by the greater amenities and enjoyments of others. Thus there are no strong psychological propensities prompting them to curtail their liberty for the sake of greater absolute or relative economic welfare. The desire for a higher relative place in the distribution of material means should be sufficiently weak that the priority of liberty is not affected.

In a well-ordered society then self-respect is secured by the public affirmation of the status of equal citizenship for all; the distribution of material means is left to take care of itself in accordance with the idea of pure procedural justice. Of course doing this assume the requisite background institutions which narrow the range of inequalities so that excusable envy does not arise. Now this way of dealing with the problem of status has several noteworthy features which may be brought out as follows: Suppose to the contrary that how one is valued by others depend upon one's relative place in the distribution of income and wealth. In this case having a higher status implies having more material means than a larger fraction of society. Thus not everyone can have the highest status, and to improve one person's position is to lower that of someone else. Social cooperation to increase the conditions of self-respect is impossible. The means of status, so to speak, are fixed, and each man's gain is another's loss. Clearly this situation is a great misfortune. Persons are set at odds with one another in the pursuit of their self-esteem. Given the preeminence of this primary good, the parties in the original position surely do not want to find themselves so opposed. It would tend, for one thing, to make the good of social union difficult if not impossible to achieve. If the means of providing a good are indeed fixed and cannot be enlarged by cooperation, then justice seems to require equal shares, other things remaining the same. But an equal division of all primary goods is irrational in view of the possibility of bettering everyone's circumstances by accepting certain inequalities. Thus the best solution is to support the primary good of self-respect as far as possible by the assignment of the basic liberties that can indeed be made equal, defining the same status for all. At the same time, distributive justice as frequently understood, justice in the relative shares of material means, is relegated to a subordinate place. Thus we arrive at another reason for factoring the social order into two parts as indicated by the principles of justice. While these principles permit inequalities in return for contributions that are for the benefit of all, the precedence of liberty entails equality in the social bases of esteem.

It is quite possible that this idea cannot be carried through completely. To some extent men's sense of their own worth may hinge upon their institutional position and their income share. If, however, the account of social envy and jealousy is sound, then with the appropriate background arrangements, these inclinations should not be excessive, at least not when the priority of liberty is effectively upheld. But theoretically we can if necessary include self-respect in the primary goods, the index of which defines expectations. Then in applications of the difference of principle, this index can allow for the effects of excusable envy ($ 80); the expectations of the less advantaged are lower the more severe these effects. Whether some adjustment for self-respect has to be made is best decided from the standpoint of the legislative stage where the parties have more information about social circumstances and the principle of political determination applies. Admittedly this problem is an unwelcome complication.

Some may want to object to this account of the priority of liberty that societies have other ways of affirming self-respect and of coping with envy and other disruptive inclinations. Thus in a feudal or in a caste system each person is believed to have his allotted station in the natural order of things. His comparisons are presumably confined to within his own estate or caste, these ranks becoming in effect so many non-comparing groups established independently of human control and sanctioned by religion and theology. Men resign themselves to their position should it ever occur to them to question it; and since all may view themselves as assigned their vocation, everyone is held to be equally fated and equally noble in the eyes of providence. This conception of society solves the problem of social justice by eliminating in thought the circumstances that give rise to it. The basic structure is said to be already determined, and not something for human beings to affect. On this view, it misconceives men's place in the world to suppose that the social order should match principles which they would as equals consent to.

The problematic of needs is acutely disturbing for the received models of human rights, thought and action. It often gets translated into a conflict between 'bread' and 'freedom'; freedom usually wins within the liberal conceptions of rights, despite the awareness that without 'bread', freedom of speech and assembly, of association, of conscience and religion, of political participation—even though symbolic adult suffrage—may be existentially meaningless for its 'victims'.

But the issues are not really "bread" and/or "freedom" in the abstract, but rather who has how much of each, for how long, at what cost to others, and why. Some people have both "bread" and "freedom"; others have "freedom" but little "bread" or none at all; yet others have half a loaf (which is better than none, surely!) with or without freedom; and still others have a precarious mix where "bread" is assured if certain (not all) freedoms are bartered[15].

Five approaches to the problems of development and redistribution are available in the Declaration of Cocoyoc (1974)[16]; the Hammerskjold Foundation's What Now—Another Development (1975)[17]; the conclusions of the 1976 ILO Conference embodied in Employment, Growth and Basic Needs; One World Problem (1976)[18]; the Bariloche Foundation Report Catastrophe or New Society? A Latin American Model (1976)[19]; The Reshaping of International Order (1976) commissioned by the Club of Rome[20]. To this must be added the major Asian effort at formulating an approach to "development" by Rajni Kothari's *Footsteps into Future* (1974)[21].

These five approaches also share the awareness that emphasis on basic survival needs may lead to a situation of conflict between human needs and human rights ("bread" *vs*. "freedom"). The 1977 ILO employment report stresses that "basic needs constitute the minimum objectives of society not the full range of desirable attributes, many of which will inevitably take longer to attain." It seeks employment strategies which will make employment "more humane and satisfying" as an "element of basic needs strategy". The Declaration of Cocoyoc goes even further when it includes in the notion of development the right to work "not simply (as) having a job but finding self-realization in work, the right not to be alienated through production processes that use human beings simply as tools".

The ILO report also supports participation as an aspect of the basic need strategy.

Clearly, it would involve too great an adherence to human rights orthodoxy to raise issues of "bread" *vs*. "freedom" for such approaches. The broad conception of human needs here involves both material and non-material human needs. The conception itself offers a latent critique of parcelling out the latter as "rights" and the former as "needs".

It has been said that a basic needs approach may be congenial to the justification of authoritarian regimes. The provision of "bread" may justify indefinite postponement of the provision of any kind of "freedom". In the absence of such freedom, even the promised "bread" may not be realized by the masses; indeed, they even lose, in the process, their power to protest at the indignity of regime-sponsored starvation. This, indeed, is a possibility which has materialized more often than not.

The problem of human rights, in situations of mass poverty, is thus one of redistribution, access and needs. In other words, it is a problem of "development"; a process of planned social change through continuing exercise of public power. As there is no assurance that public power will always, or even in most cases, be exercised in favour of the deprived and dispossessed, an important conception of development itself is accountability by the wielders of public power to the people affected by it and people at large. Accountability is the medium through which we can strike and maintain a balance between the governors and the governed.

In this perspective, the discussion of human rights becomes fused with a discussion of developmental processes. But what is "development"? "To sleep, to dream, perchance to develop; here is the rub". What is development? Many conceptions of 'development' floating around in massive literature are themselves the means of exploitation. It is at last now being asked: Development for whom? Development from whom? Development of what? Development through what? Undoubtedly, in most countries the GNP has increased; but Gross National Poverty (the other GNP) has also simultaneously increased. That is why one is more comfortable with the expression "impoverishing" societies. Undoubtedly, the reasons for all this are far too complex to permit any "whipping boy", "scapegoat" explanations.

The concept of "human-centred development" provides an example of the economic thinking which comes close to the concept of the right to development. According to a recent UN Publication "...the term 'human-centered development' has gained wider currency. It seeks to direct attention both to the final objective and to the needs. It recognizes that development projects that have ignored broader social and human considerations have often failed, and in many cases actually worsened conditions for the very people they were intended to benefit. To overcome such past failings, the people themselves, both at the grassroots and at high levels have to be involved in planning and implementation. Local resources and untapped human energies and initiatives such as those of women need to be harnessed to achieve the greatest possible impact and to ensure genuine social progress."[22]

Acceptance of such interpretations of development gives rise to the question whether the concept of the human rights to development can be helpful and if so in what way. As a concept which emerged in the framework of human rights discourse it should be helpful in linking development considerations with human rights concerns. However, these links are not simple and the right to development cannot be used as a justiciable right, *i.e.* a right upon which direct legal claims can be used. On the other hand the concept and the declaration on the right to development can be used as a means of interpretation of relevant legal norms.

The 1979 General Assembly Resolution provided a response to this problem by formulating a human right to development. The Resolution states "... the right to development is a human right and equality of opportunity for development is as much a prerogative of nations as of individuals within nations". This formulation matured into the 1986 Declaration on the Right to Development. The Declaration should be read in the light of the formulation of the New International Economic Order (NIEO) and the New International Development Strategy adopted by the General Assembly. The specific goals of this strategy are:

(1) Elimination of hunger and malnutrition;
(2) Accelerated agricultural production in developing countries;
(3) Avoidance of further environmental degradation by policies preventing deforestation, erosion, soil degradation and desertification;
(4) Reduction and elimination of poverty;
(5) Primary health care for the poorest sections of society;

(6) Well-balanced development of human settlements so as to provide greater benefits to low income groups;
(7) Eradication of illiteracy and "closest possible realization of universal primary education by the year 2000";
(8) Reduction of infant mortality and special programmes for children under fifteen years of age "living in poor rural and urban areas";
(9) Efforts at the integration of disabled in the development process; and
(10) Securing equal participation of women "both as agents and beneficiaries in all sectors and at all levels of development process".

The right to development represents the quintessence of a more humane conception of development stressing not just economic growth but values of social justice. Significantly, the alternative paradigm of human development focuses on rights as means of development rather than as ends in themselves. And the values towards which this development efforts is aimed are: human integrity (through the fulfilment of basic needs), autonomy, participation, self-reliance and dealienation.

RIGHT TO HUMAN DEVELOPMENT

The right to human development is a short hand expression for a whole variety of endowments and entitlements. Primarily, the bearer of these rights are about one thousand billion human beings of the south living 'at the margin of existence-enduring hunger, sickness, homelessness and absence of meaningful employment'. The correlated duties are addressed to the governing elite's of the South and the North and to International, Regional institutions and organisations. Indeed, part of the problem is, in this area, that most of us have been too quick to explain, and even to predict, but too slow to understand.

Whatever it may be made to mean, "development" must at least mean this: people will be given the right to be and remain human. Total and continuing destitution and impoverishment exposes people to a loss of their humanity. In no society that takes human rights seriously should there be allowed a state of affairs where human beings become sub-human—that is, when they perforce have to surrender even those sonorously recited "inalienable" rights of man, where people sell their wives, children or themselves (in bonded labour) in order to survive, or surrender their life. The expression "human rights" presupposes a level at which biological entities are bestowed with the dignity of being called human. The bearers of human rights must have an implicit right to be and remain human, allowing them some autonomy of choice in planning survival.

But needs will surely conflict with rights, argues Dr. Upendra Baxi, but whose needs? And whose rights?[23] These would be concrete questions. Should not the need for shelter for the millions of pavement and slum dwellers in Bombay have any legitimacy at all as compared with the rights of the *nouveau riche* to live in five-star splendour? Should not continued drought or famine in one State in India, which forces people to sell their children to receive food for a day, justify a nationwide ban on conspicuous consumption of food on social events? Should not the fact that more than a half of Indian villages do not have access to potable water ensure draconian policing of wanton waste of water by the urban Indians?

Questions of this genre could be multiplied. The point will remain. And the point simply is that the model of universal human rights for all human beings, without exception, has a right to be human. If only a handful enjoy human rights, and erect the general model of human rights as a way of making illegible even the script of basic human needs for the masses, we diminish the very notion of humanity from species-life (as young Marx used to describe it) to class-life. Pithily put, in order that some classes may have human rights, masses have to cease to be human. Human rights thought and action thus rests upon a confiscation of the right of all, without exception, to count as human.

A society that is so basically unjust, in this radical sense, that denies the masses their right to be human, also offers frail foundations for the continued protection of human rights, traditionally conceived.

It is true, at the level of the politics of human rights, that the human rights rhetoric offers powerful, insurrectionary devices for marginally ameliorating the plight of disadvantage, deprived and dispossessed. It is also true that our long period of time the deployment of human rights strategies, such as social action litigation in India tends towards empowering the impoverished. All that this mean is that, in historical time, human rights carry the promise of the rights of all human beings to be human. In this sense human rights thought and action is essentially millenarian promising a golden age, the reversal of the eternal looking *Kali Yuga*. But the messianic future entails bloody costs and conflicts for large masses of human beings, here and now.

Talking specially about human right, in this country, we have the shortage of them. Our system has given us so much rights (only rights) that the parallel of which is very difficuit to find in other countries. One can do whatever one wants. There is so much freedom that you are free to sell medicine in the buses or trains. All types of doctors are available there. Even if you do not have any degree or diploma in medicine you can operate someone in a *dharamshala* or in private house or do whatever you want with his body. With a few screwdrivers, a plier and some nuts and bolts one can sit on the road claiming to be a specialised auto-mechanic and can play havoc with the scooter or car of someone. Such freedoms and rights are not available elsewhere. I am not blaming these people. Perhaps it may be their compulsion. Till we are able to satisfy their basic wants, we will have to accept it.

GANDHI'S VIEWS ON HUMAN RIGHTS

Mahatma Gandhi very much appreciated this point of view. Since he was very sensitive to the feelings and needs of masses he could never stand apart from his people. Moral elevation of individual and satisfaction of needs were not antithetical for him. Rather he was of a definite opinion that human wants must precede other developments.

When Rabindranath Tagore told Gandhi that he was giving more emphasis to human wants than to moral, aesthetic and romantic aspects of human personality, Gandhi wrote back, "To a people famishing and idle, the only acceptable form in which God can dare appear his work and promise of food as wages". He further wrote, "True to his poetical instinct the poet lives for the morrow and have us to do likewise. He presents to our admiring gaze the beautiful pictures of the birds early in the morning singing hymns of praise as they soar into the sky. But I have had the pain of watching the birds who for want of strength could not be coaxed even to flutter their wings. The human birds under the Indian sky gets up weaker than when he pretended to retire. It is an indescribably painful state, which has to be experienced to be realised. I have found it impossible to soothe the suffering patients with a song from Kabir. The hungry millions ask for one poem or right—the invigorating food."[24]

Human thought, in this day and age, must now accomplish what has appeared forbidding and even impossible to liberal human rights, thought and action. And that is the endeavour to conceptualise the right to be human where the antinomy between needs and rights is dissolved. For this endeavour, we need not the Western concepts and thoughts but an authentic action plan as suggested by the Father of Our Nation, Mahatma Gandhi.

Duties and Rights

There is a well-known incident which illustrates Gandhi's attitude towards duties and rights. H.G. Wells once drew up a Charter of Human Rights and sent it to Gandhi asking for his subscription to it. Gandhi cabled him back: "Begin with a Charter of Duties of man, and I promise the rights will follow as spring follows winter."[25] His reply amounted to putting a premium on the duties of man. He thought that the "true source of rights is duty", and urged his countrymen to discharge their various duties willingly and cheerfully. He upheld the *Gita's* gospel of *nishkama karma* by giving it a fresh interpretation. Explaining its dictum of *karmanyevadhikaraste ma phalesu kadacana*, he observed: "Action alone is thine. Leave thou the fruit severely alone. *Action is duty; fruit is rig.*" This was an attempt only to "correlate every right to some corresponding duty to be first performed".[26] He believed that "those only are true rights which flow from due performance of one's duties".[27] In his scheme of the ruler-ruled relationship the discussion of rights, thus, only follows that of obligations.

In consonance with his views on the cultural inheritance of man, Gandhi also subscribed to a coterie of natural rights, describing them variously as "birth rights", "primary rights", or "inherent rights". These rights are, however, natural only in the sense in which Green uses the term "natural", that is, "they arise out of, and are necessary for the fulfilment of, a moral capacity without which a man would not be a man". In other words, these are natural in the sense of being innate.

Gandhi, thus, simultaneously subscribed to two different rights, namely, the rights which the people (the obligors) earn by first performing the corresponding duties, and the natural rights which they deserve instinctly, *i.e.* by virtue of their cultural heritage of rationality. Put together, these constitute his charter of earned rights.

Despite his conviction that "Rights accrue automatically to him who duly performs his duties", Gandhi admitted the hard reality that only those succeed in actually securing the deserved rights who shout, strive and are ready to sacrifice their all. Once reminding his countrymen of the fundamental principles of the British Constitution, he observed: "Even a mother, says an Indian proverb, does not serve without being asked much less does a British Government. We, therefore, hope that our countrymen throughout South Africa will make a careful note of this aspect of the British Constitution, and refuse to rest wild justice is granted." Elsewhere he observed: "That the genius of a democratic Constitution requires that every citizen should be as free as any other, and, if he is not, it is his duty to demand and fight for his freedom."[28]

In the course of his Satyagraha Movements, he frequently stressed the need of sacrifice for attaining the basic rights of citizenship. In South Africa, he asked Indians to "take courage in both hands and burn the obnoxious Asiatic Act with the fire of gaol going". And, in India he expressed the need of supreme sacrifice for attaining the birth-right of *Purna Swaraj* (complete independence). He said: "*Swaraj* won without sacrifice cannot last long. I would, therefore, like our people to get ready to make the highest sacrifice that they are capable of... May India live up to this *mantra.*"[29]

Gandhi did not delineate coherent characters of obligations or rights as he was not an academician. An outline of the rights that he wanted the people to earn, secure and enjoy does, nevertheless, emerge from his writings scattered over two scores of years of his active political life. For the purpose of systematic presentation the rights he advocated and fought for are classified in this section under the broad categories of political, civil, religious, economic and educational rights.

Political Rights

In Gandhi's list of political rights may be included the right to vote, right to participate in one's governance, right to liberate one's country from the foreign yoke, and the right to warn, to resist and to disobey a bad government.

He subscribed to the notion of "universal adult franchise a disciplined and politically intelligent electorate." He, however, prescribed quite a few qualifications for the people who would be entitled to vote in elections. In the first place, he wanted the voters to be within the age group of 18/21 to 50 years. Once prescribing the minimum age-limit he hoped that when the Congress government comes into power, "the large majority of men and women of 21 years and above will have been enfranchised."[30] Though he specifically wanted 21 years to be the minimum age-limit for the general body of voters, his statement recorded by *Harijan* indicates that he would not have objected to its fixing even at 18 years. The maximum age-limit, on the other hand, was prescribed by him with the sole intention of debarring the people above fifty years of age from voting. He thought that "old men like himself... were of no use as voters", and, as such, "he would have a bar against persons beyond a certain age, say fifty". The prescription by Gandhi of this maximum age-limit was the outcome of his belief in the *varnashrama* of Vedas. The Vedas compartmentalize the life of man into four stages of 25 years each, namely, the *brahmacharyashrama*, the *grihasthashrama*, the *vanaprasthashrama* and *sanyasashrama*. Accordingly, Gandhi would include in the list of voters only those citizens who belong to the second stage of life *grihasthashrama*, or are nearing it.

Secondly, he wanted the literacy test to be necessary for every voter in order to enable him "to value his freedom" before comes to exercise it. Emphasizing the necessity of such a test for every voter, he said:

> "I have come round to the view that a literacy test is necessary for two reasons. The vote should be regarded a privilege and should, therefore, carry some qualifications. The simplest qualification is a literacy test. And if the ministry appointed under the literacy franchise is sincere and solicitous about the disqualified illiterates, the much desired literacy would come in no time."[31]

And, in order speedily to wipe out unemployment, he prescribed an additional qualification of 'manual labour'. Of the literates belonging to the age group of 18-50 years, Gandhi would give the right to vote only to those who serve the state by willingly undertaking manual labour. In *Young India*, he proclaimed that by *swaraj* he meant "the government of India by the consent of the people ascertained by the vote of the largest number of the adult population...who have contributed by manual labour to the service of the state."[32]

Gandhi was eager to secure the right to vote to all those citizens, who fulfil these three qualifications irrespective of their caste, creed, sex, religion, property qualifications, or place of birth. The actual exercise of this right, he, however, would leave to the discretion of the voter. He wanted suffrage to be the citizens' 'privilege' rather than their 'duty'. He would allow the conscientious objectors to abstain from voting, for his South African *satyagraha* had taught him that "a very powerful effect, can be produced by abstaining from exercising the franchise."

Gandhi also upheld the citizens' right to participate in the conduct of government through their *bona fide* representatives. He fought for securing this right to his countrymen for he sincerely believed that like all other peoples, Indians, too, had an innate "capacity to regulate national life through national representatives". The additional ground of his demand for this right was that they were actually "fighting for" securing this instinctively deserved right. Moreover, he subscribed to the maxim: "He who pays the piper has the right to call the tune". In other words, he thought that since people send their representatives to the Assemblies "loyally to, carry out" their wishes, they have, a right to the government of their choice.

Freedom from foreign rule, he believed was a pre-condition to the attainment of self-rule or *swaraj*. He, thus, inaugurated and led as many as five Satyagraha Movements for securing this right to his countrymen. And, it was during the course of these movements that he appealed to them "to lose all, if they will save their souls and gain the freedom which is their birth right". He desired both Great Britain (the foreign ruler) and her allies—"the United Nations" to recognize India's birth right of freedom from foreign rule. At the same time he called upon Indians to exhibit a high degree of political awareness needed for securing this freedom, for he thought that "there is no room for cowards in a society... which loves freedom".

He also urged them to exercise their birth right to warn, dismiss or resist a bad government by "undergoing hardships and self-sacrifice" and by attaining a high degree of political awareness. Once, justifying the attitude of South African Indians of towards their government, he said: "we often talk of the disabilities... and we have a right to complain about them and to seek redress". He justified people's right not only to warn their government if it went wrong, but also "to protest and to carry on any agitation" against it, if it perpetuated its wrongs. In extreme cases, he also recognized their right to "remove the Government if they wished to," that is if they found it to be incorrigible. His abiding belief was that the notion of "responsible government includes the power to dismiss ministers", if they commit excesses or overstep their limits. In specific cases, he thought it to be "the birth right and duty of the people to disobey orders which on mature consideration, they regard as unjust or oppressive." He, nevertheless, insisted that they ought to earn even this instinctively deserved right by first "obeying the many laws of the state". He found the confirmation of his views in Thoreau's statement: "Mankind has the right to refuse allegiance to and resist the government when its tyranny becomes unendurable".[33] Gandhi was only eager to persuade that civil disobedience is "the inherent right of a citizen."

Shriman Narayan Agarwal suggests that Gandhi would go so far as to entitle the citizens of parliamentary democracy to claim the right to recall their duly elected representatives if they do not discharge their civic duties to the entire satisfaction of electorates.[34] In short, Gandhi upheld citizens' right to make the government and also to unmake it.

Civil Rights

Gandhi's *satyagraha* struggles were characterized by his strenuous defence of the rights which he thought the citizens would enjoy in a state which is free from foreign rule. He believed that "Civil liberty consistent with the observance of non-violence...is the breath of political and social life... the foundation of freedom... the water of life". Following were various civil rights that he specifically claimed and advocated from time to time: (i) Right to Citizenship; (ii) Right to Legal Equality; (iii) Right to the Freedom of Speech and Expression; (iv) Right to form Associations and to hold Public Meetings; (v) Right to the Freedom of Movement; (vi) Right to the Freedom of Residence, and (vii) Right to Legal Remedies.

Gandhi thought that a person ought to be recognized as a citizen by the singular fact that he was born in the state whose citizenship he seeks. He upheld the principle of *jus soli*, irrespective of the descent of the citizen. He said: "The Jews born in France are French in precisely the same sense that Christians born in France are French." Giving his own example he observed:

> "If I were a few and were born in Germany and earned my livelihood there, I would claim Germany as my home even as the tallest gentle German may, and challenge him to shoot me or cast me in the dungeon; I would refuse to be expelled or to submit to discriminating treatment."[35]

He also pleaded for the recognition of citizenship by naturalization. He urged the South African Government to define the status of Indians residing in various South African Colonies and to accord to them the rights of citizenship on the footing of equality with the original inhabitants. Claiming the right of Transvaal Citizenship for his countrymen domiciled in Transvaal, he declared: "We think we have as much right to be in this land as the Whites have. The Negroes alone are original inhabitants of this land. We have not seized the land from them by force; we live here with their goodwill."[36]

Consonant with his belief in Divine equality of men. Gandhi wanted that all should be equal in the eyes of the man-made law, irrespective of the type of their citizenship. He also desired that equal protection of laws be available to all the citizens, whatever be their caste, class, colour, material possessions, numbers, race, religion, sex or social status. He was eager to stop the exploitation of man by man, for he had realized that people "suffered because of these distinctions" and that "this sense of high and low" had vitiated their lives.

Once expressing his opposition to the distinctions based on caste or class, he observed: "I hold all classes of people—Brahman, Kshatriya, Vaishya and Shudra, Rajput, Mahar, Chammar—all alike, and I regard the distinctions based on birth as immoral."[37] He objected to the apartheid policy of the South African colonies on the ground that it entailed the regulation of immigration on the basis of the "colour" of man's skin. He further, desired that in extending equal protection of laws to all the citizens, poverty or riches should not stand in their way. Nor should this equality be denied to any one on the ground that he belongs to a particular minority group, for he believed that "Even a minority of one can expect perfect justice". He also maintained that "Freedom without equality of all, irrespective of race or religion, was not worth having".[38] Similar was his view about distinctions based on sex. He thought that in the scheme of God and nature both, man and woman, are equal. No less was he convinced that the "abolition of untouchability" was man's right. He, thus, was averse to discrimination amongst the various sections of citizens on any one or more of these grounds.

Gandhi's notion of citizen's equality extends specifically to the unrestricted use of public places and services. Gandhi at all citizens should, without any distinction, have the equal right to the use of wells, tanks, roads, schools and places of public resort maintained out of state funds or dedicated by private persons for the use of the general public.

Citizen's legal equality was the solid foundation on which Gandhi built the edifice of these civil rights. The very first of these rights was the freedom of speech and expression. He not only claimed this "natural right" for all his countrymen, but also specifically directed his individual *satyagraha* of 1940-41 against Government of India's refusal to allow the people freely to preach non-cooperation with them in their Second World War effort. He desired that "Everyone should have perfect liberty to preach by pen and tongue". His notion of this freedom was comprehensive enough to include the freedom of "Healthy, well-informed, balanced criticism". He wanted everyone to say: "it is for me to judge when to say something and when to hold my tongue". In *Young India* he observed:

> "Liberty of speech means that it is unassailed, even when the speech hurts, liberty of the press can be said to be truly respected only when the press can comment in the severest terms upon and even misrepresent matters, protection against misrepresentation or violence being secured not by an administrative gagging order, not by closing down the Press but by punishing the real offender, leaving the Press itself unrestricted. Freedom of association is truly respected when assemblies of people can discuss even revolutionary projects, the state relying upon the forces of public opinion and the civil police, not the savage military at its disposal to, crush any actual outbreak of revolution that is designed to confound public and the state representing it."[39]

He clamoured for the achievement of this freedom for his countrymen because he sincerely believed it to be the foundation of *swaraj* and *dharma* and a pre-condition of evoking the best in the opponent. He was also sure that no government, however despotic or coercive it may be, can stop the exchange of views for a long time. In *Harijan*, he observed that even if the government dared, "Inter-relation of ideas cannot be prevented". Yet, he knew that "there are reasons for speech and action, as there are reasons for silence and in action". Two restrictions he specifically put on the exercise this right. First, that the people should exercise this right in such a manner as not to influence the matters *subjudice*. And, secondly, that its exercise must not result in the outbreak of violence.

Gandhi's list of civil rights also includes the freedom of association, assembly and movement. He thought that man's instinct of sociability required that he should have freedom to form associations (including political parties) and unions of his choice. Conversely, he required the state not to prohibit the peaceful associations or assemblies in an arbitrary manner. For instance, he sent strongly-worded protest notes to the Government of India when the latter declared the Congress organization "unlawful", with the intention of suppressing the freedom movement. In 1942, he wrote to the Viceroy:

> "The whole Congress movement was intended to evoke in the people the measure of sacrifice sufficient to compel attention. It was intended to demonstrate what measures of popular support it had. Was it wise at this time of the day to seek to suppress a popular movement avowedly non-violent?... however much I dislike your action, I remain the same friend you have known me. I would still plead for a reconsideration of the Government or India's whole policy."[40]

On another occasion, he justified the demand of his associates, Jamna Lal Bajaj, for the lifting of the ban on the Jaipur Rajya Praja Mandal, by declaring that the Jaipur "civil disobedience struggle will cease, the moment the bans are lifted and the right of free association, holding public meetings, etc., is conceded." He also extolled Dr. Ram Manohar Lohia's defiance of the Goan Government's order, and proclaimed that Lohia had "thereby rendered a service to the cause of civil liberty and especially to, the Goans."[41]

In the course of Satyagraha Movements, both in South India, Gandhi and his associates stood up to condemn and defy the unnecessary restrictions imposed by the governmental authorities on their exercise of the freedom of movement. They also endeavoured to persuade the rulers, of princely States to allow Indians from other parts of the country to enter their States without let or hindrance, provided, of course, their objective was not to create lawlessness. He fought for these rights for he considered them to be essential for awakening the ignorant masses to a sense of their duty as citizens.

His right for the South African Indians' right to the freedom of residence was only a corollary to his demand for the freedom of movement. He was opposed to the South African Government's policy to confine Indians to particular locations and just because they belonged to the coloured races of Asia. He incessantly asked the Government to abrogate the legislation that imposes disabilities on them "because they wear skin".[42] He proclaimed that the imposition of such restrictions was not only "inhuman" but also "undeserved". Indians, he thought, had earned this right, in common with the inhabitants, by voluntarily and cheerfully serving South Africa land of their adoption.[43]

It was in order to check flagrant violations of the citizens' rights that Gandhi insisted on the recognition of their additional right to legal remedies. He wanted that the citizens should have a right to obtain legal and political protection against acts of violence, compulsion or intimidation. The citizens should rather have the constitutional right to get their rights enforced through the courts of law in cases of their violation. Once, deploring the absence of this right in the dealer's Licences Bill of Natal, he made the following statement:[44]

The Dealers' Licences Bill is...the worst of all. It...gives absolute power to the licensing authorities to refuse, to issue or renew licences without the right to the aggrieved party to appeal to the highest tribunal of justice. It is thus subversive of one of the most cherished principles of the British Constitution.

At the Round Table Conference, he specifically asked the Indian Princes to grant to their people the right to constitutional remedies, *i.e.* the right to get their rights enforced through the courts of law. In South Africa, he had also demanded the appellants analogous right to see the documents on record of the court, by declaring that "if a man has a right to appeal, he ought to have a right to see the documents which are on record."

Religious Rights

Gandhi was the staunch upholder of secularism and wanted the people to be true to their conscience. He advocated the people's right to profess, practice and propagate the religion of their choice, without any let or hindrance. He thought that communal animosity was a serious contravention of man's conscience, which entitles one to follow the religion of one's choice, and which simultaneously oblige him to tolerate the free exercise of this right by the fellow human beings. He said:

> "Let people's religions be different. You worship a Being a single Entity—as Allah and another adores Him as Khuda. I worship Him as Ishwar. How does any one stand to lose (by this arrangement)? You worship facing one way and I worship facing the other. Why should I become your enemy for that reason? We all belong to the human race; we all wear the same skin; we hail from the same land. When the facts are as simple as that, it will be nothing but folly and short-sightedness to bear implacable enmity towards one another."

He, thus, insisted that so long as men differ in temperament, their paths are bound to differ. Conversely, he rejected the possibility, and even the necessity, of a particular religion being one day recognized as common for all mankind. In his letter to Jamnadas Gandhi observed: "Personally, I think the world as a whole will never have, and need not have, a single religion".[45]

His abiding faith in the conscience of man implied that every individual had the right to choose his religion and to practice and profess it without let or hindrance, so long as he obeys the common law of the land. He, thus, required the state to "respect the liberty of individual nonviolent conscience, however, inconvenient it may be". He thought that "freedom of worship would become a farce if interference became the order of the day".

He also wanted that everyone should have the right to interpret, accept or reject the tenets of any religion. Once, claiming the mission for himself the right to study and interpret the message of Islam, he said: "Islam was not a creed to be preserved in a box. It was open to mankind to examine it and accept or reject its tenets".[46]

Finally, his advocacy for the freedom of religious worship and study also enabled him to uphold the analogous right of a person to "intelligent conversion", that is, to voluntary change of belief and faith. But, he was basically opposed to forcible conversation which he thought to be a flagrant violation of the man shares with God. Once, explaining the mission of his life, he proclaimed: "Love is the basis of our friendship as it is of religion. I seek to gain Mussalman friendship by right of love. And if love persists even on the part of one community, unity will become a settled fact in our national life."[47]

Economic Rights

In Gandhi's list of economic rights may be included the right to work, right to just and adequate wages, and the right to hold and dispose of property.

His discovery of unemployment as a major symptom of India's social disorganization had impelled him to ask the people to claim the basic necessities of their life only after rendering physical labour as per their capacity and choice. Conversely, he enjoined the state to guarantee the right to work to all unemployed men and women so that they may be able to earn bread by the sweat of their brow. The work ensured to each individual should, as far as possible, be of his choice. Not only that, the state should not force any citizen into work, it should also not force any one to do the work which is not of his choice. In other words, every citizen should be ensured the right to work of his choice.

In his enthusiasm to expect the state to recognise the citizen's right to have the work of their choice, Gandhi would go to the extent of requiring the state to provide to every able-bodied person a variety of employment opportunities so that he may opt for the work of his choice. He once said:

> "A variety of work should be put before the people and they should have one month's notice that if they made no choice of occupations suggested, nor did they suggest some other acceptable occupation but declined to do any work, though their bodies were fit, they would not be able to give them doles after the expiry of the notice. It was wrong for any citizen to accept rations without some physical work."[48]

The idea is that no able-bodied citizen should live on charity, and that there must always be enough occupations in a well ordered state for all those who are willing to work.

Though Gandhi allowed each individual to claim the occupation or profession of his choice, he was not radical enough to reject the traditional *varna* or class system under which each individual followed "the profession of his ancestors for earning his livelihood". He wanted to retain the *varna* system, which divided the Hindu into *brahmanas* (teachers of religion), *kshatriyas* (soldier), *vaishyas* (merchants or farmers), and *shudras* (servants or employees, misknown as "untouchables"), for he believed that every person inherits the particular characteristics and qualities of his progenitors. At the same time, he thought that *varna* does not compel anyone to follow the parental occupation against his aptitude. It rather allows each individual to determine his occupation or profession in terms of his physical ability, mental aptitude and personal choice. Such a liberal interpretation of the traditional *varna* system of the Hindu society enabled Gandhi to synchronize with it the individual's democratic right to work.

Gandhi also upheld the citizen's right to, limited hours of work. He wanted that nobody should be compelled to work for more than eight hours a day so that he has his earned rest and leisure to look after himself, his family and to render to the society whatever service he can.

Eight hours' work should secure to each worker just and adequate wages. The state should see to it that the wages for such an honest work are sufficient to ensure satisfaction of worker's basic needs of food, clothing and shelter. This should be the minimum that the state should ensure to every one irrespective of the nature of his work. Over and above this basic minimum, the wages could vary according to the needs of the worker concerned.

Gandhi also upheld the individuals analogous right to hold and dispose of the wealth he thus earns. He should be allowed to acquire, hold and dispose of property. If, however, the state wants to take over his earned property for public purposes, he should be duly compensated. Gandhi fought for securing economic rights to his countrymen in the course of his *satyagraha* movements in South Africa, Ahmedabad, Bardoli and Kheda.

Educational Rights

Gandhi attached primary importance to the problem of education. He knew that *swaraj* and democracy have no meaning in the context of a society in which the majority of the people are illiterate. He, thus, felt the imminent necessity of requiring the state to promote education and to speed up the literacy campaigns. At the same time, he was eager to relate education to the conditions of life in India. The scheme of education he hammered out is popularly known as the Wardha Scheme of Education, after the name of the place where a two-day Conference was held in October 1937 to discuss and examine his propositions.[49]

In order to enable every citizen to understand and experience the real meaning of *swaraj* and democracy, his scheme provided for the right to a seven years free and compulsory education. In the beginning, Gandhi had desired education at all levels should be optional and not compulsory. He thought that compulsion was unnecessary if people wanted education. It would rather be harmful if they did not opt to be educated. However, the stern reality of mass literacy in India ultimately led him to allow compulsory education at the primary level. On the eve of the Wardha Conference, he declared:

> "I am a firm believer in the principle of free and compulsory primary education for India. I also hold that we shall realize this only by teaching the children a useful vocation and utilizing it as a means for cultivating their mental, physical and spiritual faculties."[50]

He wanted the state to make the primary education free so that the obstacles from the way of those who cannot afford it may be removed. In other words, "education to be universal must be free". He also insisted that this state-managed compulsory and free vocational primary education should be spread over a period of seven years, between the age group of seven to fourteen, so that at the end of this period the students become self-supporting.

In his scheme of education, individual's right to higher vocational education is to be ensured by the state in collaboration with the private enterprise who would pay for the training of the persons required by them. Gandhi wanted to leave higher vocational education to be financed by the private enterprise so that the universities do not cost the state much, practically nothing beyond the cost of running a central education department. The rationale of leaving higher vocational education with the private enterprise was twofold. In the first place, he had realized that "no government can provide fully for all the education which the people need". Secondly, he would not like the state to pay from the general revenue for all higher education also, because its purpose is narrow and demand limited. He summed up his conclusions as follows:

> "(1) I am not opposed to education even of the highest type attainable in this world;
> (2) The state must pay for it whenever it has definite use for it;
> (3) I am opposed to all higher education being paid from the general revenue."[51]

Thus, he subscribed to the maxim: "He who needs the expertise shall pay for its training too".[52]

Gandhi did not deny to women the right to study any branch of human knowledge. He, however, desired that they, traditionally the master of household, should devote themselves to the education primarily of domestic affairs. The nature of women's biological and social functions being different from that of men, they should be taught management of the home, the things they should or should not do during pregnancy, and the nursing and care of children.

Gandhi made no distinction between man and woman in so far as their educational rights were concerned. He was uncompromising in upholding the equality of the sexes and was eager to restore to women their traditional and natural right to rule the home.

Gandhi also championed the right of the educationally backward classes to special treatment in matters of education so that they may also come up to the level of the educated ones and enjoy their rights equally with others. They should be free to preserve and develop their own script, language and culture.

NOTES

1. Jai Narain Sharma, "Rural-Urban Dichotomy Need for a Fresh Look", *Gandhi Jyoti*, Bhagalpur, Bhagalpur University, Year 6, No. 4, 24 July, 1989.
2. Morse Bradford and Berger Thomas, "Sardar Sarovar", *The Report of Independent Review*, Canada, World Bank, 1992.
3. Har Mohan Mathur and Marsden David (eds.), *Development Projects and Impoverishment Risks*, New Delhi, Oxford University Press, 1998.
4. *The Economic and Political Weekly*, 1989, Vol. 34, No. 1, Mumbai.
5. Upendra Baxi, "The State of Human Rights Movement in India", in Manoranjan Mohanty *et al.*, *People's Rights Social Movements and the State in the Third World*, New Delhi, Sage Publications, 1998.

6. Human Development Report 1998, *United Nations Development Programmes*, Delhi, 1998.
7. P.K. Nayak, *Resettlement at Rengali Dam*, Orissa, Bhubaneshwar (Monograph), 1986.
8. United Nations, *Resolution of the General Assembly*, 10 December 1948.
9. Jai Narain Sharma, "Human Rights *Vs*. Human Needs", in A.D. Mishra (ed.), *Perspectives on Human Rights*, New Delhi, Radha Publications, 2002, pp. 18-28.
10. Vienna Declaration and Programme of Action (A/CONF. 157/23).
11. Maurice Cranston, *What are Human Rights?* London, Longmans, 1973.
12. The original text is in Sanskrit and is taken from Mandala 5, Sukta 60, Mantra 5, which states: ajyestaso akanishtasa etc., Sam bhrataro va virdhuhu sowbhgya.
13. J.S. Mill, *Essays on Liberty*, Oxford, Blackwell, 1947.
14. J.A. Rawls, *A Theory of Justice*, London, O.U.P., 1972.
15. Upendra Baxi, *Mambrino's Helmet*, New Delhi, Har-Anand Publications, 1994.
16. Declaration of Cocoyoc, 1974.
17. *The Hammerskjold Foundations*, What Now—Another Development, 1975.
18. ILO Conference on Employment, *Growth and Basic Needs: One World Problem*, 1976.
19. The Bariloche Foundation Report, *Catastrophe or New Society? A Latin American Model*, 1976.
20. Reshaping the International Order, *RIO A Report to the Club of Rome*, London, Hutchinson, 1976.
21. Rajni Kothari, *Footsteps into the Future*, New Delhi, Orient Longmans, 1974.
22. *The World Economy: A Global Challenge*, UN Publication, 1989.
23. Baxi, Upendra, *Inhuman Wrongs and Human Rights*, New Delhi, Har-Anand Publications, 1994.
24. *Young India*, 15-10-1931, p. 307.
25. *Harijan*, 13-10-1940, p. 320.
26. *Ibid.*, 8-6-1947, p. 184.
27. *Ibid.*, 25-3-1939, p. 64.
28. *Ibid.*, 15-4-1939, p. 90.
29. *Ibid.*, 25-4-1939, p. 30.
30. *Ibid.*, 1-9-1940, p. 266.
31. *Ibid.*, 14-1-1939, p. 421.
32. *Ibid.*, 2-3-1947, p. 46.
33. *Ibid.*, 27-5-1939, p. 136.
34. Shriman Narayan Agarwal, *Gandhian Constitution for Free India*, Allahabad, Kitabistan, 1946, p. 102.
35. *Harijan*, 26-11-1938, p. 352.
36. *Ibid.*

37. *Ibid.*, 2-5-1936, p. 89.
38. *Ibid.*, 23-11-1947, p. 423.
39. *CWMG*, Vol. XXII, pp. 176-77.
40. Pyare Lal, *Gandhiji's Correspondence with the Government: 1944-47*, Ahmedabad, Navajivan Publishing House, 1959, pp. 17-20.
41. *Harijan*, 30-6-1946, p. 208.
42. *Ibid.*, 28-1-1939, p. 437.
43. *CWMG*, Vol. II, pp. 28-30.
44. *Ibid.*, Vol. III, p. 333.
45. *Ibid.*, Vol. XI, p. 125.
46. *Ibid.*, Vol. XII, p. 127.
47. *Harijan*, 23-2-1947, p. 39.
48. *CWMG*, Vol. XXI, pp. 110-11.
49. *The Hindu*, Madras, 11-2-1947, p. 4.
50. C.J. Varkey, *The Wardha Scheme of Education: An Exposition and Examination*, Mysore, Oxford University Press, 1940, p. 3.
51. *Harijan*, 9-10-1937, p. 292.
52. *Ibid.*, 9-7-1938, p. 176.

7

Nationalism and Internationalism

The process of making and breaking of a nation is complex. Considerable investigations and research in depth are required to understand as to how, as a general phenomenon, nations came into being, how long does it take them, what is the sequence of evolution and finally, what constellation of factors act together or separately to make a nation.

However, the history reveals certain general tendencies in nation-building, the following are the sequence of the stages of the formation of a nation: "open or latent resistance to political amalgamation into a common national state; minimal integration to the point of passive compliance with the order of such an amalgamated government; deeper political integration to the point of active support for such a common state but with continuing ethnic and cultural group cohesion and diversity; and finally, the coincidence of political amalgamation and integration with the assimilation of all groups to a common language and culture."[1] In some cases, it is quite possible that cultural and linguistic assimilations have long preceded the amalgamation into a single state, and political integration likewise may develop well before the ultimate decision-making powers of several governments are amalgamated into one.[2]

There is also an existential view according to which nation-building is an act of choice or rather a sequence of choices in terms of the needs inherent in an individual's personality and in his external situation. This choice has the ingredients of community consciousness, will to be a people and will to create a state and political homeland.[3]

PROCESS OF NATION-BUILDING IN INDIA

Seen in the light of the above mentioned hypotheses, the process of nation-building in India has been different from the one in Europe, where the Greek or Roman nation-state of old was deeply rooted in the culture and where nationalism in the form we know it today emerged and matured much before anywhere else.

In India, the notion of nation (*rashtra*) emerged much before in any other civilisation. But it was a geographical and cultural rather than political identity. All that existed south of the Himalaya was India, and even outside this geographical realm. The lands where Indian civilisation took its roots were also part of India. Within this greater India were many kingdoms even republics, independent of each other. True there were persistent efforts to bring this geographical and cultural India into a single kingdom but such attempts succeeded only temporarily the subcontinent of India was too large for the transport and communication technology of the time to be united into a political entity.

Nationalism in India in its modern sense thus came only as a response to the political domination of Britain. The will to statehood, *i.e.* 'to be politically independent in the sense not to be ruled from outside, to be organized in the sense to provide a constituency for a government, which exercises effective rule within it, to be autonomous, and to accord to this government such acclaim, consent, compliance and support, as to make its rule effective'[4], developed effectively and preponderantly only in the nineteenth century. Even the will to be a people was rather weak. There is considerable evidence to show that the efforts to hasten political processes leading to the formation of the nation got attenuated and received greater attention than other aspects of nationalism. In other words, political socialization took precedence or command over other equally important forms of socialization.

Take for instance the nature and scope of the nationalist struggle under the Congress. At best, it was tantamount to a series of exercises in political pelmanism—nay bad pelmanism. It all amounted, in a sense, to making the British rulers in India to concede status of equality and respect to the Indian people. The Congress was often willing to make compromises on substantive issues, provided that its point was conceded. Masses were organized, pressures were put, new centres of influence were established, in order to rouse political consciousness, to generate fearlessness and self-confidence. This ferment had various aspects and expressions for instance, peasant unrest, trade unionism, youth turmoil, etc. But the Congress did not take full cognizance of this upsurge. It was selective in picking up only gross anti-British political issues as a basis of national campaigns, (*e.g.* boycott of Simon Commission, civil rights, war issue, claim, to full independence, salt *satyagraha*, etc.) a fact, which affected the content of nationalism in India.

The theme was a parallel movement for cultural renaissance but it was not an integral part of the political movement. Quite understandably, a people suffering under colonial yoke for more than one and a half century needed these exercises to help them to develop self-confidence. The entry of Mahatma Gandhi in the freedom movement did change the situation to a great extent but necessary groundwork, both intellectual and operational, was not done to strengthen cultural and social tissues of our collective life.

Certain features of the national movement, in fact, diverted people from social realities important among them being direct mass action followed by negotiations for constitutional changes. The direct mass action became a means of effecting transfer of power in small doses. It was not conducted for the conquest of power. There was an insistent drift in the direction of legislative work or parliamentarianism. This was due to the composition and character of leadership, which was drawn from the 'Westernized' and 'semi-modernized' urban middle classes who equated freedom and independence in terms of peaceful transfer of power leading to more patronage, more influence and more authority to Indians to manage their affairs. They could not have conceived of it as a means of creating conditions precedent to bring about basic changes in social, cultural and economic relations. In spite of emphasis on mass movement, it was admitted that at a particular stage of development in late 1930s, constitutionalism had come to stay as a major aspect of India's national struggle. Whatever little was done to inject ideology (either from within or without) into the Congress movement, it not only failed but also divided the movement and promoted 'double thinking' in it.

In fact, this development exacerbated Hindu-Muslim antagonism and hindered the fruition of those processes which could have lessened the tension between the communities. Introduction of franchise and other forms of representative institutions embittered communal relations. Religion got politicized. Militant Hindu and militant Muslim nationalism grew. There were strong elements of revivalism in these movements. As India approached 1930, it became quite clear that unity was as important a question in India as was freedom. India, in fact, was heading towards partition; the making of two nations were in the offing.

There were other aspects of the process as well. Though, unintended, the British policies also helped in promoting social ferment. For instance, such factors as the emergence of a middle class, spread of education and introduction of new means of transport and communications led to the reduction of the social, psychological and spatial distances and to the creation of a sense of common collective identity and thus laid the social basis of nationalism. As a matter of fact the process of social and cultural modernization and amalgamation had already set in, independently, even if in a small way in the eighteenth and nineteenth centuries itself. There was a desire to discover the moorings and to bring certain important aspects of our collective life in tune with the times.

There were also areas (for example, in Maharashtra) where nationalist sentiments had a positive social, cultural and economic content.[5] There is also evidence to show that some groups of individuals and organizations (*e.g.* Dadabhai Naoroji, R.C. Dutt, etc. and moderates and extremists) were aware of the importance of these questions. Later on, science, socialism and modernism and Gandhian ideas of social reconstruction also began to acquire more significance.

However, all these positive elements did not acquire an independent and preponderant position. They operated at a lower key and the dominant, component remained political. The political socialization was faster and more assertive. Consequently, the tasks of thinking basically of social and cultural reconstruction, which were to become the base of the social order in free India were neglected. For instance, the work relating to forward thinking, clarification of issues and creation of a consensus about language, education, caste, and values was not effectively undertaken.

There is one more feature of the process of nation-building in India in recent times. On the whole, the sweep and scale (taken territorially) of the national movement under the leadership of the Congress was certainly of an all-India character. But, in effect, it did not reflect all the dominant trends, emphases, and attitudes of the whole area that is India. It was, very largely Indo-Gangetic in its perspectives. It may be argued that the Congress had its following in all areas and even its leadership was drawn from all parts of India. Yet, in terms of its dominant leadership major compulsions and general direction the epicentre of the Congress lay in the Hindi-speaking areas. To be more precise, it was what has been called in ancient text "The Madhya Desh" nationalism—in line with the general trends of the history of India over thousands of years. It did not cover the princely states, the Kirat desh (*i.e.* the Himalayan areas), the tribal population all over India and several other areas. It was, thus, not comprehensive enough to reflect fully the geographic and the ethnic sweep of the Indian subcontinent.

Finally, there was one more interesting aspect of Indian nationalism. In spite of the growth of sectarianism, the ethnic, cultural, religious and social differentiations which in Europe had led to the formation of nation-states, was as such accepted in India as a basis of our constitution and the national movement, and this led to the general acceptance of the ideal of a universal state-all-inclusive, non-sectarian nationalism.

Along with the growth of sectarian trends, there were elements of universalism and liberalism also. It had a world outlook. It viewed India's freedom in the context of world forces of imperialism, racialism and peace. This element was to flower into, what we call, the policy of nonalignment.[6]

GANDHI'S CONTRIBUTION TO NATION BUILDING

Gandhi realized that social evils impeded India's march to unity and *swaraj*. For this he did not depend upon the state and its political agencies. He mobilized social energies of the people. His constructive to programme was an aspect of his philosophy of nationalism and national unity. He conceived of it as a means of strengthening social aspect of our collective existence at grassroots. Take for instance his work of untouchability. He considered it as part of the movement for unity.[7] Similarly, basic education was originally evolved as a tool for social transformation by bridging the gulf between the intellectual and working classes.

The fact that he did not wait for political freedom and worked simultaneously for the reordering of society shows that he did not consider the purely political aspect of national struggle exclusively significant. This concern for the non-political aspect of our national life and his attempt to enrich it by the voluntary efforts of the people is relevant for the promotion of national unity, for, then alone, he thought, will India be able to evolve a style of living of its own.

Gandhi's ideas can also help us to achieve our definition as a nation and thus remove the badge of imitativeness and lack of identity. Freedom, to him, did not mean English rule without Englishmen. It meant conditions to be able to live according to our own genius, according to the inner law of our being. He knew almost intuitively that culture does not travel in parts. One thing leads to another. If India accepted machines and goods and ideas from the West, indiscriminately and wholesale, it will lose its soul.[8]

Consequently, he tried to persuade us to turn our gaze within and to discover our roots and sources for renewal. He tried to make us aware of the importance of being ourselves and not to be swept away by the westerly winds. His nationalism was not against an imperial system but against a value system, against a civilization which had the potency to demolish our identity. Today, India needs this inward looking tendency, it needs the *swadeshi* spirit, about which Gandhi spoke incessantly. This component of Gandhi's heritage alone can give sharpness, depth and substance to national idea.

The acceptance of this concern of Gandhi about our identity does not mean that his answers to achieve the identity are also to be accepted, we can reject his anti-science slant and anti-Western civilization proclivities.

Today, fascist forces are again gathering strength and gaining respectability. The militant and revivalist Hindu nationalist philosophy is winning considerable following. The hardline Islamic elements have turned into terrorists with global network. They hold that religion is the basis of nationalism. This view ignores the multi-religious, multi-cultural, multi linguist and multi-racial character of Indian polity. It will lead India on the road to fascism and narrow nationalism.

Gandhi was opposed to Hindu nationalism and divisive politics of Muslims. Though himself a Hindu, he did not consider it as a basis of nationality. He believed that India is a land for all. It is not only of and for Hindus. If Hindus want non-Hindus to live as slaves of Hindus they will he thought kill Hinduism itself.[9] This concern of Gandhi with all-inclusive non-sectarian secular concept of nationalism is of utmost relevance.

He believed that religion is not a factor in the creation of a nation. The followers of the respective faiths are not different nations.[10] In no part of the world are one nationality and one religion synonymous terms;[11] nor has it ever been so in India. The quarrel between Hindus and Muslims recommenced with the advent of English.[12] The way to promote national harmony is: "If everyone will try to understand the core of his own religion and adhere to it and will not allow the false teachers to dictate to him, there will be no room left for quarrelling" [13] Further, he thought that as Hindus are better able to shield themselves from attack...they should not oppose the concessions Muslims ask...and thus avoid taking our quarrels to a third party. He thought Hindus should be brave enough to trust and all will be well.[14] He argued that Hindus by their action should prove or disprove two nation theory.[15]

According to Gandhi[16], the religion of Islam was not antagonistic to Hinduism. He tried to find common grounds and points of similarities between Hinduism and Islam. To him all great religions sprang from the same source and their fundamentals like nonviolence were common to them all.[17]

He interpreted Hinduism too in the same light. "My Hinduism...includes all that I know is best in Islam, Christianity[18]...it demands the fulfilment of all cultures...It is all-inclusive. It stands for tolerance". He said that "all should forget their religious affiliations".[19]

Apart from the commonality in ethical and moral principles, Gandhi pointed to the commonality between Hindus and Muslims in the matter of basic human needs such as employment, sanitation; secondly, justice, etc.[20] Moreover, common economic intensity would tend to make Hindu-Muslim tensions less acute.[21] He thought that it could be best promoted by 'cooperating to reach a common goal[22]... bridging social distance consistently with religious belief...by going out of my way to seek common ground on political fields'.[23] 'Common birth, common distress, common manners and common bondages are...a real cohesive force. He thought all these will prove a force that will make the nation irresistible'. But he thought that if Hindu and Muslim cannot come to an agreement,[24] "we must fight till we are exhausted and come to our senses without seeking the intervention of British justice...or bayonets...."[25]

Gandhi did not think that interdining and intermarriage between Hindus and Muslims would promote unity. "It is tantamount to asking the Hindus to give up their religion... It is a reformation outside practical politics. And when that transformation comes, if it is ever to come, it will not be Hindu-Muslim unity.[26] The inter-religious marriages should follow harmony, it will be disastrous, so long as the relations are strained. They have no bearing on unity. The causes of discard are economic and political..."[27] To promote Hindu-Muslim unity, Gandhi advised the adoption of Hindustani (a mixture of Hindi and Urdu) with two scripts (Devanagari and Persian) for inter-provincial communication,[28] irrespective of whether Muslims opt for Devanagari or not.[29]

Gandhi was a successor to militant Hindu nationalist revivalist movements in the nineteenth century and he himself was a devoutly religious person. Therefore, there is a considerable amount of religion in his ideas and approach. He tried to resolve Hindu-Muslim conflict within the frame of reference of religion rather than within a militant secularist frame, thought and action. No doubt there is evidence to indicate that Gandhi did not rule out the importance of secular ideals and approaches, yet this aspect of his ideas was not militant enough and he sought to resolve communal difference mainly by exhorting each of the communities to be better religionists. He was building nationalism on the basis of harmonious coexistence and reconciliation, rather than on assimilation and amalgamation and fusion.

There can be two possible ways of looking at the answers which Gandhi evolved to deal with the Hindu-Muslim question. One is to note his shrewd understanding of the fact that in a congenitally religious society like India, no social and political question can be completely isolated from religion and, therefore, it is more politic to keep on finding out the point of equilibrium at which the two forces get suitably balanced than to discard religion outright and, thus, to alienate the people. The second is to reject the above approach outright and adopt an absolutely militantly secular stand and note the weakness of Gandhi's approach and the inadequacy of his answer, namely, in a religion oriented society, involved intensely in a process of deep political socialization, any attempt to purify politics by religion would have failed. The more Gandhi tried to press religion in the service of politics, the more rapidly did religion get politicized.

For taking up a more scientific and militantly secular approach to nationalism, we should gain a keener understanding of India's history, society and traditions. For instance, it will be necessary to decondition the mind of both Hindus and Muslims in respect of their present notions of Indian history. If we think that the secular traditions of Indian history began in the middle ages we are wrong... The most potent traditions of materialism and secularism, which cut across all religions are to be found in the ages that preceded the middle ages.

Louis Fischer says: "In modern times, the urge towards nationhood has been elemental, natural and instinctive. Gandhi is the most forceful Indian exponent of this urge."[30] Subjectively, he incarnated the very spirit of nationalism, its profound indignation against foreign enslavement and the heroic will and determination to end that enslavement. The consciousness of Gandhi was also completely free from even the faintest trace of provincial particularism or communalism. He was not a Gujarati or even a Hindu but an Indian, a nationalist *par excellence*. But his concept of nationalism had a wider connotation. In our earlier discussion on his concept of *swaraj*, we have seen that his nationalism was based on the interest of the masses as opposed to the classes. In the discussion to follow we shall see that the nationalist Gandhi did not preach jingo nationalism. On the other hand, he tried to lead India away from the path of narrow and exclusivist nationalism into a recognition of her duty as a member of the international fraternity of nations based on interdependence as a recognized principle of public life.

NATIONALISM AS GANDHI CONCEIVED

Gandhi's early initiation to nationalism, in the main a western ideology, was evident during his stay in London. It seems quite likely that Gandhi, who was born in India in an age when nationalism swept the imagination of the advanced and educated sections of the population, was influenced by it to some extent in his younger days. But his nationalism effectively dates from his South Africa days when he actually experienced the humiliation of racial discrimination. His nationalist feelings developed since his arrival in India in 1915. Intimate contact with the suffering millions of India made him a staunch opponent of foreign slavery and an ardent nationalist. The most remarkable thing that one finds is that his philosophy of nationalism was not based upon race-hatred and chauvinistic feelings. It was the stroke of his genius that blended nationalism with internationalism. His patriotism transcended geographical frontiers and was coterminus with humanity.

In 1921, he wrote: "For me patriotism is the same as humanity. I am patriotic because I am human and humane. It is not exclusive. It will not hurt England or Germany to serve India. Imperialism has no place in my scheme of life. The law of a patriot is not different from that of a patriarch. And a patriot is so much the less patriot if he is lukewarm humanitarian. There is no conflict between private and political law."[31] In his famous article, 'The Great Sentinel', he wrote: "Indian nationalism is not exclusive, nor aggressive, nor destructive. It is health giving, religious and, therefore, humanitarian."[32]

Similarly, he wrote in 1924: "I live for India's freedom and would die for it, because it is part of Truth. Only a free India can worship the true God. I work for India's freedom because my *swadeshi* teaches me that being born in it and having inherited her culture, I am fittest to serve her and she has a prior claim to my service. But my patriotism is not exclusive; it is calculated not only not to hurt another nation but to benefit all in the true sense of the word. India's freedom as conceived by me can never be a menace to the world."[33]

Here is a graphic description of nationalism as conceived by Gandhi:

> "We want freedom for our country, but not at the expense or exploitation of others, not so as to degrade other countries. I do not want the freedom of India if it means the extinction of England or the disappearance of Englishmen. I want the freedom of my country so that other countries may learn something from my free country, *so that the resources of my country might be utilized for the benefit of mankind.* Just as the cult of patriotism teaches us today that the individual has to die for the family, the family has to die for the village, the village for the district, the district for the province, and province for the country, even so, a country has to be free in order that it may die, if necessary, for the benefit of the world. *My love, therefore, of nationalism, or my idea* of *nationalism, is that my country may become free, that if need be, the whole country may die, so that the human races may live.* There is no room for race-hatred there. Let that be our nationalism."[34]

NATIONALISM SHOULD STRENGTHEN INTERNATIONALISM

Gandhi's naturalism was not chauvinistic. "I want India's rise so that the whole world may benefit. I do not want India to rise on the ruin of other nations,"[35] he said in 1925. I do want to think in terms of the whole world. My patriotism includes the service of humanity. "I would like to see India free and strong so that she may offer herself as a willing and *pure* sacrifice *for the betterment* of *the world*."[36] Speaking of his mission, Gandhi said in 1929 "My mission is not merely brotherhood of Indian humanity. My mission is not merely freedom of India, though today it undoubtedly engrosses practically the whole of my time. *But through realization of freedom of India I hope to realize and carry on the mission of the brotherhood of man.* My patriotism is not an exclusive thing. It is all-embracing and I should reject that patriotism which sought to mount upon the distress or exploitation of other nationalities. The conception of my patriotism is nothing if it is not always, in every case without exception, consistent with the broadest good of humanity at large."[37]

In 1931 he remarked: "Our nationalism can be no peril to other nations inasmuch as we will exploit none, just as we will allow none to exploit us. Through *swaraj* we will serve the whole world."[38] Similarly, he wrote in 1933: "I am a humble servant of India and in trying to serve India, I serve humanity at large.... After nearly 50 years of public life, I am able to say that today my faith in the doctrine that the service of one's nation is not inconsistent with the service of the world has grown. It is a good doctrine. Its acceptance alone will ease the situation in the world and stop the mutual jealousies between nations inhabiting this globe of ours."[39]

He told Louis Fischer in June 1942: "For the time being, India disappears from my gaze. I never wanted independence for India's sake alone. I never wished to play the role of frog-in-the-well."[40]

For Gandhi, there was no antithesis between nationalism and Internationalism. He did not preach abstract internationalism. He knew that one must be a good nationalist in order to become a true internationalist. He explained in his writings that there could be no genuine International cooperation without national independence.

In 1925, he wrote: "It is impossible for one to be Internationalist without being a nationalist. Internationalism is possible only when nationalism becomes a fact, *i.e.*, when peoples belonging to different countries have organized themselves and are able to act as one man. It is not nationalism that is evil, it is narrowness, selfishness, exclusiveness which is the bane of modern nations which is evil. Each wants to profit at the expense of, and rise on the ruins of, the other. Indian nationalism has struck a different path. It wants to organize itself or to find full self-expression for the benefit and service of humanity at large....Goa having cast my lot in the midst of the people of India, I should be untrue to my Maker if I failed to serve them. If I do not know how to serve them I shall never know how to serve humanity. And I cannot possibly go wrong so long as I do not harm other nations in the sob of serving my country."[41]

Again, in 1931: "You want cooperation between nations for the salvaging of civilization. I want it too, but cooperation presupposes free nations worthy of cooperation. If I am to help in creating or restoring peace and goodwill and resist disturbances thereof, I must have the ability to do so and I cannot do so unless my country has come to its own. At the present moment, the very movement for freedom in India is India's contribution to peace. For so long as India is a subject nation, not only is she a danger to peace, but also England which exploits India. Other nations may tolerate today England's imperialist policy and her exploitation of other nations, but they certainly do not appreciate it; and they would gladly help in the prevention of England becoming a greater and greater menace everyday. Of course, you will say that free India can become a menace herself. But lot of assume that she will behave herself with her doctrine of nonviolence, if she achieves her freedom through it and for all her bitter experiences of being a victim of exploitation."[42]

Cooperation of subject India with the Allies during Second World War was a preposterous proposition. Gandhi, though an ardent advocate of international collaboration and cooperation, did not mince words reminding Louis Fischer that "to collaborate we must be free. Slaves do not fight for freedom."[43]

Gandhi fought for and led the nation for national freedom but as has been seen above from his own writings, he did not advocate an isolated independent existence. In fact, his emphasis was on a federation of friendly interdependent states, and as national independence was the pre-condition for such an existence, he waged battle against foreign domination.

As early as 1924, he wrote: "Isolated independence is not the goal of the world states. It is voluntary interdependence."[44] Again, in the same year he said: "The better mind of the world desires today not absolutely independent states warring one against another, but a federation of friendly interdependent states. The consummation of that event may be far off. I want to make no grand claim for our country. But I see nothing grand or impossible about our expressing our readiness for universal interdependence rather than independence. I desire the ability to be totally independent without asserting the independence."[45]

Similarly, he told a gathering in Bombay in 1931: "My notion of *Purna Swaraj* is not isolated independence but healthy and dignified interdependence. My nationalism, fierce though it is, is not exclusive, not designed to harm any nation or individual. Legal maxims are not so legal as they are moral. I believe in the eternal truth of *"sic utere tuo ut alienum non loedas*."[46]

In a letter to Jawaharlal, dated 14 September, 1933, he wrote, as follows:

> "Nor have I the slightest difficulty in agreeing with you that in these days of rapid intercommunication and a growing consciousness of the oneness of all mankind, we must recognize that our nationalism must not be inconsistent with progressive internationalism. India cannot stand in isolation and unaffected by what is going on in other parts of the world. I can, therefore, go the whole length with you and say that we should range ourselves with the progressive forces of the world."[47]

Asserting this principle of international cooperation and solidarity, he wrote in 1939: "A free democratic India will gladly associate herself with other free nations for mutual defence against aggression and for economic cooperation. She will work for the establishment of a real world order based on freedom and democracy, utilizing the world's knowledge and resources for the progress and advancement of humanity."[48]

TOWARDS A WORLD FEDERATION

It may be recalled here that the democratic world federation he visualized could only be raised on the foundation of nonviolence. He envisaged the establishment of a world federation as the necessary condition for world peace. In a letter, dated Sevagram, 28-7-1942, addressed to Maurice Frydman who was very much interested in the idea of world federation, Gandhi wrote:

> "I told you that I was one with you and that I was trying to take the Congress and everybody towards world federation. I also told you if it ever comes, it will come through Sevagram or the Sevagram way; I want Free India, too, for that purpose. If I can get freedom for India through non-violent means, power of

non-violence is firmly established, Empire Idea dissolves and the World-State takes its place in which all the states of the world are free and equal, no state has its military. There may be a world police to keep order in the absence of universal belief in non-violence."[49]

In 1947, Gandhi said in reply to a question that the only condition on which the world could live was that it should be united under one central governing body composed of representatives of the component parts.[50] "I would not like to live in this world if it is not to be one world. I would certainly like to see that dream realized in my life time", Gandhi declared in Inter-Asian Relations Conference held in the last week of March 1947. "If you work with a fixed determination, there is no doubt that in our own generation we will realise, this dream."[51]

Gandhi's intense nationalism or the concept of *swadesi* fitted in quite well with his one-world idea. He repeatedly asserted that the concept of *swadesi* was not based on narrow exclusivism. The spirit of sacrifice underlying *swadesi* should go beyond a man's own community and should embrace the whole of humanity. He believed in the truth implicitly that a man could serve his neighbours as well as humanity at large at the same time, provided the service to the neighbours was in no way selfish or exclusive, *i.e.*, did not in any way involve the exploitation of any other human being."[52]

Gandhi discussed the reason why *swadesi,* which he called "the acme of universal service," implied preference for the nearest and the immediate. One may refer to *From Yervada Mandir* for a clearer exposition of the doctrine of *swadesi*.[53] "*Swadesi* recognized the scientific limitation of human capacity for service." 'Thus understood', *swadesi* serves the cause of international brotherhood.

Gandhi's, fundamental religious belief that all are equal before God explains to an extent why he adhered to the concept of human brotherhood as opposed to national exclusivism. In the memorable article, '*The Doctrine of The Sword*', Gandhi wrote: "My religion has no geographical limits. If I have a living faith in it, it will transcend my love for India herself."[54] His deep humanitarianism found its expression when he declared: "There is no limit to extending our services to our neighbours across state-made frontiers. God never made those frontiers."[55] This statement made in 1931 was not just a culled out, isolated statement to prove our point that Gandhi's supreme concern was humanity at large. In 1947, on the eve of independence, he was asked the question, 'If a neighbouring state is in want, what should 'Free India do?' His categorical answer was that "a truly Independent India was bound to run to the help of its neighbours in distress."[56]

Gandhi, like a practical Utopian, visualized, World Federation, a plan of human unity to be realized by the federal organisation of friendly interdependent states. He had a great devotion to the noble goal of international cooperation and universal harmony because, according to him, not to believe in the possibility of "permanent peace" amounts to disbelief in the "godliness of human nature". Hence he wanted that permanent peace should be secured. He also pleaded for world order and world federation. He wrote:

> "Isolated independence is not the goal of the world states. It is voluntary interdependence. The better mind of the world, desires today not absolutely independent states warring, one against another, but a federation of friendly interdependent states. The consummation of that event may be far off. I want to make no grand claim for our country. But I see nothing grand or impossible about our expressing our readiness for universal interdependence rather than independence. I desire the ability to be totally independent without asserting the independence."[57]

On July 4,1947, at a prayer speech Gandhi visualised that "if by India's effort such a world federation of free and independent states was brought into being, the hope of the kingdom of God, otherwise called Ram Raj, might legitimately be entertained.[58]

He agreed that the only condition for the survival of world civilization was the realization of world union under one central governing body composed of representatives of the constituent entities. Most probably, Gandhi had in mind the federal pattern for this central governing body.

Gandhi would like the world government to non-cooperate with the lawless, aggressive and recalcitrant forces. But a world police force may be necessary in the beginning. This police force, under the control of the world authority, would exercise its power only as the last sanction when moral and nonviolent sanctions had ceased to have effect. Thus it is clear that absolute unadulterated pacifism is not the Gandhian gospel for the contemporary world.

Speaking of Gandhi's concept of nationalism and internationalism, Dr. Dhirendra Mohan Datta observes: "Indian nationalism drew its inspiration from the dominant Indian belief in the fundamental unity of humanity in spite of its diversity, and the consequent belief in the reasonableness of human equality. So nationalism logically led on to internationalism. Love of man impelled Gandhi to be both a nationalist and an internationalist."[59] While we express our complete agreement with Dr. Datta when he asserts 'love of man as being the motive force of Gandhi's nationalism and internationalism, we fail to persuade ourselves to accept the earlier portion of his statement as valid where he traces the source of Indian nationalism. Indian nationalism is a modern phenomenon. It came into being during the British period as a result of the action and interaction of numerous subjective and objective forces and factors which developed within the Indian society under conditions of the British rule and the impact of world forces. As Asoka Mehta and Achyut Patwardhan argue: "...a historical approach is necessary for history is to a student of politics what a laboratory is to a man of science. It provides him a frame of reference with which to test the validity of political ideas. From history then we have to find out how and at what time the group-feeling called nationality first become conscious and vocal. We have, for instance, in *Atharva Veda*, which even at the lowest estimate is 4,000 years old, the famous *Prithvi Sukta* or hymns praise and gratitude to Mother Earth. The content of some of these hymns is strikingly similar to that of some of the modern national anthems. But will that justify us in attributing a feeling of nationality to the Aryan *rishis* who sang these hymns? Certainly not, for it would be absurd to call this simple love of Mother Earth patriotism or attribute any national feeling to it."[60]

Besides his deep religious convictions and seminal humanism, the advanced thought—currents and objective forces helped to Gandhi's ideas about nationalism and internationalism. His idea of internationalism was not to be viewed merely as a projection of his *advaita* faith; it was certainly there, but the political aspect should not be lost sight of. We find him recognizing the essential political bearing of the problem of internationalism and world order. It was proof of his genius that he could integrate his philosophical faith with political acumen.

His native sense of realism enabled him to discover the interconnection between creative nationalism and genuine internationalism. The goal being the establishment of world brotherhood, he realized that slaves had no place in that fraternity. As early as 1909, he could assert: "Slaves ourselves, it would be a mere pretension to think of freeing others."[61] As a practical politician, he did not think it worthwhile to mouth fashionable phrases of internationalism, but he moved in the direction of an international order of free nations by working for the establishment of a free and democratic India. It was his earnest belief that India could further the interests of internationalism only by freeing herself from the shackles of bondage. That is why he devoted almost all his energy and time for the attainment of freedom of his country. As he himself said, his patriotism was both exclusive and inclusive. Exclusive in the sense that his nationalism was not of competitive and antagonistic nature. For Gandhi, nationalism was not an end in itself but a stage, though a necessary one, in the political evolution of man. One may find parallels between Gandhi's and Mazzini's ideas about nationalism.[62] "God", Mazzini used to say, "has engraved a message on the cradle of every nation which it has to give to the world". His nationalism was not exclusive; it was informed with a moral purpose. It had meaning as a new "tie" for humanity and the emphasis was always on its "fraternal and liberal development."[63] In the name of nationality itself he denounced the narrow spirit of nationalism and "the stupid presumption on the part of each people that they are capable of solving the political, social and, economic problems alone; and their forgetfulness of the great truth that the cause of the peoples is one."[64]

Nationalism carried a distinct meaning for Gandhi; it could enlist his allegiance only when its political and moral boundaries were conterminous.

ATTITUDE TOWARDS IMPERIALISM AND FASCISM

It was in the heyday of nationalism that Mazzini came forward. But the later history of nationalism in Europe records that it had degenerated into a cult of self-aggrandizement. In countries which had already developed into nation-states, the economic development made liberalism an inadequate creed. It had either to broaden internally—by extending democracy from political rights to economic freedom of the masses—into social democracy, or expand externally as imperialism. There was thus a duality in nationalism. The western states sought a solution in imperial adventure. As J.A. Hobson records in his pioneer study, *Imperialism* (1902), Great Britain set out its sails 'in forcing bad markets and finding speculative fields of investment in distant corners of the earth, adding millions of square miles and of unassimilable population to the area of the Empire.' Imperialism, tied to the politics of power and profit, created international rivalries and the constant threat of war—the corollary of which was militarism. And militarism negates the political and social gains of democracy.[65]

Gandhi experienced this transformation of nationalism into imperialism. As is well known, he led the greatest battle against the mightiest Empire. We shall not engage ourselves in outlining the role he played in that battle; we would rather make a study of how his 'ideas evolved from a belief in imperialism's progressive character to a criticism of—its motives and an ultimate rejection of its results.

Gandhi recorded in his Autobiography that during his student days in London he developed the habit of reading newspapers like *The Daily Telegraph*, *The Daily News* and *The Pall Mall Gazette*. The last named daily was independent; under the editorship of William T. Stead and then of Edward T. Cook during Gandhi's London phase, its policy adhered to J.R. Seeley's conception of the civilizing role of imperialism throughout the world. For the following score of years Gandhi too was attached to this view of the British Empire. In the first decade and a half of his South African phase, he was generally loyal to the British Empire. In the preamble declaration of Gandhi's Indian Opinion, we read: "The Policy of the paper would be to advocate the cause of the British Indians in this subcontinent. But while it would insist upon the rights of the community, it would not be slow to point out to its responsibilities also as members of a mighty Empire. It would persistently endeavour to bring about a proper understanding between the two communities which providence has brought together under one flag."[66]

Speaking of 'Ourselves' the same issue carried the editorial note to the effect that "there is nothing in our programme but a desire to promote harmony and goodwill between the different sections of the one mighty Empire."[67]

He had warm praise for British justice. In an article in Indian Opinion, entitled 'A well-deserved Victory', dated 14-5-1904, he wrote: "…in British Dominions, no matter how high prejudices may ran, there is always a haven of safety in the highest courts of justice."[68]

Appealing to the Potchefstroom Vigilants to desist from violence and incitement, he wrote: "The history of British rule is the history of constitutional evolution. Under the British flag, respect for the law has become a part of the nature of the people." ('The Potchefstroom Vigilants and British Indians' in *Indian Opinion*, 24-12-1904).[69]

The strain of racial discrimination practised by the colonialists in South Africa had its impact on his mind. Gandhi's faith in the civilizing mission of the Empire received a severe jolt. To him, imperialism appeared as a concomitant of western industrial civilization. "Let us pray", he wrote in conclusion to his paraphrase of Ruskin's *Unto This Last*, "that India is saved from the fate that has overtaken Europe, where the nations are poised for an attack on one another, and are silent only because of the stockpiling of armaments. Some day there will be an explosion, and then Europe will be a veritable hell on earth. Non-white races are looked upon as legitimate prey by every European state. What else can we expect where covetousness is the ruling passion in the breasts of men?"[70] We see Gandhi at this period growing alive to the nature of European economic penetration. India provided the classic example. About the British East India Company he wrote in *Hind Swaraj*: "That corporation was verged alike in commerce and war. It was unhampered by questions of morality. Its object was to increase its commerce and to make money....To protect the latter it employed an army...." Napoleon is said to have described the English as a nation of shop keepers. It is a fitting description. They hold whatever dominions they have for sake of their commerce. Their army and their navy are intended to protect it...They wish to convert the whole world into a vast market for their goods.[71]

During the First World War, Gandhi had placed a moratorium, so to say, on his criticism of imperialism. But from 1920 onwards full-throated denunciation of British imperialism marked his political career.

Replying to the allegation of inconsistency against him, he wrote in *Young India* (17-11-1921):

> "I know now that I was wrong in thinking that I was a, citizen of the empire. But on those few occasions [Gandhi's service during Boer War, Zulu 'rebellion', raising ambulance corps in London in 1914 and enlistment of recruits during First World War] I did honestly believe that in spite of the many disabilities that my country was labouring under, it was making its way towards freedom, and that on the whole the Government from the popular standpoint was not wholly bad and that the British administrators were honest

though insular and dense. Holding that view, I set about doing what an ordinary Englishman would do in the circumstances. I was not wise or important enough to take independent action. I had no business to judge or scrutinise ministerial decisions with the solemnity of a tribunal. I did not impute malice to the ministers either at the time of the Boer War, the Zulu revolt or the late war. I did not consider Englishmen nor do I now consider them as particularly bad or worse than other human beings. I considered and still consider them as capable of high motives and actions as any other body of men and equally capable of making mistakes. I therefore felt that I sufficiently discharged my duty as a man and a citizen by offering my humble services to the empire in the hour of its need whether local or general.

"The whole situation is now changed for me. My eyes, I fancy, are opened. Experience has made me wiser. I consider the existing system of government to be wholly bad and requiring special national effort to end or mend it. It does not possess within itself capacity for self-improvement. That I still believe many English administrators to be honest does not assist me, because I consider them to be as blind and deluded as I was myself. Therefore I can take no pride in calling the empire mine or describing myself as a citizen. On the contrary, I fully realise that I am a pariah, untouchable of the empire. I must therefore constantly pray for its radical reconstruction or total destruction..."[72]

The excerpt is given above *in extenso*, for it lays bare the evolution of his idea about the British Empire. Another significant document that explains his evolution from 'a staunch loyalist and cooperator' to 'an uncompromising disaffactionist and non-cooperator', is his written statement before the Court in the historic trial of March 1922.[73]

In 1929, in an article in *Young India*, he indicted exploitive colonialism as the first cause of the war. "Is not the prime cause of modern wars the inhuman race for exploitation of the so-called weaker races of the earth?"[74] While talking to an American interviewer in 1940, he asked: "Why is there the war today, if it is not for the satisfaction of the desire to share the spoils?" However, Gandhi distinguished between the imperialism which he criticized scathingly and its agents who administered the decisions of the imperial government. For he regarded man above institutions and he believed in the redemption of man.

Gandhi held that imperialism had its origin in man's covetousness or greed. This belief might have been due to the influence of the Upanisadic tradition that he inherited. The parallel is to be found in Tagore who held that greed was the seed of all that polluted the sense of human unity. Dr. Paul F. Power observes in this connection: "As to Gandhi's economic interpretation of imperialism emphasizing the greed of men, such an analysis overlooks the motivating factors of prestige and adventure which have been significant in the history of Western colonialism. It should be noted also that Gandhi's economic critique of imperialism is non-Marxist in origins tracing back to the influences of Naoroji, Ruskin, Gokhale and Tolstoy. He seldom indicted capitalism as such for sustaining imperialism as have Marxists drawing from Lenin's Imperialism: The Highest Stage of Capitalism."[75]

While it is true that Gandhi's ideas about imperialism and economic ruin of national wealth were to a great extent influenced by the above mentioned thinkers, still it cannot be said for certain that 'he seldom indicted capitalism as such for sustaining imperialism'. Gandhi, it is true, did not systematically analyse the social roots of imperialism as was done by Lenin. He was not built up that way. But his unerring insight penetrated deep into the social basis of imperialism as can be illustrated from his interview to an American journalist wherein he said that 'Your land is owned by a few capitalist owners'.[76] In Gandhi's critique of Western democracy, that he charged capitalist democracies with expansionism. And what else is imperialism but loot of markets and financial investment outside one's own country? And further, 'prestige and adventure' might have played their part in the history of western colonialism, but in our opinion 'the motivating factors' were in essence economic. The factors of 'prestige and adventure' were ostensible and those sentiments were called forth to put a covering on the sordid aspect of the whole thing. Whether one agrees or not to Gandhi's analysis of imperialism and his suggested solution for the liquidation of the same, it cannot be gainsaid that he grasped the nature of the phenomenon. This comprehension, we are sure, was not a product of a theoretical analysis, rather he arrived at the truth from his experience. His method, it may be said once again, was empiric.

Italian Fascism and German National Socialism were the clearest expressions of the autocratic and intolerant nationalism. The whole philosophy of Nazism and Fascism was based on the premise of the sacrifice of the individual at the altar of the nation or the state. "Fascism", said Hitler in a speech delivered on 10 March, 1933, "is against individualist abstractions founded on a materialist basis of the type of the eighteenth century. It is not the individual but the nation which is at the centre of the Law."[77] The merging of the individual into the nation was one of the outstanding characteristics of totalitarian nationalism. As has been said, Hegel's Absolute State and Bismarckian nationalism culminated in modern totalitarianism. Jingo nationalism believed that violence was the *ultima ratio* of human endeavour.

We have seen above that Gandhi had strong repulsions, against aggressive nationalism based on force and as was only expected, he denounced Nazism and Fascism in no uncertain terms.

On his way back from the Round Table Conference, Gandhi paid a visit to Rome and called on Mussolini. The Fascist dictator asked Gandhi whether he expected to win independence for India through nonviolence and what he thought of the fascist state which he had built. With disconcerting frankness, Gandhi told Mussolini that he was only building a house of cards. Gandhi was not at all impressed by the dictator's personality: "His eyes are never still."

Gandhi's censure of Fascism was a logical extension of his anti-colonialism. The Diary of Mahadev Desai records (entry dated May 27, 1932): "Fascist propaganda is being carried on even in England. There are some Fascists in Parliament, and that Winston Churchill is a great admirer of Mussolini."[78]

In 1938, Gandhi denounced the militarist philosophy of Hitler and Mussolini: "The philosophy for which the two dictators stand calls it cowardice to shrink from carnage. They exhaust the resources of poetic art in order to glorify organized murder....They are ever ready for war."[79]

In another article, entitled 'How to combat Hitlerism', dated June 18, 1940, he wrote: "Whatever there Hitler may ultimately prove to be, we know what Hitlerism has come to mean. It means naked ruthless force to an exact science and worked with scientific precision."[80]

Gandhi considered violence as a transitory phenomenon corrected by non-violent resistance. While explaining his weapon of non-violence to two Negro visitors in 1937, Gandhi said: "A violent man's activity is most visible, while it lasts. But it is always transitory. Hitler and Mussolini on the one hand and Stalin on the other are able to show immediate effectiveness of violence. But it will be as transitory as that of Jhenghis's slaughter."[81]

Despite the worst demonstration of the naked violence of Fascism and Nazi tyranny, Gandhi did not lose his faith in the redemptive nature of man. He told a delegation of Christian leaders in December 1938: "...belief in non-violence is based on the assumption that the human nature in its essence is one and, therefore, unfailingly responds to the advances of love."[82]

The belief that powerful dictators are not beyond redemption is to be found in Gandhi's letter to Hitler dated Abbotabad, 23 July, 1939: "It is quite clear that you are today the one person in the world who can prevent a war which may reduce humanity to the savage state. Must you pay that price for an object however worthy it may appear to you to be? Will you listen to the appeal of one who has deliberately shunned the method of war not without considerable success? Anyway, I anticipate your forgiveness, if I have erred in writing to you."

"This manslaughter must be stopped. You are losing; if you persist it will only result in greater bloodshed", Gandhi wrote about May 1940 to Lord Linlithgow, the then Viceroy of India, concerning the war. "Hitler is not a bad man. If you will call it off today, he will follow suit. If you want to send me to Germany or anywhere else, I am at your disposal. You can also inform the Cabinet about this."[83]

Gandhi addressed a second letter to Hitler, dated Wardha, December 24, 1941. Needless to say, the Censor intervened and he was not allowed to publish it, nor presumably did it ever reach Hitler. He had intended to address a joint-appeal to Hitler and Mussolini and he expressed the hope that Mussolini would take the letter as addressed to him also, with the necessary changes. He wrote: "We have no doubt about your bravery or devotion to your Fatherland, nor do we believe that you are the monster described by your opponents. But your own writings and pronouncements and those of your friends and admirers leave no room for doubt that many of your acts are monstrous and unbecoming of human dignity especially in the estimation of men like me who believe in universal friendliness."[84] He continued: "We resist British imperialism no less than Nazism. If there is a difference, it is in degree. One-fifth of the human race has been brought under the British heel by means that will not bear scrutiny. Our resistance to it does not mean harm to the British people. We seek to convert them, not to defeat them on the battlefield. Ours is an unarmed revolt against the British rule....We know what the British heel means for us and the non-European rates of the world. But we would never wish to British rule with German aid." After elaborating upon his doctrine of non-violent resistance he appealed to Hitler "in the name of humanity to stop the war."[85] This letter indicates that, as in relation to British imperialism, he regarded man as above the system he upholds.

At times Gandhi's view of fascism was a paradoxical mixture of appreciation and criticism. "It is not that people would necessarily be unhappy under fascism", he said in 1934. "We may leave aside Hitler, but under Mussolini Italy is certainly better off than before. Some of the public utility works undertaken there are commendable. The standard of living has improved. But what does it all avail? There is no freedom. Whoever dares to oppose Mussolini's policy invites death. And now even killing has become unnecessary. People have adapted themselves to the new condition and are content with it. He has done the work more cleverly than Hitler."[86] Another mixed comment is to be found in his article, 'How to combat Hitlerism', referred to above. "They [the Germans] will honour Hitler as a genius as a brave man, as matchless organizer, and much more. But I should hope that the Germans of the future will have learnt the art of discrimination even about their heroes."[87] In the same letter, he urged upon the victims of Nazi oppression to defeat Hitlerism not with counter-Hitlerism but by organizing non-violent defence, and he fervently hoped that the moral force of non-violence would ultimately triumph.

NOTES

1. Karl W. Deutsch, "Nation-Building and National Development: Some Issues for Political Research" in Karl W. Deutsch, and J. William Foltz, (ed.), *Nation Building*, New York, 1963, pp. 7.8.
2. *Ibid.*, p. 8.
3. Hermann Weilemnann, "The Interlocking of Nation and Personality Structure" in Karl W. Deutsch, and J. William Foltz (ed.), *Nation Building*, New York, 1963, pp. 33-55.
4. Karl W. Deutsch, *op. cit.*, pp. 11-12.
5. Dev Dutt, "Indian Nationalism and Gandhi", in S.C. Biswas (ed.), *Gandhi Theory and Practice, Social Impact and Contemporary Importance*, Shimla, IIAS, 1969, p. 298.
6. *Ibid.*
7. M.K. Gandhi, *Caste Must Go and The Sin of Untouchability*, Ahmedabad, Navajivan Publishing House, 1967, p. 39.
8. See also A. Toyanbee's, *The World and the West.*
9. *Harijan*, 28-9-1947, p. 349. Quoted in U.R. Rao, *The Way to Communal Harmony*, Ahmedabad, 1963, p. 371.
10. M.K. Gandhi, *Hind Swaraj*, Ahmedabad, Navajivan Publishing House, 1958, p. 50.
11. *Ibid.*, 49.
12. *Ibid.*, 50.

13. *Ibid.*, 53.
14. *Young India*, 29-5-1924, p. 185. Quoted in U.R. Rao, The Way to Communal Harmony, Ahmedabad, 1963, p. 54. Gandhi was even willing to have the power transferred to Muslim League.
15. *Harijan*, 6-7-1947, p. 218.
16. He tried to promote a better understanding of Islam and remove some of the prevailing false notions about it. For instance, he thought Islam is a tolerant, liberal, peace-loving, compatible with non-violence, that sword is no emblem of Islam; that Koran makes no distinction between Hindus and Musalmans.
17. *Young India*, 18-9-1924, p. 308.
18. *Harijan*, 30-4-1938, p. 99.
19. *Ibid.*, 14-9-1947, p. 323..
20. *Ibid.*, 25-1-942, p. 13.
21. *Ibid.*, I-6-1947, p. 172.
22. *Ibid.*, 24-11-1946, p. 409.
23. *Ibid.*, 15-9-1946, p. 309.
24. *Young India*, 14-5-1919, p. 14.
25. *Ibid.*, 25-9-1924, p. 314.
26. *Harijan*, 11-5-1947, p. 147.
27. *Ibid.*, 25-5-1947, p. 165.
28. *Ibid.*, 5-10-1947, p. 356.
29. *Ibid.*
30. Louis Fisher, *A Week With Gandhi*, Bombay, International Book House, 1944, p. 97.
31. *Young India*, 16-3-1921, p. 646.
32. *Ibid.*, 13-10-1921, p. 673.
33. *Ibid.*, 3-4-1924, p. 109.
34. Mahadev Desai, *Gandhiji in Indian Villages*, Madras, S. Ganesan, 1927, p. 170.
35. *Young India*, 12-3-1925, p. 88.
36. *Ibid.*, 17-9-1925, p. 673.
37. *Ibid.*, 4-4-1929, p. 107.
38. *Ibid.*, 16-4-1931, p. 79.
39. *Harijan*, 17-11-1933, pp. 5-6.
40. Louis Fisher, *op. cit.*, p. 82.
41. Young India, 18-6-1925, p. 211.
42. *Ibid.*, 12-11-1931, p. 353.
43. Louis Fisher, *op. cit.*, p. 74.
44. *Young India*, 17-7-1924, p. 236.
45. *Ibid.*, 26-12-1924, p. 425.
46. *Ibid.*, 26-6-1931, p. 51.
47. D.G. Tendulkar, *Mahatma*, *op. cit.*, Vol. III, p. 309.
48. *Harijan*, 23-9-1939, p. 278.
49. *Gandhian Outlook and Techniques*, New Delhi, Ministry of Education, Government of India, 193, p. 274.
50. *Harijan*, 8-6-1947, p. 184.

51. *Pyare Lal, op. cit.*, p. 90.
52. *Harijan*, 23-3-1947, p. 184.
53. M.K. Gandhi, *From Yervada Mandir*, Ahmedabad, Navajivan Publishing House, 1956.
54. *Young India*, 11-8-1920, p. 263.
55. *Ibid.*, 31-12-1931, p. 427.
56. *Harijan*, 23-3-1947, p. 79.
57. D.G. Tendulkar, *Mahatma, op. cit.*, Vol. II, p. 686.
58. *Ibid.*, Vol.VIII, p. 40.
59. Dhirendra Mohan Datta, *The Philosophy of Mahatma Gandhi*, Madison, The University of Wisconsin Press, 1953, p. 144.
60. Ashok Mehta and Achyut Patwardhan, *The Communal Triangle in India*, Allahabad, Kitabistan, 1942, pp. 130-31.
61. M.K. Gandhi, *Hind Swaraj, op. cit.*, p. 47.
62. *The Modern Review*, November 1953.
63. Ashok Mehta and Achyut Patwardhan, *op. cit.*, p. 135.
64. *Ibid.*, p. 136.
65. *Ibid.*, p. 139.
66. *CWMG*, Vol. III, p. 313.
67. *Ibid.*
68. *Ibid.*, Vol. IV, p. 184.
69. *Ibid.*, p. 332.
70. M.K. Gandhi, *Unto This Last: A Paraphrase*, Ahmedabad, Navajivan Publishing House, 1956, pp. 66-67.
71. M.K. Gandhi, *Hind Swaraj, op. cit.*, pp. 28-29
72. *Young India*, 5-11-1931, p. 341.
73. D.G. Tendulkar, *Mahatma, op. cit.*, Vol. II, p. 686.
74. *Young India*, 9-5-1929, pp. 67-68.
75. Paul F. Power, *Gandhi on World Affairs*, George Allen and Unwin, 1960, pp. 67-68.
76. Ashok Mehta and Achyut Patwardhan, *op. cit.*, p. 141.
77. D.G. Tendulkar, *Mahatma, op. cit.*, Vol. III, p. 148.
78. *The Diary of Mahadev Desai*, tr. and ed., Valji Govindji Desai, Ahmedabad, Navajivan Publishing House, 1956, pp. 66-67.
79. *Harijan*, 15-10-1938, p. 290.
80. *Ibid.*, 22-6-1940, p. 172.
81. *Ibid.*, 20-3-1937, p. 41.
82. *Ibid.*, 24-12-1938, p. 38.
83. D.G. Tendulkar, *Mahatma, op. cit.*, Vol. V, p. 160.
84. G.D. Birla, *In the Shadow of the Mahatma: Personal Memoir*, Bombay, Orient Longmans Ltd., 1953, p. 302.
85. *Ibid*,, pp. 250-52.
86. Paul F. Power, *op. cit.*, p. 73.
87. *Harijan*, 24-10-1948, p. 286.

8

Doctrine of Means and Ends

Most political and social thinkers have been concerned with the desirable (and even necessary) goals of a political system or with the common and competing ends that men and women actually seek, and then pragmatically considered the means that are available to rulers and citizens. Even those who have sought a single, general and decisive criterion of decision-making have stated the ends and then been more concerned with the consequences of social and political acts than with consistently applying standards of intrinsic value. It has become almost a sacred dogma in our age of apathy that politics, centred on power and conflict and the quest for legitimacy and consensus, is essentially a study in expediency, a tortuous discovery of practical expedients that could reconcile contrary claims and secure a common, if minimal, goal or, at least, create the conditions in which different ends could be freely or collectively pursued. Liberal thinkers have sought to show that it is possible for each individual to be used as a means for another to achieve his ends without undue coercion and to his own distinct advantage. This occurs not by conscious cooperation or deliberately pursuing a common end but by each man pursuing diverse ends in accordance with the "law" of the natural identity of interests, a "law" that is justified if not guaranteed in terms of metaphysical, economic or biological "truths." Authoritarian thinkers, on the other hand, justified coercion in the name of a predetermined common end, the attainment of which cannot be left to the chaotic interplay of innumerable wills. The end may simply be the preservation of a traditional order, the recovery of a bygone age of glory, or the ruthless reconstruction of society from the top to secure some spectacular consummation in the future.

It appears to be common to most schools of thought to accept a sharp dichotomy between ends and means, a distinction that is deeply embedded in our ethical, political and psychological vocabulary, rooted in rigid European presuppositions regarding the very nature of human action. Distinctions have been repeatedly made between immediate and ultimate, short-term and long-term, diverse and common, individual and social, essential and desirable ends, as also between attainable and utopian goals. Discussion about means has not ignored questions about their moral implications and propriety, or about the extent of their theoretical and contingent compatibility with desired ends or widely shared values. But despite all these reservations, the dangerous dogma that the end entirely justifies the means is merely an extreme version of the commonly uncriticized belief that moral considerations cannot apply to the means except in relation to ends, or that the latter have a moral priority.

The term "end" has two different meanings, failure to discriminate between which, causes most of the controversy and confusion regarding the relationship between ends and means. It means, first a subjective purpose or blueprint which exists only in the mind of the subject before and during the performance of an act. It means, in the second place, the objective consequence of an act or a series of acts performed by the subject irrespective of the subjective purpose he may have in mind. For the sake of clarity, it is desirable to use two different terms for these two separate meanings of the word "end": the term "goal" to denote the subjective purpose for which an action is performed, and the term "result" to denote the objective consequence of the act. It is clear that there is a necessary cause connection only between the means and the result, which is ascertainable through inductive logic, but none between the means and the goal. Whether the goal and the result coincide or not would depend on whether the means selected are causally connected with the goal, and not on the subject's own value judgement regarding the goal itself. In other words, given a certain well-defined goal, the selection of the means is not a question of moral choice, but of efficiency. The value judgement is involved in the selection of the goal, not of the means. The means can be justified only in terms of the result, and not of the goal. The goal cannot justify the means any more than my intention of going to Delhi can justify my boarding a train for Madras (due to ignorance or inefficiency). Only my going to Madras, *i.e.* the result of my act, can justify my boarding the train for Madras. Whether I have boarded the right train or not depends not on my preference for Delhi, but on the efficiency with which I have ascertained, on the basis of empirical evidence and inductive reasoning, which train will end up in Delhi.[1]

In *Hind Swaraj* the Editor tells the Reader (who argues in favour of the forcible overthrow of British rule in India): "Your belief that there is no connection between the means and the end is a great mistake. Through that mistake even men who have been considered religious; have committed grievous crimes. Your reasoning is the same as saying that we can get a rose through planting a noxious weed. If I want to cross the ocean, I can do so only by means of a vessel; if I were to use a cart for that purpose, both the cart and I would soon find the bottom... The means may be likened to a seed, the end to a tree; and there is just the same inviolable connection between the means and the end as there is between the seed and the tree. I am not likely to obtain the result flowing from the worship of God by laying myself prostrate before Satan.... We reap exactly as we sow".[2] Years later he put the matter in a nutshell when he said: "Means and end are convertible terms in my philosophy of life".[3]

The acceptance of a broad goal, *e.g.* the ideal society or *swaraj*, was not altogether ruled out by Gandhi, as we have seen. But he regarded the preparation of a detailed and foolproof blueprint of the goal as a relatively fruitless job, because however perfect the blueprint might be, it would not be realized unless the right means were adopted. It was, therefore, mainly necessary, he argued, to concentrate on the selection of the means, keeping in view only a broad image and a sense of direction regarding the goal. Like Newman, whom he frequently quoted, Gandhi often said, as we have noted before, that one step was enough for him. He insisted that the goal could have no reality except as the actual result of the means, on which, therefore, our attention should be primarily focused. Thus in September 1933, he wrote to Jawaharlal Nehru that although he agreed with the latter regarding the goal of complete independence, he was interested not so much in elucidating and repeating this objective, as in the means necessary for its attainment. "I have concerned myself more", he wrote, "... with the conservation of the means and their progressive use. If we can take care of them, the attainment of the goal is assured. I feel that our progress towards the goal will be in exact proportion to the purity of our means."[4]

The same is true of his views on ends and means. The *karma* theory states, quite rightly it would seem from the logical point of view, that every act has its own independent result which affects both the subject and the object of the act. It further states of course, that the acts of an individual thus determine the character of the subject's "self" in this and after life—a metaphysical proposition which we have to ignore for our present purpose. The *Bhagavadgita* also states that the man has control only over his act, but none over the goal of it; an act should, therefore, be performed in a spirit of detachment, and not with a passionate attachment to a specific goal. This idea Gandhi considered to be "the centre round which the *Gita* is woven". "But renunciation of fruit", he observed, "in no way means indifference to the result. In regard to every action one must know the result that is expected to follow the means thereto and the capacity for it. He, who, being thus equipped, is without desire for the result, and is yet wholly engrossed in the due fulfilment of the task before him, is said to have renounced the fruits of his action."[5] That Gandhi was influenced by his own understanding of the theory of detached action as expounded in the *Gita,* with regard to his formulation of the relationship between ends and means, is borne out by the fact that sometimes he spoke or wrote on the subject practically in the language of the *Gita*. Thus he once observed: "As the means, so the end. There is no veil of separation between means and end. Indeed, the Creator has given us control (and that too very limited) over means, none over the end. Realization of the goal is in exact proportion to that of the means. This is a proposition that admits of no exception."[6]

If we leave aside Gandhi's references to God, and interpret what he calls the "purity" of the means as its consistency with one's own ultimate values, *i.e.* the goal, his analysis of the end means relationship would seem to be the correct formulation. But this so far as the theoretical presentation of the end-means relationship goes. The truth about whether the result of a particular will coincide with a particular goal in a given situation can be discovered only through empirical investigation and inductive reasoning, and not from theoretical formulations on the subject. And hence, the whole of Gandhian thought and Gandhi's numerous experiments in social control are in a sense a long study in the end-means relationship.

Like Gautama Buddha, Gandhi was an ethical absolutist and would not make any compromise with what he regarded as essential and fundamental moral principles. He refused to exalt the cult of expediency. He would have held that the highest morality is the highest expediency. The principle of the sacrosanct character of human conscience and the incorporation of its commands in the structure of society and politics necessarily implies the purification of means. Gandhi always claimed to adhere to the command of inner, conscience.

But he claimed no infallibility for himself and was self-conscious and humble not to be deluded by the appellation of "Mahatma". He confessed having made Himalayan blunders but never was he consciously guilty of any compromise with the purity of means.

In a spiritual organic universe, good ends cannot be achieved by evil methods. Hence Gandhi stressed the nobility of technics for the realization of the goals set by him. Both in South Africa and India, he stressed the purity of means for the realization of his political objectives. He was an advocate of the principle of pure *karma*. Only by noble actions can a blissful goal be realized. Gandhi would never subscribe to any policy and action that could lead to a compromise with truth because to him loyalty to truth is the supreme consideration. He was sanguine that political action could be made to conform to the ultimate values of the spirit. He also said: "And where the means are clean, there God is undoubtedly present with his blessings." His religious personality is apparent, in his emphasis on purity of means.

"The ultimate object of man's life is, according to Gandhi, self-realization. Self-realization means seeing God face to face, realizing Absolute Truth, attaining *moksha* or knowing oneself. He believes in the principle of spiritual unity. So the immediate service of human beings becomes a necessary part of the endeavour, because the only way to find God is to see Him in His creation and to be one with it. The individual must work not only for his own spiritual freedom but also for that of his fellow beings. Thus Gandhiji reconciles self-realization with service to society. The conception that salvation can be sought in the seclusion of solitude is not acceptable to him. Self-realization to him means realization of "the greatest good of all". "The greatest good of all", or, as he calls it in Gujarati, *sarvodaya*, also includes political progress, for political degeneration is a great hindrance to moral and spiritual regeneration. Politics, however, is only a part of this aim. Gandhiji also insists that the best way to serve all is to serve one's own country or one's countrymen or one's nearest neighbours.[7]

He rejects the utilitarian doctrine of "the greatest good of the greatest number" as the end of life. For "it means in its nakedness that in order to achieve the supposed good of 51 per cent the interest of 49 per cent may be, or rather, should be sacrificed. It is a heartless doctrine and has done harm to humanity. The only real, dignified, human doctrine is the greatest good of all, and this can only be achieved by uttermost self-sacrifice."[8] In 1926 he wrote, "He (the *ahimsaist*) will strive for the greatest good of all and die in the attempt to realize the ideal.... The greatest good of all inevitably includes the good of the greater number and, therefore, he and the utilitarian will converge at many points in their career but there does come a time when they must part company, and even work in opposite directions. The utilitarian to be logical will never sacrifice himself. The absolutist will even sacrifice himself."[9]

Closely connected with the ultimate end is the problem of means. Communists, Fascists as well as most practical politicians believe in the maxim, "the end justifies the means." That is, if the end is desirable, even means like cunning, deceit and violence are justified, if they help us to achieve the end.

In Gandhian philosophy means and ends are convertible terms. The two are inseparable and should be equally pure. That the end is high and laudable is not enough for him, the means too must be moral. In fact, the means are, to him, everything.

This emphasis on means is partly due to the fact that man can only strive, he cannot command results. We can control the means but not the end. Besides, the end grows out of the means. To quote Gandhi, "As the means so the end." "The means may be likened to a seed, the end to a tree; and there is just the same inviolable connection between the means and the end as there is between the seed and the tree. The *Gita* doctrine of *nishkama karma* (action without attachment), also teaches us that a good deed produces only a good result. So Gandhi believes that "if one takes care of the means, the end will take care of itself," and that realization of the goal is in exact proportion, to that of means. To him, "the attempt made to win *swaraj is swaraj* itself.

Further, Gandhi has personal experience of how, whenever he compromised the means, progress on the path of truth and nonviolence received a setback. The Rajkot affair is, an instance. By seeking the intervention of the Paramount power—a sign of impatience which is a form of violence he failed to convert the opponent.

Gandhi's theory seems to be the only correct view of the end and the means. The opposite theory that the good end justifies all means, even violent means, is dangerous in practice and unsound ethically. The theory permits the recourse to violence, fraud, untruth, opportunism etc., provided the end is just. But these means, instead of helping us to advance on the path of progress, lead us to regard human beings as means rather than ends, deaden our finer feelings and result in oppression and cruelty. Besides, there can generally be no certainty that a violent action is always motivated only by a good end. The tyrant and the terrorist invariably plead laudable ends when perpetrating the most outrageous crimes. Further, it is dangerous ethics to make the success of an action or policy the criterion of its propriety. There is, moreover, all the differences between what passes for success, quick results mostly short-lived, and real, enduring achievements that require a long period of gestation. Violence and deception, terror and Machiavellian diplomacy might seem to score for the time being over truth and love, justice and open dealing. But the victory is partial and transitory and the gains mere burdens. Good means alone can lead us to lasting peace and progress. History as well as contemporary experience teach us that violence engenders violence, revenge leads to counter-revenge and a war sows the seeds of further wars. The two world wars, ostensibly fought for justice and democracy, bear ample testimony to the truth of this argument.

If we believe in the ultimate aim stated above and in the fundamental unity of life, good ends will mean, in the words of Aldous Huxley, "a state of greatest possible unification". This can be obviously achieved by intrinsically unifying, *i.e.*, good means and not by separative or divisive, *i.e.*, bad, means.[10] According to Tolstoy, "All that tend to unify mankind is Beautiful. All that tend to disunite are Evil and Ugly."[11]

Gandhi's emphasis on the importance of means should not be misconstrued as implying that the end is, with him, only a secondary consideration. He believes that the means and the end are inseparably connected and is eager that the means used should in no way detract from the moral character of our end. Hence his repeated insistence that our means must be as pure as our end and that in regard to our means we must take our stand on "the firm solid ground of unadulterated good". His effort to give concrete expression, in the form of *satyagraha*, to this principle of moral approximation of the end and the means is, perhaps, the most unique contribution of our times to the philosophy and technique of revolution.

What then are the means that Gandhi prescribes for the realization of the ultimate end? Self-realization, he says, requires self-purification. Self-purification requires an ethical discipline. According to Gandhi, "...he who is not prepared to order his life in unquestioning obedience to the laws of morality cannot be said to be a man in the full sense of the word."[12] This ethical outlook is the backbone of Gandhi's political philosophy even as his ethics has for its foundation his metaphysical principles. To him the moral discipline of the individual is the most important means of social reconstruction, and it is as vital to his philosophy as the capture of political power and state machinery is to Socialism and Fascism. The content of the ethical discipline also determines the structure of the nonviolent state.

Gandhi gives us the moral principles which should be observed as vows by mankind in general. Most of these principles, which he laid down in 1916 for being observed in the *Satyagraha Ashram*, Sabarmati, are the maxims of life enjoined for thousands of years by the Hindu *shastras* as being dispensable for moral growth. The first five of these vows, *i.e., satya* (truth), *ahimsa* (nonviolence), *asteya* (non-stealing), *aparigraha* (non-possession) and *brahmacharya* (celibacy), are *yamas* or cardinal restraints. For long years before 1916 Gandhi had endeavoured to live up to these ideals, and he modified and amplified them in the light of his experience.

Vows, Gandhi thinks, are a moral discipline absolutely necessary for self-realization. They are a source of strength, for they mean unflinching determination to observe moral laws. In the absence of vows we may be unable to stand against temptations and may bend before discomforts. The refusal to take vows, moreover, is an indication of weakness and betrays a subtle desire for the things to be avoided. Vows should, however, be taken only on points of universally recognized principles. But "the taking of a vow does not mean that we are able to observe it completely from the very beginning, it does mean constant and honest effort in thought, word and deed with a view to its fulfilment. When in doubt about vows, the seeker should interpret them against himself, *i.e.*, in favour of greater restriction."[13]

Truth, the pole-star of his life and philosophy, comes first among these vows.

Gandhi distinguishes between truth as a vow or means, *i.e.*, relative truth as perceived by finite individuals in relation to a particular set of thoughts and circumstances, and Truth, as the *summum bonum, i.e.*, Absolute, Universal, Infinite Truth which exists beyond and unconditioned by space and time.

In the sense of Absolute Truth Gandhi identifies Truth with God. Truth or *Satya*, which means 'real existent', is "the only correct and fully significant name of God". Truth in perfection includes all Knowledge (*Chit*) and latter is the source of eternal *Bliss (Ananda)*.

Hence we know God as *sat-chit-ananda*, one who combines in Himself Truth, Knowledge and Bliss. Gandhi worships God as Truth only; he is devoted to none but Truth.[14]

Gandhi explicitly rejected the doctrine that the end justifies the means, and went so far as to assert that a moral means is almost an end in itself because virtue is its own reward.

The doctrine that the end justifies the means goes back to Kautilya in India and to Machiavelli in the West, and is connected with the notions of self-preservation at all costs and of *raison d'etre* and in more recent times with the attainment of a secular millennium through revolutionary action. The doctrine was implicit in *Killing No Murder,* Colonel Sexby's incitement to political assassination published in 1657. This once-famous pamphlet argued that, tyrants accomplish their ends much more by fraud than by force and that if they are not eliminated by force the citizens would be degraded into deceitful, perfidious flatterers. It is not only "lawful" and even glorious to kill a tryant, but indeed "everything is lawful against him that is lawful against an open enemy, whom every private man hath a right to kill."[15] It is no doubt possible to justify tyrannicide without going so far as to say that a worthy end legitimizes any and every means. The difficulty, however, is that few practitioners would admit to holding to this maxim in an unqualified and unconditional form.

It has been argued repeatedly that any means is legitimate that is indispensable at least for internal security or to defend society against its external enemies. The sole reason for restricting the choice of means is expediency rather than principle, prudence rather than (non-utilitarian) morality. It is taken for granted that cunning and force must unite in the exercise of power. Power may be justified as a means to a higher end but in the attempt to employ any and every means to secure and maintain power it becomes an end in itself. The idea that one, is serving some higher entity which rises far above individual life and that one is no longer serving oneself makes one no less indifferent to the morality of the means employed than the open pursuit of naked self-interest. Alternatively, we have the straightforward Machiavellian notion that the individual agent cannot escape the nature he is born with, that as *fortuna* is malicious so virtue must also be malicious when there is no other way open. If virtue is the vital power in men which creates and maintains states, *necessita* is the causal pressure required to bring the sluggish masses into line with *virtue.* If there is a moral law, it must can be flouted in the practice of politics and this infringement justified by the plea of unavoidable necessity. This line of reasoning is commoner than we like to think and is sometimes couched in such specious or emotive language that in moments of crisis many, people are hardly aware of the wider implications of a doctrine that they invoke for their special pleading in what seem to be exceptional situations. Hume thought that this doctrine was so widely practiced that it is safer in politics to assume that men are scoundrels even if we do not believe that all men are Knaves.

It is true that thinkers like Machiavelli and Bentham have been rather unfairly accused of actually holding that there is an end justifying all means to it. Bentham said only that happiness is the end justifying all means, which is more an empty than a pernicious doctrine. Again, Machiavelli never said that power justifies all means to it, but merely that the gaining of power often involves committing some very nasty crimes. A similar defence could also be made on behalf of Kautilya. The important point, however, is not the precise standpoints of Bentham, Machiavelli or Kautilya, but the dangerous uses to which their doctrines could be put. Just as Benthamites, Machiavellians and followers of Kautilya could be charged with ruthlessness (even more than their teachers), so too Gandhians also could be accused of coercive-tactics (nonviolent only in a very restricted sense) in the pursuit of worthy ends.[16] But it would be much easier to challenge such Gandhians in terms of Gandhi's fundamental tenets than to appeal to the writings of Machiavelli or Bentham against diehard Machiavellians, or Benthamite planners.

The doctrine that the end justifies the means does not even require any special justification for the Marxist who accepts no supra-historic morality, no categorical imperative, religious or secular. Engels declared in his letter to Herson Trier in 1889 that "any means that leads to the aim suits me as a revolutionary, whether it is the most violent or that which appears to be most peaceable." In his pamphlet on Socialism and War, Lenin said that Marxists differed both from pacifists and anarchists in their belief that the justification of each war must be seen individually in relation to its historical role and its consequences. "There have been many wars in history which, notwithstanding all the horrors, cruelties, miseries and tortures, inevitably connected with every war, had a progressive character, *i.e.* they served in the development of mankind, aiding in the destruction of extremely pernicious and reactionary institutions... or helping to remove the most, barbarous despotism in Europe." Whether an action is justifiable or not simply depends on what historical end it serves.

Unlike Engels and Lenin, Trotsky stressed what he called the dialectical interdependence of means and ends. He argued that the means chosen must be shown to be really likely to lead to the liberation of mankind. "Precisely from this it follows that not all means are permissible. When, we say that the end justifies the means then for us the conclusion follows that the great revolutionary end spurns those base means and ways which set one part of the working class against other parts, or attempt to make the masses happy without their participation; or lower the faith of the masses in themselves and their organization, replacing it by worship of the leaders."[17] This is clearly an improvement on Lenin, for it at least provides a criterion by which a collectivist regime or revolutionary leaders could be criticized for pushing an exclusively utilitarian creed to extremes of practical ruthlessness in perpetuating a monopoly of power and privilege.

Although Trotsky denied that the end justifies any and every means, he still insisted that a means can be justified only by its end, which for him is the increase of the power of man over nature and the abolition of the power of man over man. For Gandhi, on the other hand, the end is *satya* or truth, which requires no justification, and the means (*ahimsa* or non-coercion) must be justified not merely with reference to the end but also in itself; every act must be independently justified in terms of the twin absolutes, *satya* and *ahimsa*. It is, therefore, not permissible or possible to justify a single act of untruth or violence by appealing to the past or future possession of *satya* and *ahimsa*, though no man can wholly avoid a measure of *himsa* or *asatya* or claim to possess in their fullness absolute truth and absolute, universal love. Weakness and error are ubiquitous and inescapable, but their justification and rationalization make all the difference to our personal and political integrity. We cannot condone our untruthfulness in the present on the ground that we shall be truthful tomorrow when we are stronger or conditions are more favourable. A violent revolution cannot lead (and, in any case, cannot be justified on the ground that it is expected to lead) to a nonviolent society in the fullness of time. Further, in Gandhi's view it is not sometimes, as Trotsky suggested, but always (under the moral law of *karma*) that the end changes in character as a result of the means adopted in its attainment.

If the doctrine that the end justifies the means is invoked in the attainment of the good society through a single, violent revolution, it could also be made to justify repression in the aftermath of revolution.

In Abram Tertz's *The Trial Begins* we have the following dialogue between Rabinovich and Globov. Rabinovich holds that "every decent End consumes itself. You kill yourself trying to reach it and by the time you get there, it's being turned inside out. These Jesuits of yours made a miscalculation, they slipped up." Globov answers: "They were right. Every educated person knows that the end justifies the means. You can either believe it openly or secretly but you can't get anywhere without it. If the enemy does not surrender, he must be destroyed. Isn't that so? And since all means are good, you must choose the most effective. Don't spare God himself in the name of God… And as soon as one End is done with, another bobs up on the stage of history."[18]

In any long-term programme of social engineering, there is not just one goal and one means, but a hierarchy of goals and means. Thus in the Marxian programme of the socio-political reconstruction of the world, the ultimate goal is represented by a conception of Justice, reducible to certain ultimate values, which seem to be Liberty, Equality and Fraternity—the same value-goals as were associated with the French Revolution. These value-goals in turn are supposed to be consummated in an ideal society which is stateless and classless, and, therefore, such a society is also the ultimate Marxian goal—the concrete counterpart of the abstract value-goal (it is not a means to the value-goal, because once it is reached, the ultimate values are immediately consummated, and the value-goal is also thus simultaneously reached). This ultimate goal is to be brought about by means of the Dictatorship of the Proletariat, which in turn is to be brought into existence by means of the Revolution, and the Revolution is to be generated by means of the class struggle. The class struggle, the Revolution, and the Dictatorship of the Proletariat, are all means through which the stateless and classless society representing Liberty, Equality and Fraternity is to be brought into existence. But from another point view, the Revolution and the Dictatorship of the Proletariat are goals subsidiary to the ultimate goal of the stateless and classless society. The class struggle is the common means, running from the existing capitalist society through the Revolution and the Dictatorship of the Proletariat to the classless and stateless society. In the same way, in the Gandhian programme of the socio-political reconstruction of human society, there is the ultimate value-goal of Justice, reducible to the ultimate values of Nonviolence, Freedom and Equality and the anarchistic and rural, first-order ideal society described in Part II which represents the consummation of these ultimate values. The second-order ideal society, also described in Part II can be regarded either as a means to the first-order ideal society or a goal subsidiary to it. The Constructive Programme and *Satyagraha* are the common means running from the given social reality through the second-order ideal society to the ideal society of the first order, in a process of successive approximation. The major differences between the Marxian and the Gandhian schemes of social engineering are that (i) there is in Gandhian thought an insistence on the inculcation of the ultimate values in the lives of the social worker through self-control as a prerequisite social control, while in Marxian thought not only is there a total absence of any reference to self-control, but there is positive encouragement of group or class aggrandizement at the cost of the other sections of society; (ii) there is no sudden point of departure in the Gandhian scheme like the Marxian Revolution; the Gandhian programme of social control is a perennial and gradual one, without any sudden twists or turns in it ; (iii) the Gandhian programme is based on two separate but interrelated means of social control, one for building new social institutions and the other for the resolution of conflicts—the Constructive Programme and *Satyagraha*—while the Marxian emphasis is on only one means of social control, namely, the class struggle, and there is no reference to a simultaneous constructive effort for the establishment of new social institutions, and (iv) the Constructive Programme and *Satyagraha* are uncompromisingly nonviolent means of social control, while the class struggle is unreservedly violent.

As regards the use of force as a means of social control, those who argue in its favour do not in fact, denounce Nonviolence, Freedom and Equality as value-goals. They only maintain that these value-goals cannot be achieved the use of force, because the cause of the non-realization of these goals is itself force in one form or another, and that force can be defeated only with greater force. In other words, they argue that if the force which is allegedly used to suppress Liberty, Equality and Fraternity is eliminated or controlled through the use of greater force, then the social equilibrium will be restored and the social goal realized. The Marxists, for example, argue that the root cause of social "contradictions" is the exploitation of one class by another in all stages of historical development, with the exception of "primitive communism", which they believe to be the earliest phase of the development of human society, and the stateless and classless Communist society of the future, which they believe to be more or less the end of social evolution. In the contemporary phase of human history, they maintain, the exploiting class is the bourgeoisie, and the exploited class, which is in an overwhelming majority, the proletariat. The exploitation by the bourgeoisie, which is thus the cause of the "class contradiction", cannot be ended or mended without the use of force, argue the Marxists, not only because the bourgeoisie has the power of money, but also because the state itself is merely an instrument of exploitation in the hands of the bourgeoisie; that in fact, is the *raison d'etre* of the state, which, therefore, uses its law, the police and the armed forces to protect vested interests of the bourgeoisie and to suppress the proletariat. A violent class struggle and armed revolution are, therefore, necessary to defeat the force used by the bourgeoisie through the state in order to remove the "class contradiction" and to establish Liberty, Equality and Fraternity.

It may be argued that violence is the opposite of Non-violence (Peace, Fraternity), and that, therefore, the use of force as a means of social control is in itself a negation of Nonviolence. On the same logic a series of violent acts would simply result in greater violence, although Nonviolence may be the goal of such acts. But it will be readily seen that this is a tautological argument. We are simply defining violence as inversely related to Nonviolence, identifying the use of force with violence, and then, through this purely linguistic formulation of the relation between force and Nonviolence, making out a logical contradiction between force as a means and Nonviolence as a goal.

Similarly, when Rubashov in *Darkness at Noon*, points out that violence starts a chain of cumulative consequences, Ivanov replies that no battalion commander can stick to the principle that the individual is sacrosanct; the world has permanently been in an abnormal state since the invention of the steam engine, and the principle that the end justifies the means remains the only rule of political ethics. It is ironical that while this doctrine is increasingly taken for granted by some Benthamite planners and Kautilyan diplomats in Gandhi's India, it has been openly questioned even in the most powerful society that has adopted Marxism as a State religion. The Russian poet, Yevgeny Yevtushenko, has stated that Stalin was forgiven much in his lifetime because Soviet citizens were led to think that his acts were necessary for some higher purpose.

They steadily impressed upon us that the end justified the means. A great pain gives birth to a great "flow of energy" as Stalin once declared. But even as we lamented him, many of us recalled our kin and our friends who had perished in the prisons. Naturally, to lock up such an enormous number of people required a truly prodigious amount of "energy" But people did not ponder on the fact that the aim itself may cease to be great, if one strives after it only with great energy and without paying much attention to the means. We realized that the means must be worthy of the end. This is an axiom, but an axiom that has been proved through much suffering.[19]

Similarly, in the most affluent society that had almost elevated Pragmatism to a State religion, the American President drew a major moral lesson in a national broadcast on the Watergate Scandal (April 30, 1973):

> I have been in public life for more than a quarter of a century. A know that it can be very easy, under the intensive pressures of a campaign, for even well-intentioned people to fall into shady tactics—to rationalize this on the grounds that what is at stake is of such importance to the nation that the end justifies the means... In recent years, however, the campaign excesses that have occurred on all sides have provided a sobering demonstration of how far this false doctrine can take us. The lesson is clear: America, in its political campaigns, must not again fall into the trap of letting the end, however great that end is, justify the means.[20]

As a matter of fact, however, Gandhi himself did not regard use of force as such as a violent act. For example, killing for sustaining one's own body (not for satisfying the palate) and for protecting those under one's care he regarded as unavoidable violence and, therefore, consistent with nonviolence, while killing for the sake of those who are killed is a purely nonviolent act, according to him. In other words, although Gandhi regarded violence as inversely related to Non-violence, he did not regard the use of force as necessarily equivalent to violence. Moreover, he regarded a violent act as preferable to a nonviolent act born of cowardice which he considered to be negative violence. Thus in the first case he justifies the use of force in terms of some specific goals, which he regards as consistent Nonviolence, while in the second he regards the abstinence force as inconsistent with Nonviolence on account of the condition which has resulted in such abstinence.

Looked at from this point of view, the argument of the Marxists is not really different from that of Gandhi in kind; they only carry the argument further and state (in terms of dialectical materialism) that violence and nonviolence (Peace) are in fact only two sides of the same coin, and not really qualitatively different from each other. They would argue, in the first place, that force used against the bourgeoisie is not truly violence, because its goal is the establishment of Communism which stands for Liberty, Equality and Fraternity, while the abstinence from force which is prompted by the desire to maintain "class peace", *i.e.* the lack of class-consciousness, or fear of the bourgeoisie, is tantamount to violence. Or to take the example of the international class conflict, a war waged by a Communist state against "international imperialism" is, not an act of violence, because its goal is the establishment of international peace and the other values Communism stands for, while the abstinence from waging such a war due to fear of "international imperialism", or a desire to maintain peaceful coexistence with it, would tantamount to violence. In the second place, the Marxists extend the argument further and say that according to the law of the identity of opposites, which is an essential postulate of dialectical materialism. Peace and violence of war are in fact identical phenomena, one often shading into the other. Mao Tse-tung, for example, says: "As everybody knows, war and peace transform themselves into each other. War is transformed into peace; for example, the First World War was transformed into the post-war peace; the civil war in China has now also ceased and peace has come about. Peace is transformed into war; for example, the Komintang-Communist cooperation of 1927 was transformed into war, and the peaceful world situation of today may also be transformed into a Second World War. Why? Because in a class society such contradictory things as war and peace are characterized by identity under certain conditions."[21]

In other words, the relationship between force as a means of social control and the ultimate values of Nonviolence, Freedom and Equality is not a matter of definition; it is a relationship which has to be discovered through empirical investigation. Any distinction which one may like to draw between the rather exceptional and cases in which Gandhi regarded the use of force as consistent with Non-violence, and the large-scale use of force for bringing about a total social transformation with a view to the realization of a particular socio-political goal envisaged by a particular section of the society, however large, must also similarly rest on an empirical or rather than on purely deductive reasoning. Gandhi's argument is, of course, that the empirical result of the use of force as a means of social control is the negation of such values as Nonviolence, Freedom and Equality. He was severely critical of the traditional Western democracies, German and Italian Fascism and Soviet Communism, he believed that the ultimate values cherished by him were non-existent in any of these systems, and he attributed this fact to the readiness with which violence (both in the form of physical and in other forms like exploitation, suppression of minorities, etc.) was resorted to by the countries concerned, internally as well as externally. The use of force, he argued from such empirical evidence, always leads to a violent socio-political system, war and imperialism, dictatorship and inequality.

It is not possible here to go exhaustively into the empirical evidence regarding the result of the use of force by individuals, groups and masses of men. But it would seem from all available data that Gandhi is on very strong grounds on this question. The history of the last two thousand years tells us that very few revolutions have resulted in the realization of Freedom, very few wars in the establishment of Peace (Nonviolence), very few class conflicts in the establishment of Equality. In fact, the use of force has seldom resulted in the realization of the goal for which force was used. As an authority on Social control has observed: "Violence is answered by violence, and the result is a physical struggle. A physical struggle inevitably arouses in the minds of those directly and even indirectly concerned in it emotions of hatred, fear, rage and resentment. In the heat of conflict all scruples are thrown to the winds, all the habits of forbearance and humaneness, slowly and laboriously formed during generations of civilized living, are forgotten. Nothing matters any more, after a while, except victory. And when at last victory comes to one or other of the parties, the final outcome of struggle bears no necessary relation to the rights and wrongs of the case; nor, in most cases, does it provide any lasting settlement to the dispute. In particular, the prophets of violence fail to understand that the average person—and, therefore, most of mankind—is averse to the continued terrorization and eventually violence which is always replaced by the comparative stability of social relations in which the prophets of violence and terror have no place".[22] Many years ago Aldous Huxley had amassed a large body of empirical evidence to show that the use of force as a means of social control almost invariably leads to a result which is very different from, and in many ways opposed to, the goal ostensibly visualized originally by those who perpetrated the violence.[23] With the added evidence of another war and the post-war, cold-war, Communist China and Eastern Europe, the large number of dictatorships of various descriptions which have come into existence in many parts of the world following revolutions whose avowed goal was to end all forms of injustice, and the threat of a third world war, there would seem to be a strong case for Gandhi's contention that the use of force can never result in the achievement of Nonviolence, Freedom, Equality or similar ultimate values.

It is true that Gandhi's insistence on self-control as an essential prerequisite to social control is logically unexceptionable, and gives the Gandhian approach to social control a greater rationality than claimed by those who advocate violent social control mainly at the cost of those who are considered by the reformers as their opponents. If those who want to bring about a certain social change act of narrow sectional (and hence indirectly personal) interests, there is no guarantee that the change, if and when it comes about, will not be used in order to further these interests at the cost of others; indeed, reason and experience both tell us that social change brought about by sectional interests through revolutionary or other violent means of social control would almost inevitably lead to oppression, exploitation and tyranny in one form or another. It is only when the "rational will" of the individual or the group, as distinguished from self-interest, the desire to bring about social transformation in the common interests of all rather than the sectional interests of some, governs the nature and process of social control, that general welfare can logically be expected to follow from it. Hence it is necessary for social workers to train themselves in self-control involved in the inculcation of the universal goal values in personal life, so that they are transformed into impersonal agents of society, before they can hope to bring about social transformation in terms of these values. The necessary self-control would probably be only partially realized, as Gandhi readily admits; but logically there is no escape from the need for self-control if social control is to be purged of self-interest.

But it is necessary, in order to be able to make an objective assessment of Gandhi's ideas on ends and means, not only to examine the merits of nonviolent social control in general, but also those of the Constructive Programme and *satyagraha* in particular. The particular conclusions regarding the Constructive Programme and *satyagraha* can alone enable us to come to any general conclusions, nonviolent means of social control which Gandhi has in mind.

It is also true that the Constructive Programme is fraught with grave inner contradictions and practical difficulties. It cannot have any effect at all on societies which are already highly industrialized or in the process of rapid industrialization. It cannot hope to make any headway in a dictatorial political system in which the government is opposed to such a programme. It can exist only through the sufferance and protection of the state, and cannot thus be the long-term instrument for replacing the state with decentralized and voluntary socio-political associations. Particularly, in the second order ideal society, where the power of the state is considerably increased, the Constructive Programme will and it extremely difficult to make any progress in transforming the socio-political relations and paving the way for the ideal society of the first order.

The chief merit of the Constructive Programme lies in the fact that it tends to awaken the spirit of self-rule among the people and thus promotes Freedom in a very real sense. The constructive effort involved in the programme being entirely voluntary, and thus free, promotes Freedom in the sense of absence of compulsion. It also leads to the growth of Freedom in the sense that the discipline involved in the programme helps the acquirement of virtue and self-perfection on the part of the constructive workers. Finally, since the constructive effort enables the people to be independent of state control, at least to some extent it fosters *swaraj* or Freedom as applied to the social organization. But while the idea of the Constructive Programme is basically sound, the actual programme undertaken at any given time must be adapted to the requirements of the given situation. The specific programme laid down by Gandhi could not be the powerful means of social control he had expected it to be and although the central role assigned in it to *khadi* and village industries is fundamentally consistent with Gandhi's own long-term programme of social engineering, it has to be viewed, so far as Social Science is concerned, in the given context of the freedom movement and the economic conditions of the time. To seek to implement a given specific programme at all times, irrespective of social, political and economic changes, is to adopt an scientific attitude towards social control and progress. That has the great mistake of the Gandhian organizations in present day India like the Gandhi Smarak Nidhi and the Akhil Bharat Sarva Seva Sangh. If instead of wasting valuable national resources on highly unproductive and inefficient programme of spinning throughout the country, and depending in the process on heavy governmental subsidies and protection, these organizations had engaged themselves in organizing modern small and medium scale industries on a cooperative basis, including handloom and powerloom cooperatives, cooperative consumers' marketing and housing societies, adult education schools, etc. and identified themselves with Community Development Programme launched by the Government of India under the Five-Year Plans (which is based on the principle of constructive self-help by the people with a maximum of 50 per cent assistance by the government), they would probably have been truer to the ideals of Gandhi and rendered greater service to the country at the same time.

Gandhi's way of countering the doctrine that the end justifies the means was by asserting not merely that unworthy means could be a little great end but also that evil means can never, as a matter of fact, lead to good ends. Like the majority of Russian Populists, Gandhi was horrified by the advocacy of Machiavellian tactics and he thought that no end, however good, could fail to be destroyed by the adoption of monstrous means. His reason for believing this to be wholly and always true was his metaphysical conviction that the whole world is governed by the law of *karma*, that there is a moral order (*rta*) at the heart of the cosmos. Those who do not share this conviction, which is common to all the great religions and is especially prevalent in peasant societies, may well think that a lesser evil could lead to a greater good. This latter belief, which is no less non-empirical than the former, is taken for granted by many contemporary intellectuals, power-holders, leaders of organizations and evangelists (whether theological teleologists or secular historicists). It is hardly surprising that Gandhi, who even earlier than Benda recognized the betrayal of and alienation from the masses of narrowly based classes of intellectuals and power-seekers, appealed over their heads to the toiling masses to find recruits willing to dedicate themselves to the Constructive Programme and the development of a new social and political ethics.

Gandhi did more than base his view of ends and means on a metaphysical faith in the moral law or his account of the necessary as well as contingent connection between *satya* and *ahimsa*, (truth and nonviolence, tolerance and civility). He also rejected the moral model underlying the sharp dichotomy between ends and means. Moral life was not for Gandhi mainly a matter of achieving specific objectives, nor was politics like a field game in which a concrete objective is given in advance and known to all. No doubt, he regarded *satya* as the supreme common end for all men but its content cannot be known in advance. For Gandhi, as for the ancient Greeks, *satya* refers to the highest human activity rather than an imposed and predetermined target. He evolved his political and social ethics in terms of a theory of action under which all our thinking and activity can be corrected and justified only by reference to *satya* and *ahimsa*, which are good in themselves and not merely the means to a higher good. It is only for the sake of these goods in order that as such of them as possible may at some time exist that anyone can be justified in undertaking any social or political activity. They are the *raison d'etre* of virtue and excellence, the ultimate test of human endeavour, the sole criterion of social progress.

In stating that Gandhi rejected the sharp dichotomy between ends and means, it is obviously not suggested that the distinction is entirely false and useless. Surely, everyone (including Gandhi) would agree that it is often possible to distinguish between ends and means, and also useful to do so. The distinction is most easily made when we are considering some particular purpose that a man might have in mind before embarking on a specific action. But if, like Bentham, we say that what a man wants is to get or to maximize "happiness," then it becomes much more difficult to make a clear distinction between the end (the greatest happiness) and all 'the various things, said to be means to it. For a man's conception of happiness depends largely upon his desiring the things said to be means to it. It happens to be true that the things usually held up as supreme ends of human endeavour (happiness, freedom, welfare, etc.) are empty notions, apart from the things said to be means to them. We must distinguish between men's goals and their principles or the rules they accept. Sometimes, of course, their goal is to inculcate a principle or to observe it themselves or to get others to do so, but they have many other goals. But it seems to be more realistic to think of men as having a variety of goals, some of which matter more than others, than to think of them as having a supreme goal to which all others are subordinate, either as means to it or being willingly sacrificed whenever they conflict with it. The distinction between ends and means becomes misleading and dangerous when we dogmatize that there is a single supreme good or even a fixed hierarchy of goodness. Such dogmatism can have no place in the Gandhian dialectic, in which there is a dynamic fusion of *theoria* and *praxis* through the continual determination of the ends by the means.

Gandhi did not lay down the law for all men or impose on nature, a rigid, teleological pattern of his own. He merely argued from the proposition that all men have some idea of truth *(satya)* but no adequate conception of Absolute Truth *(sat),* to the prescription that society should regard the pursuit of *satya* as a common end. He further pointed out that in seeking the truth, we cannot help being true to our "real" natures (identical with that of all others) and this means exemplifying a measure of nonviolence in our attitudes and relations towards others. It is possible (though questionable) for people to argue that the unhappiness of some is required to maximize collective happiness, that individual citizens have to be coerced for the sake of general freedom, that the maintenance of public virtue sometimes requires subjects to choose (or support) privately corrupt but efficient and outwardly respectable rulers. It would, however, be difficult to contend that the collective pursuit of truth is compatible with the adoption of dishonest devices or the condoning of untruth. This could be advanced if a preordained, collectivist conception of truth were imposed on the members of a society. A dogmatic ideology may be propagated by dishonest and the less methods. A *satya* necessitates *himsa.*

Gandhi explicitly believed that no person or group could speak in the name of *Sat* or Absolute Truth for the very reason that all are entitled to their relative truths, to *satya* as it appears to different people. As truth in this conception is identical with integrity (fidelity to one's own conscience), Gandhi could claim that no man can pursue greater integrity as an end by adopting means involving a sacrifice of the integrity he already has. The test of one's immediate moral integrity is, nonviolence; it is a test of one's genuineness in the pursuit of truth (*i.e.*, of intellectual integrity) through one's actions in the midst of society. If we understand the concept of *satya* and accept its pursuit as a common end, we cannot make a hard and fast distinction between this end and the means towards it that we employ. On the other hand, it is particularly if we regard the promotion of happiness as the whole duty of man that we become careless about the means and violate the "laws of morality." "The consequences of this line of thinking are writ large on the history of Europe," said Gandhi in his introduction to his paraphrase of Ruskin's *Unto This Last.* For Gandhi the polis is nothing more or less than the domain in which all men, are free to gain skill in the art of action and learn how to exemplify *satya* and *ahimsa;*[24] the arena in which both the individual quest could be furthered and the social virtues displayed among the masses of citizens in a climate of tolerance and civility; a morally progressive society in which neither the state nor any social organization is allowed to flout with impunity the sacred principle that every man is entitled to his relative truth and no one can claim the right to coerce another, to treat him as a means to his own end.

NOTES

1. Jayantanuja Bandyopadhya, *Social and Political Thought of Mahatma Gandhi*, Bombay, Allied Publishers, 1969, p. 376.
2. M.K. Gandhi, *Hind Swaraj or the Indian Home Rule*, Ahmedabad, Navajivan Publishing House, 1975.
3. *Young India*, 26-12-1924, p. 422.
4. D.G. Tendulkar, *Mahatma*, Vol. III, New Delhi, Publications Division, Ministry of Information and Broadcasting, Government of India, 1972, p. 21.
5. M.K. Gandhi, *Hindu Dharma*, Ahmedabad, Navajivan Publishing House, 1950, pp. 160-162.
6. *Young India*, 17-7-1924, p. 233.
7. *Harijan*, 29-8-1936, p. 226.
8. M.K. Gandhi, *Delhi Diary*, Ahmedabad, Navajivan Publishing House, 1950, p. 201.
9. *Ibid.*
10. A. Huxley, *Ends and Means*, London, Kegan Paul, 1937, pp. 320-21.
11. *Modern Review*, January 1927.
12. M.K. Gandhi, *Ethical Religion*, Ahmedabad, Navajivan Publishing House, 1950, p. 36.
13. *Bapu's Letter to Mira*, Ahmedabad, Navajivan Publishing House, 1949, p. 43.
14. *Harijan*, 25-5-1935, p. 115.
15. Raghavan Iycr, *The Moral and Political Thought of Mahatma Gandhi*, Delhi, Oxford University, 1973, p. 364.

16. Jai Narain, *op. cit.*
17. Raghavan Iyer, *op. cit.*, p. 366.
18. *Ibid.*, p. 367.
19. *Ibid.*, p. 368.
20. *Ibid.*
21. *Selected Works of Mao Tse-tung*, Bombay, People's Publishing House, 1954, Vol. II, p. 45.
22. Roucek, *Social Control*, Van Nostrand, 1962, p. 344.
23. Aldous Huxley, *op. cit.*, p. 319.
24. Jai Narain Sharma, *Alternative Economics*, New Delhi, Deep and Deep, 2003, p. 84.

Bibliography

Primary Sources

The Collected Works of Mahatma Gandhi, Volumes 1 to 100, Delhi: The Publications Division, Ministry of Information and Broadcasting, Government of India.

Gandhi, M.K., *An Autobiography or The Story of My Experiments with Truth*, Ahmedabad: Navajivan Publishing House, 1983.

Gandhi, M.K., *Ashram Observations in Action*, (translated by V.G. Desai), Ahmedabad: Navajivan Publishing House, 1959.

Gandhi, M.K., *Constructive Programme: Its Meaning and Place*, Ahmedabad: Navajivan Publishing House, 1981.

Gandhi, M.K., *Delhi Diary*, Ahmedabad: Navajivan Publishing House, 1960.

Gandhi, M.K., *Ethical Religion*, Ahmedabad: Navajivan Publishing House, 1968.

Gandhi, M.K., *Fasting in Satyagraha: Its Uses and Abuses*, Ahmedabad: Navajivan Publishing House, 1965.

Gandhi, M.K., *From Yervada Mandir*, (translated by V.G. Desai), Ahmedabad: Navajivan Publishing House, 1932.

Gandhi, M.K., *Hindu Dharma*, Ahmedabad: Navajivan Publishing House, 1950.

Gandhi, M.K., *Hind Swaraj*, Ahmedabad: Navajivan Publishing House, 1982.

Gandhi, M.K., *Khadi Why and How*, Ahmedabad: Navajivan Publishing House, 1959.

Gandhi, M.K., *Non-Violence in Peace and War*, Volumes 1 & 2, Ahmedabad: Navajivan Publishing House, 1949.

Gandhi, M.K., *Satyagraha in South Africa*, Ahmedabad: Navajivan Publishing House, 1972.

Gandhi, M.K., *Truth is God*, Ahmedabad: Navajivan Publishing House, 1959.

Gandhi, M.K., *Caste Must Go and The Sin of Untouchability*, Ahmedabad: Navajivan Publishing House, 1967.

Gandhi's Correspondence with the Government, 1942-44, Ahmedabad: Navajivan Publishing House, 1957.

Gandhi's Correspondence with the Government, 1944-47, Ahmedabad: Navajivan Publishing House, 1959.

Mansergh, Nicholas (eds.), *The Transfer of Power, Constitutional Relations between Britain and India*, London: Her Majesty's Stationery Office, 1982, Volumes I to XI.

Speeches and Writings of Mahatma Gandhi, Madras: G.A. Natsen Company, 1933.

Selected Works of Mao Tse-tung, Bombay: People's Publishing House, 1954, Vol. II.

Encyclopaedias/Dictionaries

Kernig, C.D. (ed.), *Marxism, Communism and Western Society, A Comparative Encyclopaedia*, New York: Herder and Herder, 1973.

Monier-Williams, *Sanskrit English Dictionary.*

Seligman, Edwin R.A. (ed.), *Encyclopaedia of Social Sciences*, New York: Macmillan, 1956.

Sills, David L., *International Encyclopaedia of the Social Sciences*, London: Collier-Macmillan Publishers, 1972.

The New Encyclopaedia Britannica, Chicago: Helen Herningway Benton, 1978.

Journals/Reports/Newspapers/Magazines

Declaration of Cocoyoc, 1974.

Gandhi Jyoti, Bhagalpur, Bhagalpur University.

Gandhi Marg, New Delhi: Gandhi Peace Foundation.

Harijan, A Journal of Applied Gandhism, 1933-1955 (in 19 Volumes), New York and London: Garland Publishing, Inc., 1973.

Human Development Report—1998, Delhi: United Nations Development Programmes, 1998.

Indian Opinion, Natal, South Africa (1903-1914).

ILO Conference on Employment, Growth and Basic Needs: One World Problem, 1976.

Journal of Gandhian Studies, Allahabad: Gandhi Bhawan, University of Allahabad.

Modern Review—A Monthly Review and Miscellany, Calcutta: The Modern Review Office, 1935.

Reshaping the International Order, RIO A Report to the Club of Rome, London, Hutchinson, 1976.

Sarvodaya, Tirupur: Tamilnadu Sarvodaya Sangh.

The Bariloche Foundation Report, Catastrophe or New Society? A Latin American Model, 1976.

The Economic and Political Weekly, 1989, Vol. 34, No. 1, Mumbai.

The Hindu, Madras, 11-2-1947.

The Indian Annual Register 1919 to 1947, Calcutta: The Annual Register Office.

The Report of Independent Review, Canada, World Bank, 1992.

The World Economy: A Global Challenge, UN Publication, 1989.

United Nations. *Resolution of the General Assembly*, 10 December, 1948.

Vienna Declaration and Programme of Action (A/CONF. 157/23).

What Now-Another Development, The Hammerskjold Foundations, 1975.

Young India, 1919 to 1931, Madras: Ganesan.

Secondary Sources

Acton, John Emerich Edward Dalberg, *Essays on Freedom and Power*, London: Thomas and Hudson, 1956.

Adhikari, G., (ed.) *From Peace: Front to People's War*, Bombay: People's Publishing House, 1960.

Agarwal, Shriman Narayan, *Gandhian Constitution for Free India*, Allahabad: Kitabistan, 1946.

Aiken, Michael and Mott, Paul E. (eds.), *The Structure of Community Power*, New York: Random House, 1970.

Alexander, Horace, *Gandhi through Western Eyes*, Bombay: Asia Publishing House, 1969.

Andrews, C.F. *Mahatma Gandhi's Ideas,* London: George Allen & Unwin Ltd., 1949.

Ashe, Geoffrey, *Gandhi: A Study in Revolution*, Bombay: Asia Publishing House, 1968.

Azad, Maulana Abul Kalam, *India Wins Freedom*, New York: Longmans, Green & Co., 1960.

Bandyopadhyaya, Jayantanuja, *Social and Political Thought of Gandhi*, Bombay: Allied Publishers, 1969.

Bapu's Letter to Mira, Ahmedabad: Navajivan Publishing House, 1949.

Baxi, Upendra, *Inhuman Wrongs and Human Rights*, New Delhi: Har-Anand Publications, 1994.

Baxi, Upendra, *Mambrino's Helmet*, New Delhi: Har-Anand Publications, 1994.

Bell, Roderick; Edwards, D.V.; and Wagner, R.H. (eds.), *Political Power*, New York: Free Press, 1969.

Bentham, James, *The Machiavellians: Defenders of Freedom*, New York: Pioneers, 1943.

Bhattacharyya, Buddhadeva, *Evolution of Political Thought of Gandhi*, Calcutta: Calcutta Book House, 1969.

Birla, G.D., *In the Shadow of the Mahatma*, Bombay: Orient Longmans Ltd., 1953.

Biswas, S.C. (ed.), *Gandhi, Theory and Practice*, Social Impact and Contemporary Relevance, Simla: Indian Institute of Advanced Study, 1969.

Bondurant, Joan V., *Conquest of Violence: The Gandhian Philosophy of Conflict*, Bombay: Oxford University Press, 1959.

Bose, Nirmal Kumar, *Selection from Gandhi*, Ahmedabad: Navajivan Publishing House, 1959.

Bose, Nirmal Kumar, *Studies in Gandhism*, Calcutta: Indian Associated Publishing Co. Ltd., 1940.

Bose, Nirmal Kumar and Patwardhan, P.H., *Gandhi in Indian Politics*, Bombay: Lalvani Publishing House, 1967.

Bose, Subhas Chandra, *The Indian Struggle 1920-34*, Part 11, Calcutta Published for Netaji Publishing Society, 1948.

Brailsford, H.N., *Rebel India*, London: Leonard Stein, 1931.

Brown, Judith M., *Gandhi's Rise to Power*, Indian Politics, 1915-22, London: Cambridge University Press, 1972.

Brown, Judith M., *Gandhi and Civil Disobedience*, London: Cambridge University Press, 1977.

Brown, Mackenzie D., *The White Umbrella*, Berkeley: University of California Press, 1953.

Buckley, W.J., *Sociology and Modern Systems Theory*, Englewood Cliffs: Prentice-Hall, 1967.

Catlin, George, *In the Path of Mahatma Gandhi*, London: Macdonald & Co., 1948.

Catlin, George, *The Science and the Method of Politics*, New York: Alfred A., Knopf, 1927.

Catlin, George, *Systematic Politics*, London: Allen & Unwin, 1962.

Chirol, Valentine, *India Old and New*, New Delhi: New Delhi Publishers, 1975.

Collins, Larry and Lapierre, Dominique, *Freedom at Midnight?* New Delhi: Vikas Publishing House Pvt. Ltd., 1979.

Cranston, Maurice, *What are Human Rights?* London: Longmans, 1973.

Curtis, Michael, *Comparative Government and Politics: An Introductory Essays in Political Science*, New York: Harper and Row, 1968.

Dahl, Robert A., *Modern Political Analysis*, New Delhi: Prentice Hall of India (Pvt.), Ltd., 1965.

Datta, D.M., *The Philosophy of Mahatma Gandhi*, Madison: University of Wisconsin Press, 1953.

Desai, Mahadev, *Gandhiji in Indian Villages*, Madras: S. Ganesan, 1927.

Deutsch, Karl W. and J. William Foltz, ed., *Nation Building*, New York, 1963.

Dewan, Ram Prakash, *Wither His Highness, (ed.)* Lahore: Gandhi Publications League, 1948.

Dhawan, Gopi Nath, *The Political Philosophy of Mahatma Gandhi*, Ahmedabad: Navajivan Publishing House, 1962.

Doctor, Adi H., *Anarchist Thought in India,* Bombay: Asia Publishing House, 1964.

Doke, J.J., *M.K. Gandhi—An Indian Patriot*, Madras: Natesan, 1909.

Dwarkadas, Kanji, *India's Fight for Freedom: An Eye Witness Story—1913-37*, Bombay: Popular Prakashan, 1966.

Easton, David, *The Political System: An Enquiry into the State of Political Science*, Calcutta: Scientific Book Agency, 1971.

Erikson, Erik, *Gandhi's Truth on the Origin of Militant Non-Violence*, London: Faber and Faber, 1970.

Etzioni, A., *A Comparative Analysis of Complex Organisations*, New York: Free Press, 1975.

Finer, S.E., *Comparative Government*, London: Penguin Press, 1970.

Fischer, Louis, *The Life of Mahatma Gandhi*, Stuttgart: Tauchinty, 1953.

Friedrich, Carl J., *Constitutional Government and Democracy*, New York: Harper, 1937.

Gandhian Outlook and Technique's, New Delhi: Ministry of Education, Government of India, 1953.

Ganguli, B.N., *Gandhi's Social Philosophy; Perspective and Relevance*, Delhi: Vikas Publishing House Pvt. Ltd., 1973.

Gordon, George E., *Systematic Politics*, London: George Allen and Unwin Ltd., 1962.

Gould, James A. and Thutsby, Vincent B. (eds.), *Contemporary Political Thought: Issues in Scope*, Values and Direction, Holt Rinehart and Winston, Inc., 1969.

Gregg, Richard B., *The Power of Non-Violence*, Ahmedabad: Navajivan Publishing House, 1960.

Hobbes, *Thomas, Leviathan*, New York: Penguin, 1977.

Holmes, J.H.; Bridge, P.C. and James, F.E., *Mahatma Gandhi, World Significance*, Calcutta: C.C. Basik, The Research Home.

Holmes, W.H.G., *The Twofold Gandhi*, London: Mowbray & Co. Ltd., 1952.

Huttenback, Robert A., *Gandhi in South Africa: British Imperialism and the Indian Question 1860-1914*, Ithaca and London: Cornell University Press, 1971.

Huxley, A., *Ends and Means*, London: Kegan Paul, 1937.

Jack, Homer A., *The Gandhian Reader*, Bloomington: Indiana University Press, 1956.

Jayakar, M.R., *The Story of My Life* (in 2 Volumes), Bombay: Asia Publishing House, 1958-1959.

Iyer, Raghawan N., *The Moral and Political Thought of Mahatma Gandhi*, Delhi: Oxford University Press, 1973.

Kalelkar, Kaka, *Stray Glimpses of Bapu*, Ahmedabad: Navajivan Publishing House, 1957.

Karaka, D.F., *Out of Dust*, Bombay: Thacker & Co. Ltd., 1940.

Kornhavur, William, *The Politics of Mass Society*, Glencoe: Routledge and Kegan Paul, 1959.

Kothari, Rajni, *Footsteps into the Future*, New Delhi: Orient Longmans, 1974.

Kriplani, J.B., *Gandhi: His Life and Thought,* New Delhi: The Publications Division, Ministry of Information and Broadcasting, Government of India, 1971.

Kumar, R. (ed.), *Essays on Gandhian Politics*, Oxford: The Clarendon Press, 1971.

Kumarappa, Bharatan, *Capitalism, Socialism and Villagism*, Varanasi: Sarva Seva Sangh Prakashan, 1965.

Laski, H.J., *Grammar of Politics*, London: George Allen and Unwin Ltd., 1948.

Lasswell, Harold D., *Politics: Who Gets What When and How*, New York: McGraw Hill Book Co. Inc., 1936.

Lasswell, Harold D., Merriam, Charles E., and Smith, T.V., A *Study of Power*, Glenco Illinois: The Free Press, 1950.

Lasswell, Harold D. and Kaplan, Abraham, *Power and Society Framework for Political Enquiry*, London: Yale University Press, 1950.

Low, D.A. (ed.) *Congress and the Raj: Facets of Indian Struggle*, New Delhi: Arnold-Heinemann, 1977.

Lukes, Steven, *Power: A Radical View*, London: The Macmillan Press Ltd., 1974.

MacIver, R.M., *The Web of Government*, New York: The Macmillan Company, 1960.

Macpherson, C.B., *Democratic Theory: Essays in Retrieval*, London: Oxford University Press, 1975.

Mahadevan, T.K. (ed.), *Truth and Non-Violence*, New Delhi: Gandhi Peace Foundation, 1969.

Maine, Sir Henry Summer, *Ancient Law: Its Connection with the Early History of Society and Its Relation to Modern Ideas*, London: John Murray, Albemarle Street, 1890.

Majumdar, H.T., *Mahatma Gandhi, Peaceful Revolutionary*, New York: Charles Scribner & Son, 1952.

Majumdar, S.K., *Jinnah and Gandhi: Their Roles in India's Quest for Freedom*, Calcutta: Firma K.L. Mukhopadhyay, 1966.

Majumdar, R.C., *History of Freedom Movement*, Volume III, Calcutta: Firma K.L. Mukhopadhyaya, 1963.

Martin, Roderick, *The Sociology of Power*, New Delhi: Ambika Publications, 1976.

Marx, Karl, *Early Writings*, London: C.A. Watts & Co., 1963.

Mathur, Har Mohan and Marsden David (eds.), *Development Projects and Impoverishment Risks*, New Delhi: Oxford University Press, 1998.

Mathur, J.S. and Mathur, A.S., *Economic Thought of Mahatma Gandhi*, Allahabad: Chaitanya Publishing House, 1962.

Mehta, Ashok and Achyut Patwardhan, *The Communal Triangle in India*, Allahabad: Kitabistan, 1942.

Mehta, Ved, *Mahatma Gandhi and His Apostles*, New Delhi: Indian Book Company, 1977.

Michels, Robert, *Political Parties: A Sociological Study of the Oligarchical Tendencies of Modern Democracy*, (translated by Eden and Cader Paul), New York: The Free Press, 1962.

Miliband, Ralph, *Marxism and Politics*, London: Oxford University Press, 1977.

Mill, J.S., *Essays on Liberty*, Oxford: Blackwell, 1947.

Mishra, A.D. (ed.), *Perspectives on Human Rights*, New Delhi: Radha Publications, 2002.

Mohanty, Manoranjan *et al.*, *People's Rights Social Movements and the State in the Third World*, New Delhi: Sage Publications, 1998.

Mookerji, Radha Kumud, *Local Government in Ancient India*, Delhi: Moti Lal Banarsi Dass, 1958.

Mookerji, Radha Kumud, *Nationalism in Hindu Culture*, Delhi: S. Chand & Co., 1957.

Moon, Penderal, *Gandhi and Modern India*, London: The English Universities Press Ltd., 1968.

Morgenthau, Hans J., *Politics among Nations: The Struggle for Power and Peace*, Calcutta: Scientific Book Agency, 1973.

Mosca, Gaetano, *The Ruling Class*, New York: McGraw Hill, 1939, (Translated by Hannah D. Kahn).

Mukerjee, Hiren, *Gandhi: A Study*, New Delhi: People's Publishing House, 1960.

Nagel, Jack H., *The Descriptive Analysis of Power*, New Haven: Yale University Press, 1975.

Namboodiripad, E.M.S., *The Mahatma and the Ism*, New Delhi: People Publishing House, 1959.

Nanda, B.R., *Mahatma Gandhi: A Biography*, London: George Allen and Unwin Ltd., 1959.

Nayak, P.K., *Resettlement at Rengali Dam*, Orissa: Bhubaneswar (Monograph), 1986.

Nehru, Jawaharlal, *Mahatma Gandhi*, Calcutta: Signet Press, 1949.

Ostergaard, Geoffrey and Currell, Melvilla, *The Gentle Anarchist*, London: Oxford University, 1971.

Palmer, Norman D., *The Indian Political System*, Boston: Houghton Mifflin Company, 1970.

Payne, Robert, *The Life and Death of Mahatma Gandhi*, London: The Bodley Head, 1969.

Polak, H.S.L., Brailsford, H.N., and Pathick, Lawrence Lord, Mahatma Gandhi, London: Odhams Press Ltd., 1949.

Power, Paul F., *Gandhi on World Affairs*, London: George Allen and Unwin Ltd., 1960.

Power, Paul F. (ed.), *The Meanings of Gandhi*, The University Press of Hawaii, 1971.

Prabhu, R.K. and Rao, U.R., *The Mind of Mahatma*, Ahmedabad: Navajivan Publishing House, 1967.

Pyare Lal, *Mahatma Gandhi: The Early Phase,* Volume 1, Ahmedabad: Navajivan Publishing House, 1965.

Pyare Lal, *Mahatma Gandhi: The Last Phase,* in 2 Volumes, Ahmedabad: Navajivan Publishing House, 1956, 1958.

Radhakrishnan, S. (ed.), *Mahatma Gandhi: Essays and Reflections on His Life and Thought*, Allahabad: Kitabistan, 1944.

Rajendra Prashad, *An Autobiography*, Bombay: Asia Publishing House, 1957.

Rajendra Prashad, *At the Feet of Mahatma Gandhi*, Bombay: Asia Publishing House, 1961.

Rao, M.V. Ramana, *Development of the Congress Constitution*, New Delhi: All India Congress Committee, 1958.

Rao, U.R., *The Way to Communal Harmony*, Ahmedabad: Navajivan Publishing House, 1963.

Rapaport, Anatol, *Fights, Games and Debates*, Ann Arbor: University of Michigan Press, 1960.

Rawls, J.A., *A Theory of Justice*, London: O.U.P., 1972.

Robbinson, Richard, *Definition*, Oxford: Clarendon Press, 1954.

Robert, Geoffrey K., *A Dictionary of Political Analysis*, London: Longman, 1971.

Rolland, Romain, *Mahatma Gandhi, The Man Who Became One With The Universal Being*, (Translated by Catherine D. Groth), Agra: Shiva Lal Aggarwala & Co. Ltd.

Rose, Arnold M., *The Power Structure: Political Process in American Society*, New York: Oxford University Press, 1967.

Roucek, *Social Control*, Van Nostrand, 1962.

Roy, K., (ed.), *Gandhi Memorial Peace Number, The Viswa Bharati Quarterly,* Shantiniketan, 1949.

Russel, Bertrand, Power A New Social Analysis, London: George Allen and Unwin Ltd., 1957.

Saini, R.C. and R.K. Gupta (eds.), *Peoples Power: Indian Reality*, New Delhi: Commonwealth, 1994.

Saletore, B.A., *Ancient Indian Political Thought and Institutions*, Bombay: Asia Publishing House, 1968.

Sartori, Giovanni, *Democratic Theory*, New Delhi: Oxford and I.B.H., 1965.

Sethi, J.D., *Gandhi Today*, New Delhi: Vikas Publishing House Pvt. Ltd., 1978.

Sharma, Jai Narain, *Alternative Economics*, New Delhi: Deep & Deep, 2003.

Sharma, Jai Narain, *Gandhi's View of Political Power*, New Delhi: Deep & Deep, 1987.

Sharp, Gene, *Gandhi Wields the Weapon of Moral Power: Three Case Histories*, Ahmedabad: Navajivan Publishing House, 1960.

Sharp, Gene, *The Politics of Non-Violent Action: Power and Struggle*, Part 1, Boston: Porter Sarget Publishers, 1973.

Sharp, Gene, *The Politics of Non-Violent Action: The Method of Non-Violent Action*, Part II, Boston: Porter Sarget Publishers, 1973.

Sharp, Gene, *The Politics of Non-Violent Action: The Dynamics of Non-Violent Action*, Part III, Boston: Porter Sarget Publishers, 1973.

Shocan, Vincent, *Mahatma Gandhi: A Great Life in Brief*, New York: Alfred A. Knopf, 1955.

Shridharni, Krishan Lal, *War Without Violence: A Study of Gandhi's Method and Its Accomplishments,* Bombay: Bharatiya Vidya Bhavan, 1962.

Sitaramayya, Pattabhi, *Gandhi and Gandhism*, Allahabad: Kitabistan, 1942, in 2 Volumes.

Spratt, Philip, *Gandhism: An Analysis*, Madras: Huxley Press, 1939.

Tara Chand, *History of the Freedom Movement in India*, New Delhi: Publications Division, Ministry of Information and Broadcasting, Government of India, 1972.

The Diary of Mahadev Desai, tr. and ed., Valji Govindji Desai, Ahmedabad: Navajivan Publishing House, 1956.

Tawney, R.H., *Equality*, New York: Harcourt Brace, 1931.

Tendulkar, D.G. (ed.), *Mahatma,* in 8 Volumes, Delhi: The Publications Division, Ministry of Information and Broadcasting, Government of India, 1962.

Unnithan, T.K.N. and Yogendra Singh, *Traditions of Non-Violence*, New Delhi: Arnold-Heinemann India, 1973.

Varkey, C.J., *The Wardha Scheme of Education: An Exposition and Examination*, Mysore: Oxford University Press, 1940.

Verma, V.P., *The Political Philosophy of Mahatma Gandhi and Sarvodaya*, Agra: Lakshmi Narain Aggarwal, 1981.

Wasby, S.L., *Political Science—The Discipline and its Dimension*, Calcutta: Scientific Book Agency, 1970.

Weber, Max, *Theory of Social and Economic Organisation* (translated by A.M. Henderson and T. Parsons), Chicago: Free Press, 1947.

Weilemnann, Hermann, "The Interlocking of Nation and Personality Structure" in Karl W. Deutsch and J. William Foltz, ed., Nation Building, New York, 1963.

Woodcock, George, *Anarchism*, Penguin Books, 1963.

Wright, *Quincy A Study of War*, Vol. I, Chicago: Chicago University Press, 1942.

Zweig, Stefan, *Adepts in Self-Portraiture* (translated by Eden and Cedar Paul), London: Lassell and Company Ltd., 1929.

Index

Absolute majority, 78, 79
Absolute truth, 6, 176, 179, 182, 193
Aggression, 19, 26, 27, 158
Ahimsa, 33, 34, 36, 43, 47, 103, 179, 182, 192, 194
Alienation, 51, 191
Allied powers, 86
Anarchist philosophy, 42, 43
Anarchists, 7, 25, 41-44, 181
Armed forces, 14, 185
Attainment, 83, 90, 133, 162, 172, 174, 180, 182-83
Augustine, 7, 69, 70
Austin, 10
Autonomy, 71, 127-28

Birth rights, 130
Boer War, 164-65
Bread-labour, 12, 16
British army, 24, 40
British domination, 8
British East India Company, 164
British Empire, 8, 163, 165
British imperialism, 9, 39, 71, 164, 168
British Parliament, 83, 99
British rule, 161, 163, 168, 174
Brotherhood, 1, 118, 156
Buddha, 64

Capitalism, 43, 44, 108, 166
  elimination of, 44
Capitalist democracies, 86
Charter of Duties, 130
Charter of Human Rights, 130
Chauri Chaura, 62
Civic duties, 134
Civil liberty, 36, 134, 137
Civil rights, 134, 136-37, 148
Class domination, 44
Class struggle, 183-84
Classless society, 44, 183
Cocoyoc Declaration, 124
Codified rights, 115-16
Coercive state, 12, 41
Communist International, 86
Communitarian village, 38
Community Development Programme, 191
Compulsory education, 17, 142
Concentration of economic power, 38
Concentration of power, 50, 51, 81, 92
Conceptual framework, 58
Congress movement, 137, 148
Constitutionalism, 97, 98, 148
Constructive Programme, 51, 190-91
Constructive workers, 50, 74, 75, 190
Counter-Hitlerism, 169

Decentralization, 11, 29, 38, 50, 53, 102
Decentralization of power, 38, 51
Democracy, 1, 4, 19, 25, 28, 51, 53, 78-88, 90-97, 99, 106, 141-42, 158, 163, 178
  defining, 82
  evolution of, 93

extending, 162
foundations of, 92
imperialist, 87
nominal, 92
plebicitary, 96
Democratic power, 84
Democratic rights, 116
Democratic theory, 80
Democratic values, 81
Democratic world federation, 158
Denominational religion, 94
Denominationalism, 72
Devanagari, 153
Development model, 117-18
Dharma, 6, 136
Dialectical materialism, 110, 187
Dictatorships, 28, 44, 84, 95, 106, 110, 183, 188-89
Divine laws, 9, 70
Doctrine of Power, 31

Economic coercion, 38
Economic decentralisation, 38, 44
Economic development, 113, 162
Economic power, 38
Economic rights, 140
Egalitarian non-violent democratic order, 24
Empirical evidence, 173, 188-89
Enlightened anarchy, 11, 21, 40-42
Equal liberty, 121
Equality of political rights, 28
Ethical discipline, 178-79

Fascism, 84, 86, 151, 162, 166-67, 169, 179
First World War, 164, 187
Fischer, Louis, 51, 85, 90, 154, 156-57
Foreign domination, 31, 157
Foreign rule, 133-34
Foundation of freedom, 36, 134
Fraternity, 183-85, 187
Free democratic India, 158
Free India knowledge, 98
Free India, 91, 149, 155, 157-58, 160
Freedom movement, 137, 148, 190
Freedom of speech, 36, 124, 136
Freedom of worship, 24, 139
Freedom
economic, 162
equated, 148
eternal, 65
personal, 82
political, 116, 150
spiritual, 176
Fundamental ethics, 72, 94
Fundamental rights, 93

Gandhi Seva Sangh, 50
Gandhi Smarak Nidhi, 191
Gandhi, Maganlal, 83
Gandhian dialectic, 193
Gandhian gospel, 160
Gandhian Philosophy, 42, 177
Gandhian Political Philosophy, 93
Gandhian Politics, 73
Gandhian technique, 62
Gandhian theory, 4, 81
Gandhi's
anarchism, 25
attachment, 64
nationalism, 161
naturalism, 155
Gandhism, 10, 71
General Smuts, 60, 61
Generation of power, 44, 50, 51
Gokhale, 64, 166
Government of India Act, 98
Gram Swaraj, 38
Gross National Poverty, 125
Gujarat, 114

Harijan, 12, 23, 40, 66, 93, 95, 96, 100, 132, 137
Harijan girls, 98
Hindu nationalism, 151
Hindu Raj, 23, 40

Hinduism, 68, 151-52
Hitler, 9, 167-69
Hitlerite Germany, 86
Human communities, 117-18
Human dignity, 51, 116, 119-20, 168
Human rights, 4, 106, 113, 115-16, 118-20, 124-30
  activists, 116
  discourse, 126
  inalienable, 112
  inviolable, 119
  liberal, 130
  movements, 115
  orthodoxy, 125
  violations, 113-14
Humanity, 48, 65, 71, 73, 127-28, 154, 156-62, 168, 176

Ideal society, 7, 11, 21, 23, 40, 49, 74, 174, 183-84, 190
Imperialism, 85, 86, 99, 150, 154, 162-66, 188
Imperialist domination, 8, 39
India Congress Committee, 90, 92
Indian Independence Bill, 98
Indian National Congress, 35, 62, 75, 89, 90
Inequalities, 24, 82, 95, 122-23, 188
Intellectual property rights, 113
International brotherhood, 159
International cooperation, 156, 158, 160
International Development Strategy, 126
International Economic Order, 126
International functions, 14, 18, 20
International imperialism, 187
International peace, 187
Internationalism, 4, 11, 146, 154, 156, 161-62
Inter-religious marriages, 152
Intoxicants, 15
Invading army, 20, 27
Islam, 139, 152
Italian Fascism and German National Socialism, 166

Japan, 26
Jingo nationalism, 167

Karmayogi, 66
Kautilya, 58, 71, 180-81
Khadi, 38, 190
Khilafat movement, 68
Koodankulam village, 114
Krishna, 22
Kropotkin, 25, 42, 43

Lasswell, Harold, 48, 58, 59
Lenin, 44, 75, 86, 166, 181-82
Liberal conception, 124
Liberalism, 110, 112, 150, 162
Licences Bill, 138

Machiavelli, 58, 180-81
Malpractices, 84
Manipulation of power, 49, 75
Marx, Karl, 43, 44, 58, 86
Marxists, 44, 166, 181, 184-85, 187
Mass leaders, 3, 4
Mazzini, 162
Megalopolises, 79, 80
Metaphysics, 111
Minorities, 79, 81, 87, 88, 135, 188
Mobocracy, 97
Mob-rule, 97
Monolith Theory of Power, 34
Moral authority, 11, 23, 40, 42, 92
Moral discipline, 179
Moral laws, 1, 26, 39, 44, 179-80, 182, 192
Moral power, 37, 40, 47
Moral rearmament, 19, 20
Moral vows, 65, 66
Multinational companies, 113, 117
Mussolini, 167-68

National democratic development, 95

National Human Rights Commission, 119
National sovereignty, 43, 113
National struggle, 148, 150
Nationalism, 4, 146-49, 151, 153-56, 158, 161-63
Nationalist struggle, 83, 147
Nation-building process, 146
Natural rights, 115, 119, 130, 136
Nazi powers, 85
Nazism, 166, 168
Non-political society, 50, 74
Nonviolence, 1, 4, 5, 7, 8, 11-14, 24-28, 33, 36, 37, 41-44, 47, 81, 82, 84, 91, 92, 167-69, 185-89, 192-93
  foundation of, 92, 158
  ultimate values of, 184, 187
Nonviolent
  act, 186
  army, 28
  conscience, 139
  cooperation movements, 62
  majority, 12
  movement, 62, 63
  non-cooperation, 37, 38
  resistance, 13, 26, 28, 167-68
  society, 41, 182
  state, 11-14, 19, 28, 38, 41, 179
  strength, 9, 27
  technique, 26, 61

Parliamentary democracy, 83, 91, 96, 134
Patriotism, 9, 65, 154-56, 162
Philosophical anarchists, 42
Philosophy of nationalism, 150, 154
Political
  amalgamation, 146
  assassination, 180
  authority, 7, 8, 52, 67, 71
  coil, 48, 73
  consciousness, 147
  development, 96
  ethics, 185, 191
  inadequacies, 67
  integration, 146
  leaders, 5, 21, 86
  loyalty, 70
  movements, 63, 148
  obedience, 70, 71
  pelmanism, 147
  philosophy, 2, 3, 31, 42, 66, 71
  realism, 41
  rights, 28, 131, 162
  rulers, 10, 40
  science, 9, 57, 58
  socialization, 147, 149, 153
  theory, 3, 5, 66, 93
  thought, 6, 21, 40, 69, 71
Power
  politicians, 67
  politics, 45, 47-50, 60-63, 73, 75, 93, 163
Power, Paul F., 6, 43, 166
Powerloom cooperatives, 191
Power-seekers, 49, 74, 93, 191
Pragmatic approaches, 3, 4
Primary education, 142
Prohibitive Functions, 14, 15
Prophets of violence, 188-89
Prostitute, 82, 83, 99
Protective Functions, 14
Public-utility services, 16
Purest anarchy, 25, 26
Purification of politics, 48, 73
Purna Swaraj, 131, 158

Rabinovich, 183
Racial discrimination, 8, 39, 154, 164
Ramaraj, 11, 21-24, 40, 42, 69
Rawls, John, 111, 120
Religious
  anarchists, 26, 42
  basis of politics, 67-69, 71
  belief, 152
  code, 70
  consciousness, 69

convictions, 71, 161
dogmas, 73
duties, 6, 67
education, 72
ethics, 67
faith, 68
rights, 139
teachings, 72
truth, 73
values, 47, 73
Revivalism, 68, 148
Righteousness, 22, 23, 40
Rural development, 114
Ruthlessness, 85, 181-82

Satya, 179, 182, 192-94
Satyagraha, 10, 28, 32, 36, 52, 60-62, 67, 71, 82, 131, 133-34, 136-37, 178, 184, 190
Second World War, 36, 106, 136, 157, 187
Self-control, 184, 189
Self-government, 53, 78, 92
Self-purification, 178
Self-realization, 6, 124, 176, 178-79
Self-reliance, 38, 115, 127
Self-respect, 21, 122-23
Service of humanity, 155-56
Sevagram, 84, 158
Sikhs, 48, 74
Smuts-Gandhi agreement, 61
Social control, 58, 175, 184-85, 187-91
Social institutions, 184
Social obligations, 37
Social progress, 37, 126, 192
Social restraints, 37
Socio-political goal, 188
South Africa, 5, 9, 60, 61, 67, 84, 131, 138, 141, 164, 176
State Human Rights Commissions, 119
Stateless society, 40-44, 183
Stirner, Max, 25
Supreme power, 34, 51
Swadesi, 159

Third World, 108, 112
Tolstoy, 7, 9, 25, 42, 43, 67, 166, 178
Transvaal Citizenship, 135
Trotsky, 182
True democracy, 23, 51, 82, 91, 92
Truman's project, 108

United Nations, 19, 86, 118, 133
United States, 106-7
Universal Declaration of Human Rights, 118
Universal morality, 6
Utilitarian principles, 111

Village Swaraj, 91
Violent resistance, 27
Vocational education, 17, 142
Voluntary donations, 16

Western colonialism, 166
Western democracies, 81, 84, 85, 92, 166
Western theorists of democracy, 80

Young India, 11, 49, 62, 74, 83, 88, 89, 96, 132, 136, 164-65

Zulu rebellion, 8, 164